The Unity of the Virtues in the *Eudemian Ethics*

The Unity of the Virtues in the *Eudemian Ethics*

GIULIA BONASIO

OXFORD
UNIVERSITY PRESS

Oxford University Press is a department of the University of Oxford.
It furthers the University's objective of excellence in research, scholarship,
and education by publishing worldwide. Oxford is a registered trade mark of
Oxford University Press in the UK and in certain other countries.

Published in the United States of America by Oxford University Press
198 Madison Avenue, New York, NY 10016, United States of America.

© Oxford University Press 2025

All rights reserved. No part of this publication may be reproduced, stored in a retrieval system, transmitted, used for text and data mining, or used for training artificial intelligence, in any form or by any means, without the prior permission in writing of Oxford University Press, or as expressly permitted by law, by license or under terms agreed with the appropriate reprographics rights organization. Inquiries concerning reproduction outside the scope of the above should be sent to the Rights Department, Oxford University Press, at the address above.

You must not circulate this work in any other form
and you must impose this same condition on any acquirer.

Library of Congress Cataloging-in-Publication Data
Names: Bonasio, Giulia, author.
Title: The unity of the virtues in the Eudemian ethics / Giulia Bonasio.
Description: 1. | New York, NY, United States of America : Oxford University Press, [2025] |
Includes bibliographical references and index.
Identifiers: LCCN 2025005003 (print) | LCCN 2025005004 (ebook) |
ISBN 9780197801307 (hardback) | ISBN 9780197801338 | ISBN 9780197801314 (epub)
Subjects: LCSH: Aristotle. Eudemian ethics. | Virtue. | Virtues.
Classification: LCC B422 .D45 2025 (print) | LCC B422 (ebook) |
DDC 185—dc23/eng/20250207
LC record available at https://lccn.loc.gov/2025005003
LC ebook record available at https://lccn.loc.gov/2025005004

DOI: 10.1093/9780197801338.001.0001

Printed by Integrated Books International, United States of America

The manufacturer's authorized representative in the EU for product safety is
Oxford University Press España S.A., Parque Empresarial San Fernando de Henares,
Avenida de Castilla, 2 – 28830 Madrid (www.oup.es/en).

To Daniele, Cosimo, and Matilde

Contents

Acknowledgements ix
Introduction xiii

1. The unity of the parts of the soul 1
2. *Phronêsis* and the virtues of practical thinking 27
3. The interdependence between the character virtues and *phronêsis* 58
4. *Epistêmê* is said in many ways 85
5. The virtues of theoretical thinking in the Functional Unity of the Virtues 115
6. *Kalokagathia*: the Functional Unity of the Virtues 142

Conclusion 171
Bibliography 181
Index 197

Acknowledgements

This book develops ideas that I first discussed in chapter 2 of my doctoral dissertation entitled 'Happiness and Superlative Value in the Eudemian Ethics' that I wrote under the supervision of Katja Vogt at Columbia University. I am deeply grateful to Katja Vogt for support and help not only during my years at Columbia University, but also as I was writing the book: her feedback and comments were fundamental as I developed my ideas. In chapters 1, 5, and 6 of this book I discuss ideas that first appeared in my article 'Kalokagathia and the Unity of the Virtues in the *Eudemian Ethics*' published in *Apeiron* in 2020. These chapters contain sections of the original article of 2020 that are included, developed, and integrated in the book. I am grateful to the editors of *Apeiron* for permission to include these parts of the article in the book. My chapter 'Complete Virtue', published in G. Di Basilio (ed.), *Investigating the Relationship between Aristotle's Eudemian and Nicomachean Ethics*, appears as the last part of chapter 6. I am thankful to the editors at Routledge for permission to reprint this chapter as it constitutes an important step in the development of the argument that I offer in this book.

My thanks go to Christopher Rowe for making his edition of the *Eudemian Ethics* (*EE*), as well as his notes on the edition that are now published in *Aristotelica*, available to me while he was still working on them. I believe that thanks to his new edition of the *EE* we are in a much better position to interpret this text that for long time was understudied. I am in debt to Christopher Rowe and to Anthony Kenny for all their work on the *EE* that influenced my thoughts on this treatise.

A supportive environment at Durham University encouraged me to proceed in my work. I am very grateful to all my colleagues in the Department of Classics and Ancient History. A Junior Guest Professorship that I held for four months at the University of Zürich in the autumn of 2022 was fundamental for completing the book. I am thankful to the Zentrum Altertumswissenschaften of the University of Zürich for providing this wonderful opportunity and, in particular, to Christoph Riedweg and the team at the Seminar für Griechische und Lateinische Philologie for being the perfect academic hosts during my stay. While in Zürich, I taught a seminar on Aristotle's ethics where I benefitted from discussions of some of the ideas that I developed in the book with students. I wish to thank the Collegium Helveticum where I was a Senior Fellow in 2022 for offering exciting opportunities to discuss my ideas in an interdisciplinary setting and for providing a truly pleasant and beautiful environment for research.

I am grateful to audiences and organizers of conferences and workshops in the United States, Canada, Europe, and the United Kingdom where I presented material from the book. I am especially thankful to the participants of the workshop on 'New Works on Aristotle's Ethics' that took place in Lisbon in 2024. I benefitted from discussions of ideas, feedback, and comments, at times in conversation and at times in writing, from many scholars. These include F. Buddensiek, E. Diamond, T. Irwin, D. Jagannathan, M. Malink, A. Marmodoro, F. Masi, P.-M. Morel, J. Moss, K. M. Nielsen, M. B. Noé, C. Olfert, A. Price, O. Primavesi, C. Rapp, M. Rashed, C. Viano, and G. Williams. C. Bobonich, C. Gartner, and M. Jimenez provided comments on a paper on *epistêmê* and *phronêsis* in the *EE* and in the *Protrepticus* that I was writing while writing the book: these comments helped me refine my thoughts about this relation as I discuss it in chapter 4. S. Sauvé Meyer shared with me her forthcoming paper entitled 'Clarifying the Human Soul and Its Virtues: *EE* 1219b26-1220a20' that will be published in H. Lorenz, B. Morison, *Aristotle's Eudemian Ethics, Book II*. This paper helped me think about the unity of the parts of the soul that I develop in chapter 1.

I am thankful for comments by anonymous readers and by Larry Jost that helped me clarify my proposal and revise the book. My thanks go to Peter Ohlin who was my first contact with Oxford University Press and guided me through the process of submitting the manuscript, to my project editor Meredith Taylor, and to the team at OUP for supporting this project.

On a more personal note, I am deeply thankful to my parents for support and to my husband for continuous encouragement and help during all the stages of this process. This book is dedicated to him and to our two children who joined our family as I was writing this book.

Introduction

The unity of the virtues (UoV) is accepted by several leading schools in antiquity.[1] However, the precise formulation of this thesis varies greatly. The UoV can be understood as unity of virtue in the singular: the virtues, on this view, all are the same thing, virtue. All virtue terms are co-referential. What looks like a plurality of virtues is reducible to one virtue, wisdom, or knowledge. Some scholars think that this is how the UoV is conceived by Socrates and Plato.[2] Alternatively, the UoV is understood as unity of the virtues in the plural, and as the claim that when agents possess one virtue, they must possess them all. This thesis has been referred to also as reciprocity of the virtues or mutual entailment.[3] Another dispute concerns the question of what counts as 'the virtues'. What

---

[1] See Plato, *Protagoras* 329b–34c; *Laches* 190c–d, 198a–9e; *Meno* 73e–74d, 78d–79e, 349a–62a; *Gorgias* 506d–7c; *Republic* IV, 428a–44e; *Statesman* 306a–11c; *Laws* 631c–d. The Stoics: see Arius Didymus, in Stobaeus, *Anthology* II, 5b5; Diogenes Laertius, *Lives* VII, 1262; Plutarch, *On Stoic Self-Contradictions* 1046e–f. Epicurus: see Diogenes Laertius, *Lives* X, 1417–22. For an overview of conceptions of the unity of the virtues/unity of virtue from antiquity on, see Collette-Dučić and Delcomminette 2014.

[2] The question of whether we should speak about virtue in the singular or about virtues in the plural comes up in Plato's dialogues. In the *Meno*, Socrates says that even though the virtues are many, all of them have one and the same form (72c–d). In the *Republic*, Plato argues that justice is the harmony of all the parts of the soul (443d). In this sense, all the virtues are forms of justice. In the *Laches*, virtue is conceived as a whole with parts and the parts are virtues such as courage (190c–d). In the *Protagoras*, Socrates asks Protagoras whether the virtues are like parts of gold or like parts in a face (329d). With regard to the view presented in the *Protagoras*, scholars debate on whether Plato offers a coherent view that the virtues are like the parts in a face, or whether he thinks that they are like the parts of gold; cf. Devereux 1992, 765–89. For the first view, see Sedley 2014, 65–91; for the second view, see Vlastos 1973, 221–69. For the idea that the virtues are all names for knowledge of good and evil, see Penner 1973, 35–68. This identity thesis has been defended by Taylor 1976, 103; Irwin 1977, 86–90; Ferejohn 1982, 1–21; Ferejohn 1983–4, 377–88; Schofield 1984, 83–95. For a recent perspective on the UoV in Plato, see Jenks 2022.

[3] See Irwin 1988a, 61–78; Annas 1993.

is included when we say that the terms for 'the virtues' all refer to the same thing, virtue, or when we say that someone who has one virtue must have 'all' of them?

With regard to Aristotle, scholars tend to invoke the model of mutual entailment and argue that 'all virtues' refers to *phronêsis*—practical wisdom—and the virtues of character. In other words, the UoV is standardly understood as a unity of *phronêsis* and all the character virtues.[4] In discussing the UoV scholars focus almost exclusively on the *Nicomachean Ethics* (*NE*). A reconstruction of the UoV in the *Eudemian Ethics* (*EE*) has yet to be done. In this book, I examine the UoV in Aristotle's *EE*. I agree with traditional views on Aristotle's ethics in an important respect: like other scholars, I hold that Aristotle subscribes to the view that if one has one of the character virtues, one must have all of them together with *phronêsis*, and if one has *phronêsis*, one must have all the character virtues. I characterize this relation in terms of Ontological and Functional Interdependency. That is, *phronêsis* comes about only when agents have all the virtues of character and vice versa. *Phronêsis* cannot function—it cannot fulfil its tasks—without the virtues of character and vice versa. In addition, I ascribe a view to Aristotle that has so far not been considered 'Aristotelian': a UoV that is more comprehensive than the unity of practical wisdom and the character virtues, which is traditionally ascribed to the *NE*. I call this more comprehensive unity Functional Unity. All the virtues of Aristotle's *EE* form a unity in the sense that they function—namely, are exercised—together.[5]

With this proposal, I aim to shed light on philosophical options that Aristotle formulated and defended at least at some point during his philosophical career. I contribute to a deeper understanding of a treatise that, in spite of increased attention, is still less well-known

---

[4] Irwin 1988a, 61–78; Dahl 1984; Walker 1993, 44–60; Badhwar 1996, 30–29; Cooper 1998, 233–74; Halper 1999, 115–44; Kent 1999, 109–24; Natali 1989; Gardiner 2005; Russell 2009; Annas 2011, 83–100; Russell 2014, 203–21. For a detailed discussion of the role of the virtues of thinking, see DePaul and Zagzebski 2003; Kosman 2014.

[5] For a discussion of how to understand 'all the virtues', see chapter 6.

than the *NE*. On my reading, the account of the UoV that I reconstruct is critical for our appreciation of the coherence of the *EE*'s philosophical proposal. As I show, Aristotle's argument in favour of the Functional Unity of the Virtues is developed throughout the entire treatise, including the common books, namely those books that the *EE* has in common with the *NE*.[6] A reconstruction of this argument does not challenge traditional readings of the *NE* directly. However, it provides a distinctive lens through which the *EE* is elucidated, and potentially also a lens through which dimensions of the *NE* may be reassessed. What is more, in my reconstruction of the Functional Unity of the Virtues, I propose a new perspective on how we conceive of the virtues and their development. My analysis differs from the traditional focus on mutual entailment as it stresses the interaction and co-functioning of all the virtues. In this light, we must develop all the virtues contemporaneously and in conjunction.

I.1 Parts, wholes, and the unity of the virtues

In the *EE*, Aristotle talks about the virtues in terms of parts and wholes. This is especially evident in *EE* II 1219a38, where Aristotle says that virtue can be a whole (*holê*) or a part (*morion*). At

---

[6] These books are *EE* IV = *NE* V; *EE* V = *NE* VI; *EE* VI = *NE* VII. For centuries these books were treated as if they were original components of the *NE*. Jaeger (1948) argued that the books belonged to the *NE*. In the 1970s, Rowe published a study of the development of Aristotle's thought in the *EE* and in the *NE* that agrees with Jaeger on the question of the common books (Rowe 1971). A few years later, in 1978, Kenny argued that the common books were an original part of the *EE*. He based his argument on a stylometric analysis of the common books and of the undisputed books of the two ethics. The analysis brought to light stronger similarities between the style of the common books and that of the undisputed books of the *EE* (Kenny 1978, 2016). However, there is still no agreement among scholars on this matter. For an overview of the manuscripts' tradition, cf. Harlfinger 1971 and Rowe 2023, preface. In favour of reading the common books as part of the *EE*: Jost 1983; Hutchinson 1995, 195–232; Crisp 2000; Bostock 2000; Schofield 2002; Bobonich 2006, 12–36; Zanatta 2012; Inwood and Woolf 2013; Jost 2014a, 410–25. Against the idea that we should read the common books as part of the *EE*, see Frede 2019; Primavesi 2007. On the relation between the *NE* and the *EE*, see Di Basilio 2022.

1219a39–40, Aristotle defines happiness as activity according to complete virtue.[7] As I see it, this complete virtue is *kalokagathia*—literally, the virtue of being-beautiful-and-good—which is explicitly mentioned only at *EE* VIII 1248b12.[8] *Kalokagathia* is characterized as a virtue that is a whole; its parts are all the virtues. In my reconstruction of the UoV, as Aristotle conceives of it in the *EE*, I distinguish among three unities, each with a different scope:

1. The unity of the practical virtues: That is, the unity of those virtues related to *praxis* (action), namely *phronêsis* and the

---

[7] *Eudaimonia* is translated as 'happiness' for lack of a better term: I use this translation for the sake of clarity insofar as it is ingrained in the literature on the topic. Some other possible translations are 'flourishing' and 'well-being'. Some important contributions on Aristotle's notion of happiness are: Hardie 1968; Nagel 1972, 252–59; Cooper 1975; McDowell 1980; Dybikowski 1981, 185–200; Kraut 1989; Kenny 1992; Broadie 1993; Sherman 1998; De Luise and Farinetti 2001; Destrée 2003; Lear 2006; Pakaluk and Pearson 2011; Reeve 2012; Destrée and Zingano 2015.

[8] At 1248b11, I read *ekaloumen* with Rowe (2023). See chapter 6, footnote 15. The translation of *kalokagathia* is contested, and perhaps no translation is entirely ideal. Possible translations are 'fine and good' and 'noble and good', which (among other things) speak to the idea that *kalos* is quite broad and can be used in any number of contexts, just as 'fine' and 'noble'. I prefer to translate *kalokagathia* as 'being-beautiful-and-good'. My translation of *kalos* as 'beautiful' does not point to aesthetic beauty or appearance. Rather, it points to another kind of beauty that Aristotle invokes in relation to theoretical activities and theoretical objects. Depending on a given sentence, 'fine' can also be a translation of *agathos*. That is, 'fine and good' does not convey clearly that the Greek term *kalokagathia* consists of two different terms insofar as *agathos* can be translated also as 'fine'. By comparison, I take 'being-beautiful-and-good' to be more transparent; each term maps onto one Greek term. In other words, 'beautiful' has the advantage of distinguishing the Greek *kalos* from *agathos*. 'Noble' is distinct from 'good', but 'being-noble-and-good' does not convey the innovation of Aristotle's *kalokagathia*. Namely, Aristotle breaks with the Greek tradition of thinking about *kalokagathia* as the mark of those of noble birth. For Aristotle, *kalokagathia* is not by birth but is acquired by developing all the virtues. Second, and relatedly, 'fine and good' could be a way of glossing just one value term, perhaps *agathos* in a context where a complex kind of positive value is conveyed. By contrast, the translation 'being-beautiful-and-good' renders explicit that we are concerned with two value properties—beauty and goodness—that for the ancients characterize what is excellent. In particular, with my translation I wish to stress that beauty, as well as goodness, has a prominent role in the life of the *kalos kagathos*: this agent has all the virtues, including the virtues of theoretical thinking. The *kalos kagathos* is concerned with theoretical activity and theoretical objects, which, for Aristotle, are distinctively beautiful. Cf. chapters 5 and 6. My translation is in line with Dirlmeier (1984), who translates the term with the German expression 'die Schön-und-Gutheit'. Similarly, Donini (1999) translates it as 'bontà e bellezza morale'. Inwood and Woolf (2013) translate it as 'nobility'.

virtues on which *phronêsis* depends. I argue that *phronêsis* is a dependent virtue: it depends on *euboulia* (good deliberation), *sunesis* (comprehension), *gnôme* (consideration), practical *nous* (intelligence), and the virtues of character. I endorse the traditional view that *phronêsis* and the character virtues mutually entail each other. I characterize the relation between *phronêsis* and the character virtues in terms of Ontological and Functional Interdependency. *Epistêmê* (knowledge) co-functions with *phronêsis* in the practical domain.
2. The unity of all the virtues of theoretical thinking: These virtues are *epistêmê*, theoretical *nous*, and *sophia* (theoretical wisdom). *Epistêmê* and theoretical *nous* are parts of *sophia*: in order to have *sophia*, we need to have these parts.
3. A full unity of all the virtues as parts of *kalokagathia*: When agents possess all the virtues, they have *kalokagathia*. They enjoy happiness as this is described in EE II 1219a39–40. On my reading, all the virtues form the Functional Unity of the Virtues. When they are part of this unity, the virtues function at their best and fulfil their full potential; they interact and co-function.

As I explained, the UoV has been traditionally understood in two ways: (i) UoV as unity of virtue (singular); the plurality of virtue-terms is explained as co-referentiality; (ii) UoV as mutual entailment that may comprise all the virtues or, more narrowly, *phronêsis* and the character virtues. With regard to *kalokagathia*, I defend a third way of understanding the UoV: I call it Functional Unity. The relation between *kalokagathia* and its parts is 'all-or-nothing' in the sense that agents cannot possess *kalokagathia* unless they possess all its parts.[9] Agents may possess some parts of *kalokagathia*

---

[9] I will further qualify this claim in chapter 6 when I explain the idea of a 'relaxed' all-quantifier.

without possessing *kalokagathia* and all its other parts. However, the parts of *kalokagathia* function at their best and fulfil their full potential when they are possessed together with all the other parts of *kalokagathia* and when they start to interact and co-function with these other virtues. When they are possessed together with other virtues (some or all of them), the virtues take up additional tasks. I call this Additive Functionality. In this sense, the relation between *kalokagathia* and its parts is different from the mutual entailment of the character virtues and *phronêsis*. In the latter, we cannot have one or some character virtues without *phronêsis*, and we cannot have *phronêsis* without all the virtues of character.

I.2 Co-functioning and functional unity

The UoV is typically not discussed in terms of 'functions' of the virtues. Against this trend, I argue that we can better understand the *EE*'s proposals if we think of virtues having functions. This idiom also permits the description of virtues that are exercised as virtues that 'function' in this or that way.[10] Thinking about the virtues as functioning in one way or another allows us to capture what I see as an important dimension of Aristotle's view: the virtues co-function.

According to my reconstruction of the Functional Unity of the Virtues, the relation of co-functioning among the virtues takes two forms. One relation of co-functioning obtains when virtues interact

---

[10] The idea that the virtues 'function' is suggested by Aristotle's discussion of virtue in the function argument as well as by other relevant passages in the *EE*. At *EE* II 1218b38–a1, Aristotle defines virtue as a state, disposition, or capacity of what has a function or a use. He explicitly says that virtues have functions (1219a27–8) and that there is an activity (*energeia*) of a given virtue (1219a31–3). Cf. 1219a6–7; 1220a7–8, 1220a30–32; *EE* V = *NE* VI 1139a16–7; *NE* II 1106a15–7.

and co-function when they are part of other virtues. The second relation of co-functioning holds when virtues fulfil tasks that are useful for the well functioning of other virtues. For example, theoretical *nous* qua part of *sophia* provides the starting points of theoretical thinking fulfilled by *sophia*. In this sense, it co-functions with *sophia* as one of its parts. This exemplifies the first relation. The second relation holds, for example, between *phronêsis* and *sophia*. *Phronêsis* is not a part of *sophia* but fulfils important tasks that benefit the tasks of *sophia*: *phronêsis* commands and prepares the ground for the sake of *sophia*. The virtues achieve their full functionality when they function together.

The second relation of co-functioning is compatible with the idea that some virtues can be possessed without possessing all the virtues. For example, comprehension (*sunesis*) and consideration (*gnôme*) qua virtues on which *phronêsis* depends can be possessed without all the other virtues on which *phronêsis* depends and without *phronêsis*. Some forms of *epistêmê* as well as some forms of expertise (*technê*) can be possessed without all the other virtues. However, when the virtues—let's say when comprehension, consideration, some forms of *epistêmê*, and expertise—are possessed together with all the other virtues, they take up additional functions. For the purpose of this investigation, I set *technê* aside: *technê* is a virtue of thinking and is discussed in *EE* V. However, it is not fundamental for the Functional Unity that I reconstruct. Possessing or lacking *technê* does not affect in fundamental ways the Functional Unity of the Virtues; the virtues can fulfil their full potential and interact in relevant ways even when *technê* is absent.

As they are discussed in the *EE*, some virtues are possessed only together with other virtues: this is the case for *nous*. Practical *nous* provides the starting points of practical thinking and is a virtue on which *phronêsis* depends; theoretical *nous* provides hypotheses and starting points of theoretical thinking and is a part of *sophia*.

In *De Anima* (*DA*), Aristotle says that *nous* is separable which suggests that it can be possessed on its own, outside the UoV.[11] But there is no evidence of *nous* as a self-standing virtue in the *EE*.

There is no direct evidence that *phronêsis* and the virtues on which it depends (practical *nous*, good deliberation, comprehension, consideration, and the character virtues) can be possessed without the virtues of theoretical thinking, which are *sophia* and its parts (theoretical *nous* and *epistêmê*). Even if we concede this, *phronêsis* and the character virtues are somehow defective when they are possessed without the virtues of theoretical thinking. Namely, they do not function in the same way as when they function with the virtues of theoretical thinking. As Aristotle says, *phronêsis* commands for the sake of *sophia*. That is, it prepares the ground for *sophia*. What is more, the highest activity of *sophia*—contemplation of divine objects—is the final cause of the activity of *phronêsis*. In this sense, *phronêsis* and the character virtues are simply not the same virtues when they are possessed without the virtues of theoretical thinking: they do not have the same functions.

Finally, in the *EE*, there is no direct evidence in favour of the possibility of possessing *sophia* and the virtues that are its parts—*epistêmê* and theoretical *nous*—without *phronêsis* and the virtues on which *phronêsis* depends. *Sophia* requires *phronêsis* (as well as the character virtues and the virtues of thinking on which *phronêsis* depends) to function at its best. That is, we are in the best conditions to engage in theoretical activity when our soul is in harmony and all its parts function as they should. These conditions are provided by *phronêsis* and the virtues on which *phronêsis* depends: for this reason, Aristotle says that *phronêsis* commands for the sake of theoretical activity.

---

[11] Cf. *DA* 430a17.

I.3 An on-off unity of the virtues

In developing this reconstruction of the Functional Unity of the Virtues, I situate my proposal vis-à-vis some options. First, as I argue, the Functional Unity of the Virtues that Aristotle develops in the *EE* is not scalar. According to the scalar interpretation of the UoV, agents may have the virtues to greater or lesser degrees. As I show, one may have certain virtues without the other virtues that are part of the Functional Unity of the Virtues. However, the difference between possessing some virtues (without possessing all of them) and possessing all the virtues that are part of the Functional Unity of the Virtues is not a matter of having these virtues to greater or lesser degrees. Rather, virtues that are possessed outside the Functional Unity of the Virtues simply do not function in the same way as when they are possessed as part of the Functional Unity of the Virtues. We may even say that they *are not the same* virtues when they are possessed outside the Functional Unity of the Virtues: they are deficient versions that do not have the same functions as when they are part of the Functional Unity of the Virtues.

Second, the Functional Unity of the Virtues that I propose is not additive, or more precisely, it is not additive in the sense in which this option is often understood. According to the additive construal of the UoV, the activities of the virtues are not modified by the interaction with other virtues. Rather, the thought is that one acquires the virtues separately and one by one. As I show, the additive interpretation is a non-starter. It ignores the interaction and connection among the virtues. Even though I reject the additive option, I speak of Additive Functionality with regard to the version of the UoV that I defend. When the virtues are part of the Functional Unity of the Virtues, they have additional functions that originate from the interaction and co-functioning of the virtues with the other virtues. That is, the Functional Unity of the Virtues admits Additive Functionality in the sense that the virtues acquire new functions from the interaction with other virtues.

Third, as I show, the Functional Unity of the Virtues that Aristotle develops in the *EE* is on-off with respect to Aristotle's most ambitious ideal of excellence. When agents have all the virtues that are parts of the Functional Unity, they have *kalokagathia*. *Kalokagathia* comes about only if a threshold is met.[12] If an agent has all the virtues that are part of the Functional Unity and these virtues interact and co-function in relevant ways, then *kalokagathia* comes about. The *EE*'s best agent, I argue, *has* all the virtues.[13] I propose that the best agent, as Aristotle conceives of this agent in the *EE* is the *kalos kagathos*: the person who possesses the superexcellence of being-beautiful-and-good (*kalokagathia*). The agent who possesses *kalokagathia* possesses the character virtues and all the virtues of practical and theoretical thinking. For this reason, the *kalos kagathos* enjoys happiness as defined at the beginning of the *EE*.[14]

I.4 Some remarks on methodology

Regarding the methodology that I adopt in this book, I focus on the *EE* and conceive of the common books (*EE* IV = *NE* V, *EE* V = *NE* VI, *EE* VI = *NE* VII) as part of the *EE*. My proposal is compatible with the idea that the common books may also be part of the philosophical argument of the *NE*. I reconstruct the philosophical proposal of the *EE* and read the *EE* as a continuous argument. This methodological approach is not pursued in the literature on

---

[12] Cf. chapter 6.
[13] For a discussion of the difference between the *phronimos* and the *kalos kagathos*, see Drefcinski 1996, 139–53; Curzer 2005, 233–56; Sluiter and Rosen 2008; Hoffman 2010; Hursthouse 2011, 38–57; Irwin 2022, 188–207; Wolt 2022, 1–23.
[14] *EE* II 1219a39–40. Relevant Greek terms are often employed in the masculine form; for this reason the transition to feminine or plural forms (as today we often employ in philosophical discussions) can be confusing. Moreover, Aristotle's own views on women and men make it unlikely that he thinks of an account of the best agent as gender neutral. Nevertheless, for the most part I seek to employ gender neutral expressions. And I certainly believe that people of all genders can possess the Functional Unity of the Virtues.

Aristotle's ethics which tends to focus on the *NE*.[15] Scholars often turn to the *EE* to analyse passages or sections of this treatise for the purpose of comparing them with the *NE*. In my reconstruction of the UoV, I aim to clarify (and at times, in minimal ways, to reconstruct) the Greek text as well as to show how the reconstruction of the philosophical proposal of the *EE* can generate new ideas in contemporary debates in ancient philosophy, the history of philosophy more broadly, ethics, philosophy of mind, philosophy of action, moral psychology, and epistemology. Unless I explicitly indicate a departure from it, for *EE* I–III, VII–VIII, I use the Greek text edited by Rowe (2023a), and the line numbers that are used in Rowe's edition. Regarding the relative chronology of the *EE* and the *NE*, I suspend judgement as I do not think that there is enough evidence to argue for the priority of one treatise over the other.[16] For the translation of the *EE*, including the common books, I refer to and modify the translation by Inwood and Woolf (2013). Regarding the other texts by Aristotle that I quote in the book, I indicate in the footnotes whether the translations are mine or by other authors.

I.5 Overview of the chapters

Even though I develop a unified argument throughout the book, the chapters can be read independently (chapter 3 presupposes the argument developed in chapter 2). The introduction of the book orients readers who turn to individual chapters.

In chapter 1, I prepare the ground for the Functional Unity of the Virtues by turning to the *EE*'s psychology: I show that there are four ways in which the parts of the soul are unified. First of all, Aristotle specifies that the soul is divisible only theoretically or in account,

---

[15] One exception is Buddensiek 1999.
[16] On the relative chronology of the two treatises: Jaeger 1948; Gauthier and Jolif 1959; Monan 1968; Dirlmeier 1984; Rowe 1971; Kenny 1978, 2016; Jost 1983; Schofield 2002; Green 2010; Zanatta 2012; Di Basilio 2022.

but de facto is not divisible: that is, there is psychological unity. Second, there is a hierarchical unity of the parts of the soul that corresponds to a hierarchy of the virtues attributed to each part. The part of the soul that possesses reason, and to which the virtues of thinking belong, commands the part of the soul that listens to and obeys reason and to which the virtues of character belong. Third, there is teleological unity insofar as the distinctively human parts of the soul, the virtues that belong to them, and their activities contribute to the final end of theoretical activity. In addition, there is unity among the sub-parts of the part of the soul that has reason: these are the scientific and the calculative sub-parts. These two sub-parts participate in the same activity of *theôrein*, are about processes (*geneseis*), aim at the truth, and can grasp wholes. Fourth, the parts co-function and interact because the soul as a whole has one function that is living: that is, there is functional unity. To argue in favour of this point, I reconstruct the so-called Function Argument that Aristotle offers at the beginning of *EE* II, and I show that it provides evidence in favour of the Functional Unity of the Virtues.

In chapter 2, I show that *phronêsis* is a dependent virtue. I argue that *phronêsis* depends on practical intelligence (*nous*), good deliberation (*euboulia*), comprehension (*sunesis*), and consideration (*gnôme*). *Phronêsis* and the virtues on which it depends (including the virtues of character that I discuss in chapter 3) constitute what I call the unity of the practical virtues. For *phronêsis* to come about, all the virtues on which *phronêsis* depends must be in place and interact in relevant ways. I call this relation Ontological Dependency. I show that *phronêsis* is about the truth (in ways that need to be specified) because the virtues on which it depends are about the truth. I call this relation Truth Dependency. I argue that some of the tasks of *phronêsis* are tasks of the virtues on which it depends. I call this relation Functional Dependency. These three forms of dependency are compatible, on the one hand, with Additive Functionality. On the other hand, they are also compatible with the idea that the tasks of *phronêsis* cannot be reduced to the sum of the tasks of the virtues on which it depends: when the unity of the practical virtues comes about, additional tasks emerge: the commanding task, the transformative task, and the ability to grasp the good as a whole. I show that *phronêsis* has three emerging tasks that are not tasks of the virtues on which it depends. These tasks emerge when all the virtues on which *phronêsis* depends are in place and interact in relevant ways.

In chapter 3, I argue that there is Ontological and Functional Interdependency between *phronêsis* and the virtues of character. I show that the virtues of character are merely natural virtues when they are possessed without *phronêsis* and the virtues of practical thinking on which *phronêsis* depends. Only when agents possess all the virtues of character as well as the virtues of practical thinking on which *phronêsis* depends, they have *phronêsis*. *Phronêsis* and the character virtues cannot fully function unless they are possessed together. Differently from the character virtues, one may have one or some natural virtues without possessing them all. I show that natural virtues are capacities for experiencing affections in a certain way, do not require decision, are by nature, and are not stable. Insofar as character virtues are states and require decision, they must be possessed with practical wisdom. I discuss some challenges that have been moved or that may be moved to the unity of all the character virtues. On the view that I defend, the virtues of character are individuated on the basis of the emotions involved and the types of pleasures and pains, and they are all parts of a unified state of the soul that aims at the *kalon*.[17]

[17] The translation of *kalon* is controversial. Irwin (1985) and Broadie and Rowe (2002) translate 'fine'. Ross (1925) and Crisp (2000) translate 'noble'. According to Konstan (2014), there is a difference between *kallos* and *kalon*. Konstan argues that *kalon* can express physical beauty, but this usage is rare, while *kallos* refers primarily to physical beauty. For the relevant semantic range in Aristotle, see *EE* 1230b21–31a4; *NE* 1123b3–11; *Physics* 246b; *Politics* 1254b38–55a6; *Sophistical Refutations* 164b20–6; *Rhetoric* 1372a12–8. For a discussion of *kalon* in Aristotle, see Monan 1968; Rogers 1993, 355–71; Cooper 1999b, 81–114; Irwin 2010, 381–96; Irwin 2011, 239–53; Kraut 2013, 231–50; Tutuska 2013, 159–79; Crisp 2014, 231–45; Lear 2015, 116–37.

In chapter 4, I argue that *epistêmê* is said in many ways and must be part of the Functional Unity of the Virtues. I distinguish two accounts of *epistêmê* as these are discussed in the *EE*: (i) according to what I call the Understanding Account (UA), *epistêmê* is demonstrative understanding of what is necessary and eternal; (ii) according to what I call the Knowledge Account (KA), *epistêmê* is explanatory knowledge, can be demonstrative as well as nondemonstrative, and its objects are contingent. With the KA, I aim to capture all the many ways in which *epistêmê* is said that do not fall under the UA. A distinction between the UA and the KA clarifies that while we do not need theoretical understanding of the good to act as the good person acts, and relatedly, we do not need demonstrative understanding of the good, explanatory knowledge plays a fundamental role in the practical domain. We need this knowledge for actions and choices. Knowledge/ *epistêmê* that has a role in the practical domain is different from *phronêsis*. I individuate four criteria for acquiring, possessing, and using *epistêmê*—I call them Use Criterion, Nature Criterion, Distortion Criterion, and Teaching Criterion—and I show that these criteria do not apply to *phronêsis*. The two virtues do not function in the same way. *Epistêmê* according to the UA must be included in the Functional Unity of the Virtues insofar as it is part of *sophia*. *Epistêmê* according to the KA must be included in the Functional Unity of the Virtues insofar as explanatory knowledge fulfils important tasks in the practical domain and co-functions with *phronêsis*.

In chapter 5, I develop three arguments—what I call the Inclusion Argument, the Cooperation Argument, and the Teleological Argument—to show that the virtues of theoretical thinking— theoretical *nous*, *epistêmê*, and *sophia*—must be included in the Functional Unity of the Virtues. According to the Inclusion Argument, in order to achieve happiness, we need not only the virtues of character and the virtues of practical thinking, but also the virtues of theoretical thinking. According to the Cooperation Argument, *phronêsis* and the virtues on which it depends accomplish tasks that are fundamental for the virtues of theoretical thinking to fulfil their full potential. That is, when agents have these virtues, their souls are in the best conditions for theoretical activity. What is more, theoretical activity benefits from the activities of the virtues of practical thinking and the virtues of character. According to the Teleological Argument, the virtues of theoretical thinking and their activities are the final cause of the activities of all the other virtues and their activities. The virtues of theoretical thinking and their activities move everything in the soul qua final cause; they are the aim and the beneficiary of the activities of the other virtues. I conclude the chapter by highlighting that there is no evidence that the virtues of theoretical thinking can be possessed without the other virtues that are part of the unity. Even if this is possible, these virtues do not function in the same way when they are part of the Functional Unity of the Virtues and when they function in isolation.

In chapter 6, I argue that Aristotle considers *kalokagathia* a virtue composed by parts and that these parts are all the virtues discussed in the *EE*. I explain that *kalokagathia* is an on-off state: when we have all the virtues and the virtues interact in relevant ways, we have *kalokagathia*. I provide evidence in favour of the idea that *kalokagathia* is the complete virtue that Aristotle refer to (without calling it *kalokagathia*) in the *EE*'s definition of happiness. Qua complete virtue, it must comprise all the virtues discussed in the treatise. Based on the *EE* and relevant passages from the *Physics* and the *Metaphysics*, I develop a set of criteria for virtue's completeness. By reference to the long-standing discussion about inclusive versus dominant readings, I set up the Inclusion Criterion: virtue is complete only if it includes the character virtues and the virtues of thinking. By reference to wholeness as defined in the *Physics* and in the *Metaphysics*, I defend the

Wholeness Criterion: complete virtue must be a whole. Insofar as Aristotle argues that what is complete and whole must have a limit, I propose the Limit Criterion: complete virtue must have a limit. Only *kalokagathia* satisfies all the criteria for being the complete virtue mentioned in the definition of happiness.

1
The unity of the parts of the soul

As Aristotle conceives of it in the *EE*, the soul has parts. As I argue, there are four ways in which the parts of the soul are unified:

- psychological unity (or unity of one soul): the soul is divisible only theoretically or in account but de facto is not divisible;
- hierarchical unity: the parts of the soul are structured in a hierarchy of commanding and subordinated parts;
- teleological unity: the activities of the parts of the soul are for the sake of theoretical activity;
- functional unity: all the parts of the soul contribute to the function of the soul which is living.

In this chapter, I explain what the parts of the soul are and which of these parts are relevant for the unity of the parts of the soul and for the unity of the virtues (UoV) that I defend in the book (section 1.1). I discuss whether it is possible to separate the parts of the soul and explain that the soul is one and de facto not divisible (section 1.2). I show that for Aristotle, there is a hierarchy of the parts of the soul and a teleological unity of the parts of the soul (section 1.3). I argue that the parts of the soul to which the virtues of thinking belong are unified (section 1.4). I show that there is functional unity, namely the soul as a whole has one function (section 1.5). I conclude with a reconstruction and an analysis of the so-called Function Argument (section 1.6).

1.1 The parts of the soul

In *EE* II 1219b30–32, Aristotle says that in the human soul there are two parts that share in reason: one part has reason and another one is able to obey and listen to reason. He further divides the part that has reason into scientific and calculative. Aristotle is interested in the parts of the soul that share in reason insofar as they are properly human. Regarding the irrational parts of the soul, at *EE* II 1219b24, he refers to the perceptual and desiderative parts of the soul. And at *EE* II 1219b39–41, he adds that there is a vegetative part (*phutikon*) of the soul, a nutritive part (*threptikou*), and a generative part (*auxêtikou*), which are not uniquely human.[1] These parts are not uniquely human insofar as other beings have these parts of the soul such as plants and non-human animals. This multiplicity of parts characterizes other works of Aristotle, for example, *DA*. Given this multiplicity of parts of the soul, scholars try to unify the soul via partial physical overlap, teleological subordination, focal meaning, analogy, and so forth.[2] Some scholars conceive of the soul as a set of capacities, others as a unitary nature.[3] Similarly, scholars debate on what the parts of the soul are.[4] According to the standard view, the parts of the soul are capacities.[5] But more recently, scholars offered

---

[1] For a defence of the MSS reading *orektikou* instead of *auxêtikou*, see Sauvé Meyer (forthcoming). *Auxêtikou* is Bonitz's emendation; cf. Rowe 2023b, 27.

[2] For a survey of this discussion, see Frey 2015, 137–60.

[3] Against the view that it is a set of capacities, see Corcilius and Gregoric 2010, 81–119. Cf. *DA* 433b1–4: Aristotle says that if we consider the capacities, the parts of the soul would become many: *threptikon, aisthêtikon, noêtikon, bouleutikon, orektikon*. Leunissen (2010, 49) defines the soul as a 'non-aggregative unity of teleologically organised functions that make the body alive'.

[4] Both in *DA* and in the *EE*, Aristotle does not clarify whether the parts of the soul are capacities, and what the status of the parts is. He calls them capacities (*dunameis*) at *DA* 413a22–b11. And he refers to them as parts (*moria*) at 413b14–5. In the *EE*, at 1219b30–32, he calls them parts, and at 1219b35, he refers to them as capacities (*dunameis*). Leunissen (2010, 51, footnote 10), argues that the terminology *moria-dunameis* should not be taken too literally. She suggests that 'aspects' may be a better translation. Barnes shows that *morion* is used interchangeably with *dunamis* and *archê* (Barnes 1971, quoted by Corcilius and Gregoric 2010, 83).

[5] Cf. Sorabji 1974, 63–89.

persuasive arguments that show that this standard view is not accurate. Corcilius and Gregoric focus on *DA*, and show that all the parts of the soul are capacities, but not all the capacities of the soul are parts.[6] They propose a criterion according to which only those capacities whose definition make no reference to other capacities also count as parts of the soul. According to their view, the nutritive capacity, the perceptual capacity, and the thinking capacity qualify as parts of the soul.[7] These capacities/parts are fundamental insofar as we have to assume their existence to 'provide a satisfactory account of the soul on which the science of living beings will be based'.[8] This proposal connects the parts of the soul to types of life-activity such as nutrition, perception, and thought.[9] Establishing whether the division of the parts of the soul in the *EE* is in line with the one in *DA* exceeds present purposes. However, Corcilius and Gregoric's proposal that only those capacities whose definition does not refer to other capacities are parts of the soul seem to capture also Aristotle's view of the parts of the soul in the *EE*. In other words, the parts of the soul must be distinguishable in account.

At *EE* II 1219b22–23, Aristotle says that the nutritive part of the soul is not part of virtue as a whole: this is because in the context where the passage occurs, Aristotle talks about the function of the human soul and the virtue corresponding to this function. Virtue as a whole includes all the virtues of thinking and all the virtues of character and coincides with *kalokagathia*, or so I argue. The nutritive part is shared also with non-human animals and plants and is not part of *kalokagathia*. For the purpose of my analysis, I focus on

---

[6] Corcilius and Gregoric 2010, 84.
[7] As Corcilius and Gregoric explain, Aristotle considers the locomotive capacity as possible part of the soul, but this capacity is not separable in account albeit being different in account. For this reason, it does not fully qualify as part of the soul.
[8] Corcilius and Gregoric 2010, 113.
[9] For a different account that still rejects the standard view, see Whiting 2002, 141–200. Whiting argues that separability in place is the criterion to individuate the parts of the soul.

the parts of the soul that share in reason. However, I concede that it is not possible to fulfil the function of the human soul and to exercise the virtues if the nutritive part of the soul or the perceptual part do not function well. In this sense, a minimal account of the unity of the parts of the soul—rational and irrational—suffices: namely, there is a unity of the parts insofar as the human soul has a rational part that cannot function without the irrational parts such as the nutritive and perceptual parts.

1.2 Psychological unity

Aristotle specifies that the soul is divisible only theoretically or in account, but de facto is not divisible: that is, there is psychological unity.

> (T1) Since we are looking for human virtue, let us assume that there are two parts of the soul that share in reason (*ta logou metechonta*), but not both share in reason in the same way. One does so by giving commands, the other because it is by nature such as to obey and listen. Let us exclude any part that is nonrational in some other sense. It makes no difference if the soul is or is not divisible into parts; it still has different capacities (*dunameis*), that is, those we have mentioned—just as the convex is not separable in a curve from the concave, nor is the straight from the white. Yet the straight is not white, except incidentally and not in its own substance. Any other part of the soul, if it exists, for example, the vegetative, has been excluded. By contrast, the parts we have mentioned are peculiar to the human soul. Hence the virtues of the nutritive and generative (*auxetikou*) part are not human virtues. For insofar as one is human, reasoning (*logismon*) must inhere, that is, principle of command and action; but reasoning commands not reasoning but desire and affections, so a human soul must have these parts. And just as

good physical condition is composed of the virtues of the parts, so too is the soul's virtue qua end.[10]

First of all, as Aristotle says, the vegetative part (*phutikon*) of the soul is of no interest for his analysis. That is, we should not linger over the irrational parts of the soul.[11] We should focus on the part of the soul that shares in reason, which is divided in the part that commands and the part that obeys and listens (*peithesthai kai akouein*) to reason.[12] As Aristotle explains, this last part is *alogon*—non-rational—in a different way from how the vegetative, nutritive, and generative parts are irrational. This explanation that this part is *alogon* 'in a different way' (*eterôs*) suggests that *alogon* does not refer to the idea that this part of the soul is fully irrational, but indicates that this part of the soul does not possess reason in itself.[13] This is why I translate *alogon* as non-rational when it refers to the part of the soul that obeys and listens to reason. Later on in *EE* II, this part is also characterized as the part that follows reason.[14]

---

[10] *EE* II 1219b29–20a4. At 1219b39–40, I read with Rowe: ἀνθρωπίνης δὲ ψυχῆς τὰ εἰρημένα μόρια ἴδια. At 1219b41–20a1, I read with Rowe: εἰ ἡ ἄνθρωπος, λογισμὸν ἐνεῖναι καὶ ἀρχὴν καὶ πρᾶξιν.

[11] In *EE* II 1219b40–41, Aristotle says that the virtues of the nutritive and generative parts of the soul are not proper of human beings. The manuscripts of the *EE* has 'nutritive and desiderative' parts. Bonitz changed ὀρεκτικοῦ in αὐξητικοῦ. I use 'irrational' for the parts of the soul that we share with animals. I use 'non-rational' for the part of the soul that shares in reason by listening and obeying. The virtues of character belong to this part of the soul.

[12] *EE* II 1219b32. Cf. Sauvé Meyer (forthcoming), who argues that Aristotle employs a *logos*-criterion to demarcate the parts of the soul.

[13] It is called *alogon* at *EE* II 1220a11 and at 1221b31. Aristotle mentions the non-rational part of the soul at *EE* VII 1246b14, as well as at 1246b21–2, where he discusses the idea that *phronêsis* cannot be distorted and that the non-rational part of the soul cannot distort the rational part of the soul. Aristotle refers to *hai alogou hexeis* at 1246b35, which are presumably the virtues of character (Rowe does not accept Susemihl's *tou*, and I agree that there is no need for it). And he mentions the *alogou* part of the soul at *EE* VIII 1249b24–5, where he says that the best *horos* of the soul is being as little aware as possible of this *alogon* part of the soul. Rowe reads *allou*, but I think that *alogou* is more plausible insofar as it is in line with other occurrences in the *EE* where Aristotle refers to the non-rational part of the soul. In any case, even if we read *allou*, the reference is to the non-rational part of the soul. In favour of *allou*, cf. Reeve 2021, note 719.

[14] *EE* II 1220a11.

In T1, Aristotle specifies that his argument does not depend on whether the soul is divisible in parts (*meristê*) or not (*amerês*). He compares the parts of the soul to the convex and the concave in a curve and to the straight and the white in a line.[15] The first example concerning the inseparability of the convex and the concave in a curve illustrates the case in which the parts are not de facto divisible. They are conceptually distinguishable or, in other words, they are only divisible when we give an account or when we talk about them (*tô logô*).[16] Similarly, in any given line, the straight and the white are inseparable (*adiachôriston*). However, the straight is white only by accident. The first example occurs also in the *NE*.[17] The second example seems to suggest that straight and white are two capacities/ *dunameis* of the substance. The concave and the convex are two capacities/*dunameis* of the curve. We cannot separate the concave and the convex in a curve, and in a similar way, the parts of the soul cannot be separated. That is, the soul is not divided *in re*. The division of the soul into parts is a division in account, in the sense that it helps us understand the soul.[18] This suggests that even though we cannot 'pull apart' the parts, we can distinguish them in terms of the accounts we give of them and accordingly, we can distinguish them with respect to what each of them is. And yet, in agents who possess all the parts of the soul, the parts interact and co-function. The parts co-function in the sense that they are exercised together. Ultimately, there are activities such as living that are activities of the whole: the soul. Of course, the activity of living depends on the parts of the soul that a given individual possesses: for example, the activity of living of plants is different from the activity of living of human beings and this is connected to the parts that compose the soul of plants vs. the parts that compose the soul of human beings.

---

[15] *EE* II 1219b35–7.
[16] *NE* I 1102a30–5.
[17] *NE* 1102a31.
[18] See a similar remark at *NE* 1102a30–2.

There are living beings with souls that differ from human souls; as Aristotle conceives of them, plants have the nutritive part of the soul, but they entirely lack the rational part. Aristotle thinks that in human beings, some parts of the soul may fail to work properly. As he argues in *Politics* 1260a5–14, slaves lack the deliberative capacity, and children have not fully developed this capacity yet.[19] The passage at *EE* V = *NE* VI.13 1144b8–9, where Aristotle says that children and beasts can have the natural virtues without *nous*, may be quoted as evidence of the possibility of having only some parts of the soul.[20] The case of *nous* is somehow special, and in *DA*, Aristotle seems to suggest that it is separable. However, there is no direct evidence in favour of this separability in the *EE*. And at 1144b8–9, Aristotle does not seem to refer to the theoretical *nous* that according to *DA*, may be separable. Overall there seem to be little evidence that human beings can entirely lack some parts of the soul. But it seems possible that some parts of the soul may not function well or may not be fully developed as in the case of children, slaves, and women. There can be cases in which agents have all the parts of the soul, but the interaction among the parts is defective as in the case of the akratic agent. At given occasions the akratic agent fails to do what she recognizes as best. In effect, this means that even in agents who are not perfectly virtuous there is some measure of cooperation between the parts of the soul. Again, akratic agents can serve as an illustration. Though they fail to do what reason tells them is best, it is by reason that they determine what is best and they try to have affective attitudes that obey reason. In order to have a well-functioning soul we need to have all the parts that compose an adult fully functioning human soul and the parts should interact

---

[19] On the deliberative capacity of women, see Karbowski 2014, 435–60.

[20] Additional evidence that the parts of the soul are separable along these lines is provided by the difficult claim that *nous* is separable (*NE* 1178a24; *DA* 430a17). I discuss the case of *nous* in chapter 2. In the *EE*, Aristotle may not conceive of *nous* as separable. I am thankful to Larry Jost for pointing out to me the parallelism between the *EE* and *DA* with regard to the expression *holê psuchê*, which is found at *EE* II 1224b26, 28, and in *DA* 402b10, 406b2, 411a30, b15, 27.

in relevant ways. In an analogous fashion, in order to have the UoV, we need to have all the virtues and the virtues should interact in relevant ways.

1.3 Hierarchical and teleological unity

In the soul, there is a hierarchical relation among the irrational parts of the soul and the parts of the soul that share in reason. A similar relation unifies the parts of the soul that share in reason: there is a part that commands and a part that obeys and listens. The virtues of character, as Aristotle points out, belong to the part of the soul that obeys and listens to reason; the virtues of thinking belong to the part of the soul that commands.[21] This hierarchical structure unifies the soul insofar as it shows that the parts of the soul need to work together to achieve a common end and need to rely on one another to fulfil fundamental tasks. For the virtuous person, it is on account of the virtues of thinking that reason lives up to its commanding nature. And it is on account of the virtues of character that the part that can obey and listen in fact obeys and listens to the commands of reason. But even for the person who is not virtuous and for the vicious, there is a hierarchy of the parts of the soul and some level of interaction—albeit not a perfect one—among the parts of the soul that share in reason. Insofar as the virtues belong

---

[21] *EE* II 1220a5–11. Sauvé Meyer (forthcoming) notices that Aristotle does not neatly assign the virtues to one or the other part of the soul in *NE* 1103a3–4. Cf. 1221b27–34. Lorenz (2009, 192) argues that in the corresponding passage in *NE* 1.13, Aristotle does not say that the virtues of character belong to the non-rational part of the soul. Cf. Buddensiek 2022, 45. The idea that the virtues of character belong to the desiderative part of the soul should be ruled out insofar as Aristotle clearly explains that they belong to the part of the soul that shares in reason and that is properly human, while the desiderative part is shared with animals. At 1219b41, Sauvé Meyer (forthcoming) reads *orektikou*. She argues that the part of the soul able to obey and listen to reason is a distinctively human kind of *orektikon*. In the *EE* (cf. 1221a13, 1234a25), Aristotle often refers to the virtues of character in their natural form, as opposed to when they are possessed with *phronêsis*, as *pathê/pathêmata*. Cf. the division of the virtues at *EE* V = *NE* VI 1139a26–30.

to the parts of the soul that share in reason and these parts are unified, also the virtues are unified:

(T2) There are two kinds of virtue, one of character and the other of thought. For we praise not only the just but also the discerning and the expert. We have laid down virtue or its function as praiseworthy; these are not themselves active, but they do have activities. Since the virtues of thought are with reason (*meta logou*), these sorts of virtues belong to the part that has reason (*tou logon echontos*), which is the command-giving part of the soul insofar as it has reason. The virtues of character belong to the nonrational part that by nature follows the part that has reason.[22]

At *EE* II 1220a1–2 and *EE* VIII 1249b7–12, Aristotle says that there is something in the soul that commands and that we must subordinate to it.[23] He explains that this subordination is for the sake of the theoretical capacity/the divine (*theos*).[24] This idea suggests that the parts of the soul are teleologically unified insofar as they all contribute to the final end of theoretical activity.[25] This proposal shares some elements with Leunissen's proposal. According to Leunissen, the higher capacities of the soul contribute to the function of the lower capacities: in this sense, there is teleological subordination. This structure of higher and lower capacities unifies the soul.[26] Leunissen distinguishes two final ends: living and living well. Some capacities or parts of the soul are for living well—for example, higher capacities of thinking—but they contribute also to the aim

---

[22] *EE* II 1220a5–11.
[23] At *EE* II 1220a1, Rowe reads: λογισμὸν ἐνεῖναι καὶ ἀρχὴν καὶ πρᾶξιν. Susemihl reads: ὡς ἀρχὴν καὶ πρᾶξιν. Allen reads: ὄρεξιν instead of πρᾶξιν. I agree with Sauvé Meyer's argument (forthcoming) that there is no need to modify καὶ insofar as both ἀρχὴν and πρᾶξιν are mentioned as properly human at 1222b15–21.
[24] *EE* VIII 1249b7–16. I translate *theos* as 'divine'; see my discussion in chapter 5.
[25] I discuss these passages in more detail in chapter 5.
[26] Leunissen 2010, 59. Johnson argues that the lower capacities function for the sake of the higher capacities (Johnson 2005, 9). He shows that there is teleological subordination but it is bottom-up while Leunissen conceives of it as top-down. Cf. Frey 2015, 144.

of lower capacities which is simply living. Johnson proposes a different teleological view according to which simple capacities are ultimately for the sake of more complex ones.[27] Leunissen's top-down proposal and Johnson's bottom-up proposal develop a line of thought that is central to my argument, namely that all the parts of the soul are unified by being teleologically oriented toward a common final activity.

1.4 Unity of the parts of the soul that possess reason

Aristotle divides the part of the soul that possesses reason in two sub-parts: the calculative part (*logistikon*) and the scientific part (*epitaktikon*).[28] The virtues of thinking and the sub-parts of the soul to which they belong are also unified insofar as they participate in the same activity of *theôrein* and they are all about processes (*geneseis*):

> (T3) When we distinguished the virtues of the soul we said that some were virtues of character and some virtues of thought. We have dealt with the virtues of character; let us now discuss the others, after first saying something about the soul. Earlier, then, it was said that there are two parts of the soul, one rational (*to te logon echon*) and the other non-rational (*alogon*). Now we should make a similar division with regard to the rational part, and let it be postulated that there are two rational parts, one by which we contemplate the kinds of existing things whose starting points cannot be otherwise and the other by which we contemplate things which admit of being otherwise. For corresponding

---

[27] Johnson 2005, 174. Cf. Walker 2018.
[28] In T1, *logismos* refers to the part of the soul to which all the virtues of thinking belong. Aristotle seems to use *logismos*, *logos*, and *logistikon* at times in a broad sense and at times in a more restricted sense.

to things that differ in kind there are also parts of the soul, different in kind, which naturally correspond to each kind of thing, if it really is the case that they have knowledge in accordance with a kind of similarity and suitability. Let one of these be called 'scientific' and the other 'calculative', deliberation and calculation are the same and no one deliberates about things which do not admit of being otherwise. Consequently, the calculative is a single, distinct part of the rational part.[29]

The scientific sub-part is about contemplating things whose principles do not admit of being otherwise. The calculative sub-part is about contemplating things whose principles admit of being otherwise.[30] The virtues of theoretical thinking belong to the scientific sub-part while the virtues of practical thinking belong to the calculative sub-part. Aristotle specifies that these two rational sub-parts are differentiated by the principles of the objects that they contemplate. This reference to the principles is left unexplored in the ethics. A passage in *Parts of the Animals* (*PA* 640a2–5) may help us clarify the matter. Aristotle explains that in the theoretical sciences, the principles are necessary. The necessity of the principles of the theoretical sciences can be hypothetical necessity, for example, in the case of natural sciences, as well as the necessity of what is always or for the most part the case. In *PA* 640a2–5, Aristotle explains that in the natural sciences, we start with what is going to be—health or human being—and not with what is always and by necessity. That is, hypothetical necessity is 'something necessary if some goal is to be attained'.[31] The scientific sub-part of the soul that we employ in theoretical sciences has to do with what is necessary, while the

---

[29] *EE* V = *NE* VI 1138b35–39a15.
[30] Scholars often regard the division between practical and theoretical wisdom as one of the main differences between Aristotle's ethics and Plato's ethics. However, this division is not entirely foreign to Plato's own thought. In *Statesman* 258e, Plato divides knowledge in practical and theoretical.
[31] Cooper 1987, 244.

calculative sub-part has to do with practical science: with the contingent and with human action. However, these sub-parts are more similar and connected than what this initial distinction may suggest. First of all, Aristotle uses the verb *theôrein* for the activity of both parts of the soul.[32] *Theôrein* should be understood in a generic sense of rational activity.[33] The two sub-parts of the soul engage in the same activity: what differentiates them are the principles of the objects and the objects that they contemplate. Second, they are both about *geneseis*—processes. The reference to *geneseis* should be read in connection with the occurrence at 1214a27-9 (*geneseis apo tês dianoias*).[34] That is, the virtues of thinking are about *geneseis* insofar as there are *geneseis* that proceed from thought. Some processes have principles that are necessary and eternal such as the divine; other processes have principles that can be otherwise: we may even say that these are human principles. Principles are substances able to generate different things, processes, and activities. And they can be human and contingent, or eternal and divine.[35] In *EE* II 1223a1-3, Aristotle says that necessary things have necessary starting points, and contingent things have contingent starting points. This division corresponds to the division of the virtues of thinking on the basis of their starting points that we find in T3. In this light, we should read the passage at 1139a8-10. That is, the calculative sub-part of the soul has to do with the truth about objects whose principles are contingent (human). The scientific sub-part of the soul has to do with the truth about objects whose

---

[32] Cf. Aubenque 2014, 56.
[33] Cf. On *theôrein* and *theôria*, see Nightingale 2004; Roochnik 2009; Jirsa 2017; Ward 2021. I discuss this distinction in more detail in chapter 5. Cf. *EE* II 1226b27.
[34] Cf. Dirlmeier 1984, 259.
[35] At 1222b16-17, Aristotle says that all substances (*ousiai*) are principles (*archai*) and they are able to generate (*gennan*). At 1222b23, he refers to *theos* as a principle and to other principles that are necessary and immutable such as the principles in mathematics. At 1248a27, Aristotle refers again to *theos* as what moves everything in the cosmos. At 1222b29, he says that a human being is a principle of movement (movement is a type of *genesis*). In a similar way, at 1139a31, *prohairesis* is called an *archê*: it is a human *archê* and a principle of actions.

principles are necessary (principles of theoretical sciences). Both sub-parts aim at the truth and are able to grasp the whole.[36] Given the fact that they engage with the same activity and they collaborate, the two sub-parts are unified.

1.5 Functional unity of the parts

The so-called Function Argument (*EE*-FA), which Aristotle proposes at *EE* II, brings evidence in favour of what I call the functional unity of the parts of the soul. According to the Function Argument, the soul as a whole has one function or task, and all its parts contribute to it in fundamental ways. The Greek word that is usually translated as function is *ergon*. The Greek term conveys the idea that the *ergon* of something is its job, or its task. In other words, it is what something does when it is active in its characteristic and distinctive fashion. 'Function' is not an ideal translation of *ergon*. At the worst, it may suggest that human beings have a function in such a way that someone is using us for something; this idea must be set aside explicitly.[37] However, to translate *ergon* differently would ultimately be confusing, simply because 'function' as a translation of *ergon* is very well established.

Frey provides a persuasive argument for the unity of the soul: he argues that the soul is a natural unity that is the beginning and the end of its natural movement of living.[38] His argument focuses on Aristotle's notion of the soul in *De Anima* and in the biological works. It develops the notion of natural continuity: both mixtures and living organisms possess natural continuity. Frey defines

---

[36] At *EE* V = *NE* VI 1140a27–8, Aristotle says that practical wisdom does not deliberate about the good part by part (*kata meros*), but it deliberates about the good that is conducive to the good life as a whole (*holôs*). Aristotle stresses that the practically wise person knows the particular as well as the universal (1141b14). Cf. Aubenque 2014, 57.
[37] See Hardie 1968, 23.
[38] Cf. Frey 2022, 88–103.

'natural continuity' as the capacity of a thing to have in its own one right movement. As Frey points out, in *Metaphysics* 1016a5, Aristotle shows that being continuous (*sunechês*) is one of the ways to be one. Mixtures are one and they are continuous insofar as they have a unitary nature and they are principles and ends of their natural movement. In a similar sense, the soul has a unitary nature and natural continuity. More specifically, as Aristotle explains in *DA*, the human soul has an activity or function that is living. In *DA* 411b1–10, Aristotle asks precisely whether living (*zên*) must be attributed to the entire soul or only to some parts. According to the *EE*-FA, living is the function of the soul as a whole.[39]

The *EE*-FA has been reconstructed by Hutchinson, Woods, Simpson, and more recently by Lee.[40] There is some consensus on the idea that the argument starts at *EE* II 1218b31 and ends at 1219a40 with the definition of happiness. However, some scholars argue that it continues until 1220a4, and that it includes the division of the soul in parts.[41] Woods points out that there is what he calls a Subsidiary Argument that runs from 1219a18 to 1219a28.[42] This argument leads to the first conclusion of the FA at 1219a28–29, and it is embedded in the main argument although distinct from the rest. Simpson argues that the *EE*-FA has all the premises necessary to derive the conclusion, but they are not brought together in an explicit or implicit way. He calls the argument a 'proof of happiness'.[43] What seems to be agreed upon and what emerges also from my reconstruction is that not all the premises are then used in the argument. Here is my reconstruction of the argument:

---

[39] *EE* II 1219a25.
[40] Hutchinson 1986, 39–45; Woods 1992, 83–8; Simpson 2013a, 233–7; Lee 2022, 191–214.
[41] Hutchinson 1986, 43–51. See the discussion in Buddensiek 2022, 35. Buddensiek does not think that we should include as part of the argument the section on the parts of the soul.
[42] Woods 1992, 83–8.
[43] Simpson 2013a, 237.

First set of premises:

1. Among goods, some are internal and some are external to the soul (premise).
2. Goods internal to the soul are better than external goods (premise).
3. Among goods in the soul, there are states, capacities, activities, and movements (premise).

Virtue and function:

4. If something has a use and a function, the virtue is its best state (by induction or *epagôgê*). For example, there is a function and a use of the cloak, the virtue of the cloak is its best state.
5. By analogy with other things, also the soul has a function.
6. Virtue is the best state of the soul (from 4 and 5).
7. The best state has also a best function (premise).
8. Function is the end (*telos*) (premise).
9. The end is best qua end (premise).
10. Therefore the function qua end is better than the state (from 8 and 9).

Function of the soul and of its virtue:

11. Some things have a use which is distinct from the function (e.g. architecture, medicine). Other things have a function which is the same as the use (e.g. seeing, mathematical knowledge) (premise).
12. When the function is the use of something, the use is better than the state of something (from 10 and 11).
13. The function of something is the same as the function of its virtue (by induction).
14. The function of the virtue is an excellent version of the function of something (e.g. the function of the virtue of shoemaking is making excellent shoes) (from 4).

15. The function of the soul is to make something alive (premise).
16. The use of living is being awake; being asleep is some sort of inactivity (premise).
17. The function of the soul and the function of its virtue must be the same (from 13).

Happiness is the function of the virtue of the soul:

18. The function of the soul qua living is an activity (from 11).
19. The function of the virtue of the soul is excellent living (from 14, 15, and 17).
20. The function of the virtue of the soul is happiness. Happiness is the final good (*teleon agathon*) (from 2, 4, 7, 8, 9, and 19) (first conclusion based on the notion of function).[44]

Happiness is the best thing of the soul:

21. Activities are better than states and dispositions (from 12, provided that use is understood as synonymous with activity).
22. The best activity belongs to the best state (from 7, with the same proviso as in 21).
23. The activity of virtue is better than virtue (from 10).
24. The activity of the soul's virtue is the best thing (from 21, 22, and 23).
25. The activity of the soul's virtue is happiness (premise).

---

[44] This is often considered Part 1 of the FA. I translate *teleon* as 'final' to stress the connection with the step in the argument where Aristotle says that functions are ends. In 27–31, I translate *teleia* as 'complete' because in this section of the argument Aristotle focuses on the idea that virtue has all its parts. This notion is fundamental for Aristotle's remark in *EE* VIII.3 that complete virtue is *kalokagathia*: the virtue composed by all the other virtues. Lee (2022, 191–214) makes a similar choice and translates *teleon* both as 'final' and as 'complete'.

26. Happiness is the best thing of the soul (from 24 and 25) (second conclusion based on the notion of activity).[45]

Happiness is activity of complete virtue in a complete life:

27. Happiness is complete (premise).
28. Activity of something complete is complete (premise).
29. Activity of something incomplete is incomplete (premise).
30. Happiness is activity of complete virtue (from 25, 27, and 28).
31. Happiness is activity of complete virtue in a complete life (from 27 and 30) (third conclusion based on the notion of completeness).[46]

I offer a detailed discussion of this reconstruction in the next section. For the moment, it is sufficient to stress that the *EE*-FA provides evidence in favour of the unity of the parts of the soul insofar as it shows that Aristotle conceives of the soul as a whole, with its own virtue and function. What is more, in the *EE*-FA, Aristotle speaks of the virtue of the soul in the singular: as I interpret it, this virtue is the complete virtue mentioned in the conclusion of the argument (31), which is a whole that has all the other virtues as parts. The *EE*-FA is fundamental for the argument that I develop in the book insofar as it leads to the definition of happiness which is the final good/best thing of the soul. In the final definition of happiness (31), Aristotle provides the connection between happiness, which is the best fulfilment of the function of the soul, and complete virtue, which I understand as *kalokagathia* (which is explicitly mentioned only at *EE* VIII 1248b12). Happiness cannot come about without complete virtue, which on its turn, as I show in the

---

[45] This is often considered Part 2 of the FA.
[46] This is often considered Part 3 of the FA. The *EE*-FA does not provide reasons why happiness is activity of a complete life. For a discussion of the notion of complete life in the *EE*, see Vinje 2023.

book, includes all the virtues. In this sense, already in the definition of happiness we have the UoV.

1.6 Function and activity in the Function Argument

Aristotle begins the Function Argument with a distinction among different goods. He distinguishes goods in internal and external to the soul. In a similar way, Aristotle distinguishes states, capacities, activities, and movements. Throughout the FA, he says that the activity (*energeia*) and the function (*ergon*) of something is better than its disposition (*diathesis*) and state (*hexis*). This is important for the second conclusion of the argument—as I call it—that happiness is the best thing of the soul insofar as it is the best activity of the virtue of the soul and the best fulfilment of the function/*telos* of the soul. In a recent contribution, Lee argues that in the *EE*, Aristotle derives the definition of happiness without recurring to the problematic notion of function.[47] As I show in my reconstruction, both the notion of function and the notion of activity are necessary for Aristotle to establish (i) that happiness is the final good (*teleon agathon*) (20), (ii) that is the best thing (*to ariston*) of the soul (26), and (iii) that is activity of complete virtue (31). More precisely, as my reconstruction shows, the notion of function is necessary to conclude that happiness is the final good (20); the notion of activity is connected with that of function and is necessary to conclude that happiness is the best thing of the soul (26).[48] And together the

---

[47] In his reconstruction of the argument, Lee (2022, 191–214) shows that Aristotle proceeds via divisions. According to Lee, the definition of happiness of the *EE* is based on the division of goods and on the idea that some goods are better than others. For Lee, completeness is necessary to identify an indivisible species that individuates happiness.
[48] Buddensiek (2022, 38) says that the notion of *ergon* is responsible for the notion of *energeia* and that *ergon* 'has a share in accounting for the goodness of the *ariston prakton*'. In the *EE*-FA, Aristotle uses the notion of function and the notion of activity interchangeably as it is clear from my reconstruction. Some steps of the argument

notion of function and the notion of activity are necessary to conclude that happiness is activity according to complete virtue (31). At the beginning of the FA, Aristotle introduces right away the definition of virtue. At *EE* II 1218b38–19a1, he says that virtue is the best disposition, state, or capacity of what has a use or a function. Differently from what happens in *NE* 1105b25, where Aristotle says clearly that virtue is a state (*hexis*), this definition of virtue does not establish whether virtue is a state, a disposition, or a capacity. However, later in the FA and in the text, Aristotle often refers to virtue as a state.[49] He introduces the premise that best states have also best functions. Aristotle says that functions are better than states because they are ends. According to this distinction, functions are better than virtues which are states. In the Function Argument in the *Nicomachean Ethics* (*NE*-FA), we do not find any reference to the idea that functions are ends.[50] Buddensiek argues that the Eudemian specification that functions are ends (*teloi*) is necessary for Aristotle to argue that happiness is the highest practical good (*ariston prakton*) and that is better than virtue insofar as virtue is a state.[51] In agreement with Buddensiek, I think that specifying that happiness is a function and an end allows Aristotle

concerning function are necessary to derive conclusions about activity. However, we cannot conclude that happiness is the best activity simply via the notion of function.

[49] In *EE* II 1222a11, virtues of character are called *mesotêta*. In the final definition of virtue offered at 1227b6–7, virtue is a state (*hexis*). Cf. 1220b29, 1222a6.
[50] See *NE* 1097b22–98a18.
[51] Buddensiek 2022, 38. Buddensiek shows that the *EE*-FA is compatible with weakly founded inclusivism, as he calls it. This is the idea that all the parts of the soul, their virtues, and their activities should be included in happiness. Buddensiek explains that Aristotle is preoccupied with the idea that all the parts of the soul that are properly human, including the part of the soul that listens to and obeys reason and to which the virtues of character belong, should be included in the activity of happiness. This preoccupation explains why Aristotle does not specify in the *EE*-FA what the constitutive activity of happiness is. I think that the theory of mutual entailment according to which practical wisdom cannot occur without the virtues of character shows that the part of the soul to which the virtues of character belong is involved in the activity of reason. But since at the beginning of *EE* II, Aristotle has not referred to or explained yet the theory of mutual entailment, I find Buddensiek's explanation compelling.

to establish that it is better than virtue. This step is essential to derive the conclusion that happiness is the final good (20).

Aristotle says that artefacts have functions and virtues. The virtue of an artefact is its best state.[52] Aristotle uses the example of the cloak to explain this point: the cloak has a function or a use. Let's say that it has the function to cover or to keep warm. An excellent cloak—that is, a cloak that possesses virtue—is in the best state to exercise its function. An excellent cloak covers and keeps one warm. Differently from the *NE*-FA, in the *EE*-FA, Aristotle compares the function of the human soul to artefacts. In the *NE*-FA, Aristotle shows via an analogy with other things and subsequently with an elimination argument that the function of human beings is reasoning.[53] He starts out with an analogy: for a flute-player, a sculptor, a craftsman, and anyone who has some characteristic function or activity, the good resides in the function.[54] In a move that scholars have called rhetorical, Aristotle says that the same must apply to human beings—or else we are by nature 'do-nothings', a thought that comes across as absurd.[55] In the *NE*-FA,

---

[52] Not only do objects and individuals have functions, but processes and activities have functions as well. Happiness is the best activity and the best function for human beings. Aristotle distinguishes two types of functions in relation to processes and activities. Processes have an end-product. Conversely, activities do not have an end-product. The function is the end-product of the process, such as the house in the case of building, or health in the case of medicine. In the case of an activity, the activity itself is its function, such as seeing in the case of sight or studying in the case of mathematical knowledge.

[53] In the *NE*-Function Argument, Aristotle talks of human beings rather than of their soul, as he does in the *EE*. This difference is at times taken to suggest that in the *NE*, Aristotle considers what constitutes a human being as a whole, which is the compound of body and soul. Alternatively, the notion of human being is here used in the sense of synecdoche, where the whole is mentioned, while only a part of it is actually invoked. That is, though Aristotle speaks of human being, he is concerned with the human soul. As I see it, the *EE*'s focus on the soul as a whole stresses the unity of the parts of the soul. On use and function employed as synonyms, cf. *Metaphysics* 1050a22–24; Beere 2009, ch. 13.

[54] Irwin calls this move analogical; see Irwin 1988b.

[55] Nussbaum (1988a, 145–84) argues that for Aristotle parts of the body and parts of the soul have functions, but there is no function of the whole. Broadie says that an inductive argument from the examples of the flute-player and so forth would be weak; see Broadie and Rowe 2002, 35. Cf. Kraut 1979, 467–78; Whiting 1988, 33–48; Achtenberg 1991, 59–72; Lawrence 2006, 37–57; Barney 2008, 293–322; Korsgaard 2008, ch. 2.4.

Aristotle rules out living as possible function of human beings insofar as it is shared by plants and animals. He proposes an isolation argument: he aims to distinguish the function of human beings from the rest. Namely, he wants to find the distinctive (*idion*) function of human beings. This is not a concern for the Aristotle of the *EE*, who does not aim to find a distinctive function of the human soul.

Aristotle explains that certain things have a function and a use, and that the two are distinct (11). For other things, the function coincides with the use. He employs the following examples: the use of the builder's expertise is building, and its function is a house; the use of medicine is healing, and its function is health. And yet, there are things for which the use is the function. The examples are sight whose function/use is seeing, and mathematical knowledge whose function/use is studying. Use translates the Greek *chrêsis*.[56] Aristotle employs examples of *energeiai* as cases in which the function is the use.[57] This is preparatory for (25), where Aristotle says that happiness is an activity. What emerges from the FA regarding the activity of the soul is in line with *Metaphysics* 1050a23–b2, where Aristotle says that the soul has an activity/use that is living. In the context of the *Metaphysics*, this remark concludes a discussion of why *energeia* is prior to *dunamis*. Aristotle distinguishes the product which is the end of a process from the activity (*energeia*) which is the end of an activity. That is, for activities, there is no

---

[56] In his commentary on the *EE*, Woods (1992) argues that *chrêsis* has to be understood as synonymous with activity. According to Woods, insofar as Aristotle shows that living a life means employing capacities, the notion of use should be understood along the lines of Aristotle's notion of *energeia*. The notion of use has an important role in debates in the Academy. In particular, the distinction between possessing something—function, capacities, virtues, goods—and actually using it is standardly invoked. In *Republic* 335d, Plato says that what is used well benefits us; the same idea is found in the *Meno*. In *Meno* 88a–c, Plato says that goods and virtues are good only if used in the correct way. He then specifies that they are good when they are used with *phronêsis*. In *Euthydemus* 278e3–81e, and in *Clitophon* 408b, Plato says that it is not enough to possess things, but we need to know how to use them in order for them to benefit us.

[57] This is why Woods (1992, 89) says that the use of a capacity that has no purpose beyond its use is called an activity.

end external to the activity itself; the activity is its own end. To illustrate this point in the *Metaphysics*, Aristotle uses the examples of building and sight that we find also in the *EE*-FA. The activity (*energeia*) and use (*chrêsis*) of the soul is living and happiness is considered the best fulfilment of the function.

At (13) Aristotle explains that the function of something coincides with the function of its virtue. The function of the soul and the function of the virtue of the soul must be the same in substance—living—but different in quality. The virtue of the soul allows the soul to fulfil the function at the best, namely, it allows the soul to live the best life which is happiness. As it is presented, the function of the soul is very basic: it is simply living. Aristotle says that there is a use (*chrêsis*) of the soul which is being awake.[58]

> (T4) Let the function of the soul be to make a thing be alive and let the function of being alive be a using that is being awake—sleep is a kind of idleness and rest. Hence, given that the function of the soul and of its virtue must be one and the same thing, its virtue's function would be an excellent life. This, then, is the complete good, which is what happiness is.[59]

Sleep is said to be some sort of idleness and rest.[60] On the reading that I defend, in T4, we do not have a reduplication of the function—that is, it is not the case that there is a function of the soul which is living and a function/use of living that is being

---

[58] *EE* II 1219a25; I follow Rowe (2023) in retaining the MSS τοῦ which refers to ζῆν. Woods proposes to emendate the MSS: he translates 'but that is an employment and a waking state'. He argues that only if we understand the passage in this way, we have the premise that we need, namely that the function is the use. I agree with Rowe that the emendation is not needed and that it is clear from the argument that function and use are employed interchangeably. This reading is shared by Lee (2022, 191-214) who proposes to read the τοῦ δὲ as demonstrative: 'the function of living which is a use and being awake'. As I see it, the specification of the use as 'being awake' clarifies that what matters is what we do when we are awake and not what we do when we are alive but asleep.
[59] *EE* II 1219a24-9.
[60] Cf. *EE* II 1219a26; 1219b20-1.

awake. Rather, the specification that there is a use that is being awake stresses the importance of being active. In *EE* II 1219b9–11, Aristotle clarifies that what matters is the actuality rather than the potentiality. That is, he says that praise is given for virtuous actions (*erga*). Aristotle explains that we praise those who actually win and not those who only have the capacity to win. What is more, good people are not different from bad people when they are asleep.[61] These clarifications suggest that specifying that the function is a use which is being awake is not redundant and does not reduplicate the function. This step is indeed fundamental insofar as it distinguishes the function of the soul, that is, living—which is fulfilled even during sleep and when we do not act—and an active use of the function which involves activity and requires that we are awake. This specification is necessary to derive the conclusion that happiness is the best thing of the soul insofar as it is activity (26). While this is compatible with the idea that the happy agent is happy even during sleep, it is not because of what this agent does during sleep that she is happy. Conversely, for happiness it matters what the agent does when she is awake.

Aristotle connects living with being awake not only in the *EE*, but also in *DA* 412a24, where he says that having a soul involves being able to be awake or asleep. However, the capacity of being awake or asleep is not necessary in order to have a soul insofar as plants do not have this capacity and yet, they have a soul.[62] In *DA* 412a25, Aristotle says that being awake is analogous to contemplation (*theôrein*), while sleeping is analogous to the possession of knowledge without its use.[63] The comparison between the discussions of being awake versus being asleep in *DA* and in the *EE*-FA highlights

---

[61] *EE* II 1219b19–20.
[62] In *DA* 412a14–5, Aristotle defines life as the power of self-nourishment and of independent growth and decay.
[63] The example of contemplation is a standard example used in the Academy to clarify that there is a distinction between the possession and the use of knowledge. Cf. Broadie and Rowe 2002, 389.

that it is not enough to have a capacity in potentiality in order to fully have it, but it is necessary to bring it to actuality by using it.

As (25) and (26) show, the notion of activity is fundamental to conclude that happiness is the best thing of the soul insofar as it is activity of the soul's virtue and activity/function of what is best is best. Aristotle uses the results of (20) and (26) to conclude that happiness is activity of complete virtue insofar as activity of something incomplete must be incomplete (31). There is no justification in the FA of why happiness must be activity in a complete life.[64] As I see it, Aristotle employs the double meaning of *teleion*. In the case of virtue, he refers to a virtue that is complete which I interpret as *kalokagathia*, the virtue that has all the other virtues as parts and that is explicitly mentioned only at 1248b12. But in the case of life, he refers to a life that is complete in the sense of directed teleologically toward its natural end, which is theoretical activity.[65] Right after the conclusion of the FA, Aristotle comes back to the notions of activity and use:

> (T5) That we formulate well the genus and definition of happiness is supported by views that we all hold: (a) doing well and living well are the same as being happy; (b) each of these, both life and action, is a use and an activity (*chrêsis esti kai energeia*), since a practical life is a life of use (*hê praktikê chrêstikê estin*)—the smith makes a bridle, the rider uses it.[66]

In this passage, Aristotle endorses views that people hold: first of all, he says that being happy is doing and living well. Second, he adds that life and action are a use and an activity. A life that is active rather than inactive involves using things (e.g. virtues and goods) and being awake. Only if we are awake and active can we engage

---

[64] On *teleion* in relation to life, see Vinje 2023.
[65] I discuss this in detail in chapter 6. On complete virtue, cf. Bonasio 2022, 172–88.
[66] *EE* II 1219a41–b5.

in those activities such as virtuous activity and contemplation that constitute happiness.[67] T5 specifies that happiness is doing well (*eu prattein*).[68] This clarifies that happiness is the highest practical good for human beings.

The EE-FA raises difficulties in relation, for example, to the many premises that Aristotle offers and to the soundness of the argument—some of these problems, as scholars discuss, affect also the NE-FA. What matters for present purposes is that Aristotle speaks about the function and activity of the soul as a whole.[69] In this sense, the FA provides evidence of what I call Functional Unity of the parts of the soul: that is, the soul as a whole has one function—living—and one best function—excellent living or happiness. All the parts of the soul contribute to this one and best function. The Functional Unity of the parts of the soul is not confined to excellent agents who achieve the best function. The souls of agents who are not excellent fulfil the function of living even though not excellently. That is, there is Functional Unity of the parts of the soul for excellent agents as well as for non-excellent agents.

1.7 Conclusions

In this chapter, I laid out a preliminary step to the UoV that I defend in the book. That is, I argued that the parts of the soul are unified in four ways. I explained that there is psychological unity, hierarchical unity, teleological unity, and functional unity. I showed that

---

[67] One may argue that gods are happy and that non-human animals may display some kind of virtuous behaviour. However, as Aristotle defines happiness and virtuous activity, they are distinctively human.
[68] Cf. *EE* II 1219b1-3. The idea that happiness is a use occurs also in other Aristotelian treatises, but only in the *EE*, this idea is developed via the FA. In *NE* 1098b32, Aristotle says that it makes a difference whether happiness resides in possessing or in using virtue. Cf. *Politics* 1332a9; *Magna Moralia* 1208a9.
[69] Sedley argues in favour of a similar point with reference to Plato's *Republic*. He shows that virtue is attributed to the whole (Sedley 2014, 78–90).

the soul is not de facto divided. The parts of the soul have a hierarchical structure characterized by a part that commands and a part that obeys and listens. All the parts of the soul that share in reason aim at the same end. Aristotle divides the parts of the soul that are uniquely human in a part that has reason and a part that does not have reason, but is able to obey and listen to reason. I argued that these parts are unified. And I explained that even their sub-parts—the calculative and the scientific sub-parts—are unified insofar as these sub-parts engage in *theôrein*, aim at the truth, grasp the whole, and their objects are processes.

In the second part of the chapter, I turned to the Functional Unity and to the reconstruction and analysis of the Function Argument. I argued that the parts of the soul are unified insofar as the soul as a whole has one function, that is, living. As this chapter shows, the four ways of unifying the soul that I individuated stress that the soul should be conceived as a unity: insofar as the virtues correspond to the parts of the soul, they are also unified. This last unity is what I turn to in the rest of the book.

2
Phronêsis and the virtues of practical thinking

Phronêsis is the most widely discussed Aristotelian virtue. Scholars argue that practical wisdom, as I render the Greek *phronêsis*, is the virtue of the good or best agent.[1] In defending their view, they often focus on the relation between *phronêsis* and the virtues of character. I agree with the traditional view that *phronêsis* has a special relation with the virtues of character. On the view that I defend throughout the book, I conceive of the relation between *phronêsis* and the virtues of character in terms of interdependency (I discuss this in chapter 3). In addition, I argue that *phronêsis* depends on four virtues of thinking: practical intelligence (*nous*), good deliberation (*euboulia*), comprehension (*sunesis*), and consideration (*gnômê*). I call practical intelligence, good deliberation, comprehension, and consideration 'virtues of practical thinking'.[2] The dependence between *phronêsis* and the virtues of practical thinking is the focus of this chapter. In this chapter and in chapter 3, I show that there is a unity of the practical virtues which is constituted by the character virtues, *phronêsis*, and the virtues of practical thinking.

---

[1] For the view that the best agent of the *NE* is the *phronimos*, see Cooper 1975; McDowell 1979, 121–43; Woods 1986, 145–66; Wiggins 1988, 237; Reeve 1992. In Bonasio (2020, 27–57), I argue that the *kalos kagathos* is the best agent of the *EE*. Wolt seems to agree with this view (Wolt 2022, 1–23). According to the view that I defend, the *kalos kagathos* has *phronêsis* as well as all the other virtues of Aristotle's ethics. I disagree with Wolt's view that in the *EE*, *phronêsis* is about choosing things that are good by nature, and that in the *NE*, *phronêsis* takes up the role of *kalokagathia*.

[2] *Technê* is a virtue of practical thinking, but it is not a virtue on which *phronêsis* depends. *Nous* can be practical or theoretical: *phronêsis* depends on practical *nous*, while theoretical *nous* is included as part of *sophia*.

The unity of the practical virtues is included in the full unity of the virtues (UoV) that I call Functional Unity.[3] The unity of the practical virtues differs from the full UoV insofar as it does not include the virtues of theoretical thinking.

For *phronêsis* to come about, all the virtues on which *phronêsis* depends must be in place and interact in relevant ways. I call this relation Ontological Dependency. I argue that this dependency is incompletely conceived if the relation between one particular virtue and *phronêsis* is studied in isolation. Rather, in order to understand in which sense *phronêsis* is a dependent virtue we should focus on the relation between *phronêsis* and all the virtues on which it depends. In detailing this dependency, I show that *phronêsis* is about the truth (in ways that need to be specified) because the virtues of practical thinking on which it depends are about the truth. The virtues of practical thinking on which *phronêsis* depends grasp the truth, contribute to relevant steps to grasp the truth, or are states of correctness, as Aristotle calls them. I call this relation Truth Dependency. I argue that some of the tasks of *phronêsis* are tasks of the virtues on which it depends. I call this relation Functional Dependency. However, the virtues on which *phronêsis* depends take up additional tasks when they interact. This is according to the principle of Additive Functionality. For this reason, the tasks of *phronêsis* cannot be reduced to the sum of the tasks of the individual virtues on which it depends: when the unity comes about, additional tasks emerge. I show that *phronêsis* has three emerging tasks that are not tasks of the virtues on which it depends. These tasks emerge when all the individual virtues on which *phronêsis* depends are in place and interact in relevant ways. I call them the commanding task, the transformative task, and the ability to grasp the good as a whole.

---

[3] For a different view, see Russell 2009. Russell argues that the UoV follows from mutual entailment: he argues that since *phronêsis* is inseparable from the virtues and all the virtues require *phronêsis*, then all the virtues must be possessed together. For a discussion of the full unity, see chapter 6.

When scholars discuss the relation between *phronêsis* and the virtues of practical thinking, they often conceive this relation in terms of part/whole. In what follows, I situate my contribution in the debate on whether *phronêsis* has parts. In the argument that I develop in the chapter, I conceive of the relation between *phronêsis* and the virtues of practical thinking in terms of dependency and not in terms of part/whole (section 2.1). I explain the definition of *phronêsis* in the context of my argument that *phronêsis* is a dependent virtue (section 2.2). I show that *phronêsis* is a dependent virtue and discuss how we should understand this dependence (section 2.3). I analyse the virtues of practical thinking on which *phronêsis* depends (section 2.4) and the emerging tasks of *phronêsis* (section 2.5).

2.1 Does *phronêsis* have parts?

The idea that some virtues of thinking are constituents of other virtues has been explored among others by Taylor, Dahl, Russell, Kenny, and Louden.[4] Taylor argues that *phronêsis* is constituted by practical intelligence (*nous*) and good deliberation (*euboulia*).[5] Dahl shows that good deliberation is a part of *phronêsis*.[6] Russell argues that practical wisdom is 'a whole family of skills of practical intellect', including intelligence and the so-called minor virtues of thinking such as good deliberation, comprehension, and consideration.[7] According to Russell, *phronêsis* is more than its parts because

---

[4] Kenny 1978, 2016; 170; Dahl 1984, ch. 3; Louden 1997, 103–18; Russell 2009, 2014, 203–20; Taylor 2016. McDowell argues that *phronêsis* is the outcome of moral education: even though his proposal does not show that *phronêsis* has other virtues as constituents, it is relevant insofar as it shows that *phronêsis* is somehow the result of a process: McDowell 1998, 190. For a recent view that shows that virtues can be part of other virtues, see Karbowski 2019, 159. Karbowski argues that *epistêmê* is a part of *phronêsis*.

[5] Taylor 2016.

[6] Dahl 1984, ch. 3.

[7] Russell 2014, 203–20.

of its all-encompassing conception of the good and of the end.[8] On his view, *phronêsis* comes in degree: that is, one can be more or less practically wise. Kenny argues that there are two main virtues of thinking—*phronêsis* and *sophia*; the other virtues of thinking are parts of them.[9] For Kenny, there is a parallelism between the structure of *phronêsis* and the structure of *sophia*: *phronêsis* is constituted by *nous* (of the end), *logos* understood as *euboulia*, and *nous* (of particulars), while *sophia* is constituted by *nous* (of axioms), *logos* understood as *epistêmê*, and *nous* (of particulars).[10] In this sense, Kenny conceives of *nous* as a constitutive part of *phronêsis*. *Nous* has a double role in relation to *phronêsis*: it provides the starting points of practical thinking and the 'stopping points'.[11] That is, it deals with the major premise of practical thinking that has a reference to the end, and with particulars that need to be grasped via some sort of perception.[12] Kenny argues that the two parts of the rational part of the soul which are the calculative part (*doxastikon* or *logistikon*) and the scientific part (*epistêmonikon*) correspond respectively to *phronêsis* and *sophia*.

Kenny shows that evidence in favour of the idea that *phronêsis* has parts comes from passages in *EE* V = *NE* VI.[13] In *EE* V = *NE* VI 1139a14–5, Aristotle refers to the virtue—in the singular—of the calculative part of the soul (*logistikon*). And in 1140b26, he explains that *phronêsis* is the virtue of the part of the soul that deals with opinion (*doxastikon*). Here *logistikon* and *doxastikon* are two names for the same part of the soul. Yet, *phronêsis* is not the only

---

[8] Cf. *EE* V = *NE* VI 1140a28.
[9] Kenny provides the following passages as evidence in favour of this view: *EE* V = *NE* VI 1139a16, 1140b26, 1143b15–7, 1144a2–3, 1145a4. Cf. Kenny 2016, 172.
[10] Kenny 2016, 171.
[11] Kenny 2016, 171.
[12] Taylor (2016) and Kenny (2016, 173) argue that *phronêsis* is constituted by *nous* plus *euboulia*.
[13] The passages to which I refer in this paragraph are all quoted by Kenny 2016, 166. Cf. Gauthier and Jolif show that Plutarch, Aspasius, and Pseudo-Alexander of Aphrodisia report only two virtues of thinking: *phronêsis* and *sophia*. This interpretation is supported by Prantl and rejected by Zeller (cf. Gauthier and Jolif 1959, 451).

virtue of this part of the soul. Good deliberation, comprehension, and consideration belong to this part of the soul insofar as they concern things whose principles are contingent and changeable rather than necessary and eternal.[14] That is, they cannot belong to the *epistêmonikon* (scientific) part of the soul to which *sophia* and the theoretical virtues belong. Hence, either Aristotle refers mistakenly to *phronêsis* as the only virtue of the *logistikon/doxastikon* part of the soul, or good deliberation, comprehension, and consideration should be conceived as parts of *phronêsis*, or so Kenny argues. As Kenny notices, in his discussion of the two parts of the rational part of the soul, Aristotle refers consistently to two virtues: *phronêsis* and *sophia*.[15] According to Kenny, this speaks in favour of the idea that the other virtues of thinking should be conceived as either parts of *sophia* or of *phronêsis*.

On the view that I defend, and this becomes clear as I develop the overall argument of this book, *phronêsis* and *sophia* are the two main virtues of which the other virtues are either parts (in the case of *sophia* and its parts) or virtues that must be possessed together with *phronêsis* because *phronêsis* depends on them. On their turn, as I argue in chapter 6, *phronêsis* and *sophia* as well as all the virtues, are included as parts of *kalokagathia*. The view that I defend in this chapter agrees with Louden, Kenny, and Russell on the idea that the *phronimos* needs to have *nous*, as well as good deliberation, comprehension, and consideration.[16] However, I conceive of these virtues not as subordinate qualities of *phronêsis*, as Louden suggests, but

---

[14] *Technê* and practical *nous* belong to this part of the soul as well: *technê* has to do with production which is not necessary and eternal. *Nous* belongs to both parts of the soul insofar as it is responsible for the starting points of practical thinking which are not necessary and eternal, but it is also a part of *sophia* which deals with what is necessary and eternal. While Aristotle discusses all the other virtues of thinking in *EE* V, he does not dedicate a section to *nous*, but he refers to it only with reference to the starting points of practical thinking and to the fact that *nous* is a part of *sophia*.
[15] *EE* V = *NE* VI 1143b15–7; 1144a5. As I argue in chapter 1, Aristotle suggests that the soul is not truly divided and that the division of the soul is a way to understand and to study the soul in a more effective way.
[16] This idea appears in the *Epinomis* (976 b–c). The authenticity of the dialogue is controversial; cf. Jaeger 1948.

rather as virtues on which *phronêsis* depends. As I show, *phronêsis* forms a unity with the virtues on which it depends; agents must possess these virtues in order to have *phronêsis*.[17] Of course, this way of conceiving the relation between *phronêsis* and the virtues on which it depends is compatible with the idea that the virtues of practical thinking may be parts of *phronêsis*.

2.2 The definition of *phronêsis*

Aristotle dedicates *EE* V = *NE* VI 1140a24–b30 to the discussion of *phronêsis*.[18] In 1140b5–6, he offers the following definition:

(T1) Practical wisdom is a state of truth, accompanied by reason, practical with regard to what is good and bad for human beings.[19]

I discuss aspects of this definition more extensively throughout the chapter. For the moment, I flag some elements that are relevant for my argument. Aristotle calls *phronêsis* a true state (*hexin alêthê*) at 1140b5. At 1140b20–1, he says that it is a state with true *logos*.[20]

[17] Louden argues that *phronêsis* is constituted by *nous*, as well as by *euboulia*, *sunesis*, and *gnômê*. He calls *euboulia*, *sunesis*, and *gnômê* subordinate qualities of *phronêsis*. Cf. Louden 1997, footnote 8: 'On my reading, *euboulia*, *sunesis*, and *gnômê* are all in principle independent intellectual virtues concerned with conduct. They are subordinate qualities that constitute aspects of *phronêsis*, but in some individuals they may be present independently of *phronêsis*.' As he argues, these virtues constitute stages in the development of *phronêsis*. According to Louden, Aristotle does not explain how to recognize the *phronimos*. By retracing who possesses these virtues we can find the *phronimos*. Louden explores further a line of thought that can be found already in Hardie: namely, that *euboulia*, *sunesis*, and *gnômê* are subordinate qualities of *phronêsis*. Cf. Louden, 1997, 103–18; Hardie, 1968 (quoted by Louden). See also Stewart, 1892, ii 84.

[18] The entire book has often been considered a book about *phronêsis*. Natali (2017) argues that in this book, Aristotle answers the question of what *orthos logos* is. Aristotle's answer is that it is *phronêsis*.

[19] *EE* V = *NE* VI 1140b5–6: ἕξιν ἀληθῆ μετὰ λόγου πρακτικὴν περὶ τὰ ἀνθρώπῳ ἀγαθὰ καὶ κακά.

[20] Aristotle uses a different formulation to describe *technê*: at 1140a10, he calls it a state with true *logos*. Scholars discuss how to explain this difference: Alexander of Aphrodisia describes *phronêsis* as a state with true *logos* (*Metaphysics* 981b25; Comm. in Ar. Graeca,

Virtues of thinking are states (*hexeis*) as the virtues of character. However, while the virtues of character are about feeling pleasure and pain in the things that we ought, the virtues of thinking are about the truth.[21] Even though *phronêsis* is about the truth, the *phronimos* is Aristotle's good agent characterized most of all by good deliberation and virtuous actions. *Phronêsis* has a double nature: it is about good thinking (including deliberation) and it is about being habituated well. On the view that I defend, this double nature of *phronêsis* is due to the virtues on which it depends: it is about good thinking insofar as the virtues on which it depends are virtues of thinking such as practical intelligence, good deliberation, comprehension, and consideration; it is about being habituated to feel pleasure and pain in what we ought insofar as the virtues on which it depends are the virtues of character. In chapter 3, I characterize the relation between *phronêsis* and the virtues of character in terms of interdependency.

Aristotle says that *phronêsis* is accompanied by reason (*meta logou*).[22] He soon specifies that it is not truly accompanied by reason, but it is correct reason (*orthos logos*).[23] *Phronêsis* is not truly accompanied by reason because in that case, we could forget it as we forget certain states (*hexeis*). But we cannot forget *phronêsis*. Even though states are inherently stable, we may forget or lose these states in extreme circumstances. This is widely accepted with respect to the virtues of character, which Aristotle describes as states

---

t.1, 7 quoted by Gauthier and Jolif 1959, 461). Eustrate and Grossateste changed *alêthê* in *alêthous* (*cum ratione vera*), Susemihl changes it in *alêthous* as well.

[21] Cf. *EE* V = *NE* VI 1139b12.

[22] Gauthier and Jolif (1959, 459) point out that the expression *meta logou* is not technical as is common in ordinary language. They argue that we should not assign a technical meaning to it. They refer to Plato's usage of this expression (*Protagoras* 324 b; *Theaetetus* 206 e).

[23] *EE* V = *NE* VI 1144b28–30. The same remark occurs at *EE* II 1220a8–9, where Aristotle says that all the virtues of thinking are accompanied by reason. At 1220a10, he specifies that they belong to the rational part of the soul that is the part that has reason. This parallelism stresses the continuity between *EE* II and *EE* V = *NE* VI.

and thereby stable. *Phronêsis* cannot be forgotten, as Aristotle says. Accordingly, it must be more stable than the virtues of character. On the view that I defend, it has this special kind of stability because it results from the interaction between states that are already stable such as the virtues of character.

As Aristotle explains, *phronêsis* is practical as opposed to demonstrative (*apodeiktikê*) or productive (*praktikê*): *phronêsis* grasps the truth via actions that should lead to the highest good—happiness— rather than via contemplation.[24] It is about the good and the bad for human beings as opposed to the good for the entire cosmos or for other non-human beings.

2.3 *Phronêsis* as a dependent virtue

Suppose that *phronêsis* were not a dependent virtue. In this case, it would be possible to establish the distinctive task of *phronêsis*. This task would set *phronêsis* apart from other virtues such as good deliberation and intelligence.[25] Aristotle suggests that we look at the *phronimos* to establish the task of *phronêsis*.[26] At *EE* V = *NE* VI 1140a31, Aristotle says that the *phronimos* is *bouleutikos*, that is, this agent is an excellent deliberator. Excellence at deliberating seems the distinctive task of *phronêsis*. But at 1142a34–b33, Aristotle says that the virtue of *euboulia* is about excellent deliberation. Hence, *phronêsis* and *euboulia* seem to have the same task. Either *phronêsis* and *euboulia* are one and the same virtue, or the distinctive task of *phronêsis* is not excellent deliberation. We should consider a third option: if *phronêsis* and *euboulia* are two virtues, one could depend

---

[24] On *phronêsis* and contemplation, see *EE* V = *NE* VI 1139a26–7; *EE* II 1226b26–27. Pericles—the paradigmatic *phronimos*—and excellent politicians, who are also examples of *phronimoi*—engage in contemplation: *EE* V = *NE* VI 1140b8–10; *EE* I 1216b38–39. Cf. Gauthier and Jolif 1959, 562.

[25] In *DA* 403a10–1, Aristotle uses a similar method to individuate what is proper and distinctive of the soul.

[26] *EE* V = *NE* VI 1140a24–5.

on the other and they may function together. Either *phronêsis* depends on *euboulia* or the other way around. As some scholars argue, the most distinctive trait of the *phronimos* is having *euboulia*.[27] However, being *phronimos* seems to require more than just *euboulia*. And even though excellent deliberation is what characterizes the *phronimos*, this agent must be good also at other tasks. Let us suppose that it is *phronêsis* that depends on *euboulia* rather than the other way around. References to the *phronimos*—the agent who has *phronêsis*—are undoubtedly more numerous in the *EE* than references to the agent who has *euboulia* (or to the virtue of *euboulia*). Either excellence in deliberation is all that it takes to be *phronimos*, or *phronêsis* depends on good deliberation, as well as on other virtues and their related tasks.[28] However we conceive of the best agent, the *phronimos* is a good agent. For this to hold, the *phronimos* should possess all the virtues to which Aristotle assigns important roles for leading a good life. And these virtues include *euboulia* insofar as there cannot be good action without good deliberation. The idea that the *phronimos* must possess *euboulia* paves the way for the hypothesis that *euboulia* is not the only virtue involved in the tasks of *phronêsis*.

The case of *euboulia* is paradigmatic of a relation that *phronêsis* has with the virtues on which it depends: that is, the virtues on which *phronêsis* depends are required for *phronêsis* to come about. That is, an agent cannot have *phronêsis* unless she has the virtues on which *phronêsis* depends. The agent who does not have *euboulia* cannot possibly be *phronimos* as good deliberation is fundamental for *phronêsis*. In a similar way, one cannot have *phronêsis* unless one has the virtues of character.[29] This is the case for all the virtues on which *phronêsis* depends. In this sense, I speak of dependency and

---

[27] Segvic (2011, 160–86) argues that what makes a person *phronimos* is most of all *euboulia*.
[28] For a different way of conceiving of the relation between the *phronimos* and the *kalos kagathos*, cf. Wolt 2022, 1–23.
[29] *EE* V = *NE* VI 1144b31–4.

of unity of the practical virtues.[30] However, agents may have comprehension, consideration, and practical *nous* without possessing *phronêsis*. This is so because these virtues come in two forms: natural virtues and proper virtues. At 1143b5–9, Aristotle says that we develop comprehension, consideration, and *nous* by nature as we age. For this reason, it is plausible that agents have these virtues in their natural form and lack *phronêsis*, which does not come about by nature and requires practice and habituation. When these virtues are possessed without all the other virtues that form the unity of the practical virtues, they do not have the same tasks. That is, when there is the unity of the practical virtues, these virtues interact and take up additional task: within the unity, they fulfil their full potential as proper virtues.

I explain these three kinds of dependency—Ontological Dependency, Truth Dependency, and Functional Dependency—that are in place between *phronêsis* and the virtues on which it depends together as I discuss the role of the virtues of practical thinking on which *phronêsis* depends. To reiterate: these virtues of practical thinking are practical intelligence, good deliberation, comprehension, and consideration. In terms of priority, the virtues of practical thinking on which *phronêsis* depends are prior to the unity of the practical virtues in the sense that they can be separated and possessed without possessing *phronêsis*. However, *phronêsis* is prior to the virtues on which it depends in the sense that when agents possess *phronêsis* they possess also all the virtues on which it depends.[31] Conceiving of *phronêsis*

---

[30] This relation of dependence is similar to the relation between justice and the other virtues in Plato's *Republic* IV. That is, justice comes about when all these other virtues are in place and depends on them, but at the same time it is more fundamental than the single virtues on which it depends. In the *Laches*, the virtues are parts of a whole unified through *phronêsis*. A similar view is defended in the *Meno*. It is controversial whether in the *Protagoras*, the virtues are parts of a whole. All that I am suggesting is that Plato and Aristotle share an interest in the idea that virtues depend on other virtues and form a unity with them. Cf. Vlastos 1973, 221–69; Devereux 1992, 765–89; Gavray 2014, 39–65; Sedley 2014, 65–91.

[31] Cf. This is in line with different ways of understanding priority as Aristotle outlines them in *Metaphysics* 1028a30–5.

as a dependent virtue sheds light on long-standing debates on what the tasks of *phronêsis* are. For example, scholars debate on whether *phronêsis* is about ends or means. They debate on what it means that *phronêsis* is a true apprehension (*hupolêpsis*) of the end.[32] According to Functional Dependency, Aristotle may say that *phronêsis* is about means to reach a certain end, but in another way, it is also about ends insofar as one or more of the virtues on which it depends are about ends. The practical syllogism is paradigmatic of the relation between *phronêsis* and the virtues on which it depends in the sense that in order to grasp the practical syllogism, agents need to have *phronêsis* and the virtues on which it depends. In this sense, it is not possible to isolate the tasks of each individual virtue insofar as in order to grasp the whole syllogism, the virtues need to interact and additional tasks emerge from this interaction. All the virtues that are part of the unity of the practical virtues are involved in the steps of the practical syllogism and contribute to its being true.

2.4 The virtues of practical thinking on which *phronêsis* depends

My argument that *phronêsis* is a dependent virtue starts from the premise that the most distinctive task of *phronêsis* is the same task of *euboulia*. But insofar as all the tasks of *phronêsis* except what I call the emerging tasks are also tasks of other virtues, we should suppose that *phronêsis* depends on all these other virtues whose tasks are the ones of *phronêsis*.

Evidence that the tasks of practical intelligence, comprehension, and consideration (in addition to good deliberation) are the same ones of *phronêsis* is provided at 1143a25-9. In this passage, Aristotle

---

[32] *EE* V = *NE* VI 1145a5-6; 1142b33. Cf. Gauthier and Jolif 1959, 452.

says that these virtues deal with the same things as *phronêsis*, that is, they deal with final stages and with particulars:

(T2) All these states tend reasonably toward the same thing. For we attribute consideration, comprehension, practical wisdom and intelligence to the same people when we say that they also have consideration and intelligence and that they are practically wise and they have comprehension. For all these capacities deal with the final stages and the particulars.[33]

The passage provides evidence that consideration, comprehension, practical wisdom, and intelligence are connected, but it may be quoted as evidence in favour of one objection to the view that I am defending. Namely, in the passage, Aristotle does not mention good deliberation, which is one of the virtues on which *phronêsis* depends, or so I argue. Good deliberation is also about the final stages and the particulars—as the other virtues mentioned in T2. It seems plausible that the agent who has consideration, comprehension, and practical wisdom has also good deliberation.[34] The context where the passage occurs may offer some possible explanations of why good deliberation does not figure in the list. First, the passage occurs after the accounts of good deliberation, comprehension, and consideration that Aristotle develops at 1142a30–1142b35. Given this progression, Aristotle may give it for granted that good deliberation goes together with practical wisdom. Second, Aristotle introduces the passage in T2 with *legomen*—'we say'.[35] This suggests that in this passage, Aristotle reports what people say rather than his own view. People say that the same agent has *phronêsis*, intelligence, comprehension, and consideration. That is, this is an *endoxon*. Aristotle endorses the *endoxon* by explaining that it is

---

[33] *EE* V = *NE* VI 1143a25–9.
[34] This agent has also the virtues of character. Aristotle has already established that the virtues of character must be possessed with practical wisdom. For this reason, in T2, he does not need to mention the virtues of character.
[35] *EE* V = *NE* VI 1143a26.

reasonable to say that all these virtues tend toward the same thing. Namely, they are unified by the same object and by the same aim. These virtues are about the final stages of practical thinking. And they are about particulars. Of course, in T2, *nous* has to be understood as practical rather than theoretical insofar as theoretical *nous* does not deal with particulars, but with universals. Insofar as it is an *endoxon*, Aristotle may not explain his own view that good deliberation is also about the same things as these virtues. According to this reading, the passage provides evidence that these virtues must be possessed together with *phronêsis*.[36] I now turn to each of the virtues of practical thinking on which *phronêsis* depends starting with practical *nous*.

Scholars debate on what provides the starting points of practical thinking: (i) starting points are provided by habituation; (ii) starting points are acquired via dialectic as they are *endoxa*; (iii) starting points are provided by *nous*.[37] In a way, these three views are compatible as there are starting points of different kinds and are provided in different ways. What matters to assess whether *nous* is a virtue on which *phronêsis* depends is whether (iii) is a plausible view.[38] In favour of this, Aristotle says:[39]

(T3) One who deliberates always does so for the sake of something; there is always some aim that the deliberator has for the attainment of which he targets what is useful. It follows that no

---

[36] Cf. Louden 1997, 102–18.
[37] Cf. in particular *EE* V = *NE* VI 1144a7–8 and *EE* VI = *NE* VII 1151a15–19; the debate is vast, I quote only some positions that have influenced my work: (i) is defended by Greenwood 1909, 43–59; Gauthier and Jolif 1959, 563–78; Hardie 1968, 224–27; Irwin 1975, 569–76; Wiggins 1980, 221–37; Dahl 1984, 30–99; Cooper 1975; Broadie 1994, 217–54; Reeve 1992, 56–66 and 84–7; McDowell 1998, 30–2; Aubenque 2014. The second position (ii) is defended by Irwin 1978, 252–72. The third position (iii) is defended by Burnet 1900, 263, 325; Achtenberg 2002, 124–42; Moss 2011, 153–99 and 2014, 221–41.
[38] One possible objection to my view of conceiving of *nous* as a virtue on which *phronêsis* depends relies on the passage at 1145a4, where one version of the MSS read διὰ τὸ νοῦ μορίου ἀρετὴν εἶναι. Rackham and Natali accept this reading. Another version reads τοῦ instead of τὸ νοῦ. This is the version proposed by Bywater, accepted by Inwood and Woolf, and that I adopt in this chapter.
[39] For pros and cons of (i) and (ii), see Taylor 2016.

one deliberates about the end; that is rather the starting point and hypothesis, just like hypotheses in the theoretical sciences (we discussed these briefly at the beginning, and in detail in the *Analytics*).[40]

The passage touches on a number of controversial issues: scholars debate whether there are two types of *nous* (practical and theoretical) and how these two forms of *nous* function.[41] These issues are too large for present purposes. The important point is that *nous* is fundamental for practical thinking: it concerns the starting points of practical thinking. As in theoretical sciences, *nous* provides the hypotheses, in the practical domain, it provides the starting points. Hypotheses and starting points of deliberation function in similar ways. Hence, it is plausible that *nous* attends to both of them. In T3, Aristotle refers to a discussion in *Posterior Analytics*, which is most likely the passage at 72b18–25.[42] In this passage, Aristotle argues that there is no demonstration of starting points (*archai*). We know them only hypothetically, and we assume that they are true. In the case of starting points of practical thinking, as in the case of theoretical thinking, we assume as hypothesis that the goal is achievable and that is good for us.

Starting points cannot be derived by demonstration, but they need to be grasped as if it were by perception.[43] In *EE* V = *NE* VI 1141a3–8, Aristotle offers an argument by exclusion to show that *nous* is responsible for the starting points. In *Posterior Analytics* 100b5–11, Aristotle says that except *nous* there is nothing more precise (*akribesteron*) than *epistêmê*. *Epistêmê* cannot grasp the starting points: so, it must be *nous* that grasps the starting points of *epistêmê*.[44] At *EE* V = *NE* VI 1141a3–8, Aristotle says that *nous*

---

[40] *EE* II 1227a6–10.
[41] On practical and theoretical *nous*, see *DA* 432b27.
[42] At 1227a6–11, Aristotle refers to a previous discussion. Donini (1999, footnote 123) suggests that the reference may be to 1214b7–9 or to 1226b10–12.
[43] See the comparison between *nous* and sight at *EE* = *NE* VI 1144b10–13.
[44] For the role of *nous* in providing the *archai* of *epistêmê*, see *Posterior Analytics* 88b36 and 100b12.

apprehends the starting points (*archai*) because there is no other virtue that can fulfil this task. The passage occurs right after the discussion of *phronêsis* at 1140a24–b30, and before the discussion of *sophia* that starts at 1141a9. Yet, Aristotle seems to refer to starting points of *epistêmê* as these are mentioned at 1140b34.[45] These starting points cannot be derived by *epistêmê* because the object of *epistêmê* is derived by demonstration, and there is no demonstration of first principles. Starting points cannot be derived by *technê* or by *phronêsis* insofar as their object is what can be otherwise and starting points cannot vary.[46] *Sophia* cannot provide starting points for the same reason for which *epistêmê* cannot provide them. This argument by elimination shows that is *nous* that provides the starting points insofar as none of the other virtues that are always right and that are about the truth can provide the starting points. These passages do not clarify whether *nous* provides not only the starting points of *epistêmê*, but also those of practical thinking, which is my focus in this chapter. Some clarifications on this are provided at 1143a35–b5, where Aristotle says that *nous* is about what is final in both directions, which suggests that is about the end and also about the starting points:[47]

(T4) Intelligence is directed at what is final in both directions, since there is intelligence (and not *logos*) about the primary terms and the final ones. On the one hand, intelligence tracks demonstrations which involve terms that are unchangeable and

---

[45] Broadie calls these *archai* 'explanatory starting points' and 'starting points from which' the demonstration starts. Broadie 2002, 370.

[46] Natali (1999, 504–6) argues that principles can be grasped via induction (1139b31) or via intellectual intuition, as Aristotle says in the passage that I am discussing. Induction is an activity and not a state. Natali argues that there is no conflict between these two ways of grasping the principles. Cf. Karbowski 2019, 156: 'Aristotle repeatedly describes the starting points of deliberation as definitions or statements of essence, i.e. formal causes (*Physics* II.9, 200a34–5; *PA* I.1, 639b14–9; *Metaphysics* VII.7, 1032b15–21).'

[47] Kenny calls it a judgement and argues that this final judgement can be called itself *nous* (Kenny 2016, 171).

primary; on the other hand, it is occupied with action-oriented demonstrations which involve the final stage, the contingent, and the other premise, these being the starting points of that for the sake of which one acts. Universals emerge from particulars, so it is of these that one has to get perception, and this perception is intelligence.[48]

Aristotle says that *nous* knows what is last in both directions. There is *nous* and not *logos* of starting points and of end points.[49] I take it that in the passage, Aristotle is not singling out two kinds of intelligence: one at work in the theoretical domain and another in the practical. Conversely, intelligence is one virtue that realizes its full potential in the practical domain as a virtue on which *phronêsis* depends, and in the theoretical domain as part of *sophia*. In the theoretical domain, *nous* has to do with the first and unchanging principles of demonstrations. In the practical domain, *nous* has to do with what comes last in practical matters which is what can be otherwise and 'the other premise' (of the syllogism).[50] These are the starting points of practical thinking that lead to the end that we aim to achieve.

Scholars debate on what the practical matters mentioned at 1143b3 are: they argue that they are states, premises, demonstrations, or reasoning.[51] They discuss what the other

---

[48] *EE* V = *NE* VI 1143a35–b5. Translators often stress the two types of intelligence. I prefer to render the opposition as 'on the one hand' (*men*) and 'on the other hand' (*de*). Cf. Natali 1999; Inwood and Woolf 2013.

[49] Kenny (2016, 170) argues that there are two practical forms of *nous* that are referred to in this passage, one general and one particular.

[50] The view that there are two forms of *nous* is discussed by Grant (1874). Gauthier and Jolif 1959; Schollmeier 1989, 130–1. Kenny (2016, 170–1) argues that there are four forms of *nous*: universal practical, particular practical, universal theoretical, and particular theoretical.

[51] Eustrace (378, 8) interprets them as states, Burnet (1900, 280) and Irwin (1985, 166) as premises, Rackham (1934, 361) as inferences, Greenwood (1909, 115) and Gauthier and Jolif (1959, 538) as demonstrations, and Tricot (1990, 305) as *logismois* (reasoning). Dirlmeier (1984, 466) and Mazzarelli (1979, 283) interpret them as things that concern action. All these interpretations are quoted by Natali. Natali (1999, 511) seems to endorse this last interpretation. Broadie (2002, 378–9) argues that these

premise mentioned at 1143b4 is.[52] Some interpreters think that Aristotle is referring to induction at 1143b5. What matters for present purposes is that Aristotle says that *nous* has a fundamental role in the practical domain. This role has to do with starting points of practical thinking and with the end points that need to be grasped by *nous* as if it was some sort of perception.[53] Of course, insofar as the virtues of characters must be possessed together with *phronêsis* as I argue in chapter 3, the virtues of character co-function with *nous* in providing the end points.

With regard to the truth, *phronêsis* cannot be a true state without *nous*. That is, *phronêsis* cannot be a true state if the starting points of practical reasoning are false. This point is further elucidated at *EE* VIII.2 1247a27-9. In this passage, *nous* is listed together with nature and with divine protection (*epitropeia*) as possible cause of getting things right.

(T5) If it is necessary that to get things right is by nature or due to intelligence or to some divine protection, and if the other two are not the case, the fortunates would be such by nature.[54]

In this section of the text, Aristotle discusses the role of fortune in a happy life. In particular, he discusses the question of why fortunate people seem to achieve the same results as wise people (1248a35-6). Three things are listed as causes of getting things right: nature,

---

practical matters refer to practical reasoning and that what comes last is the decision and the particular situation.

[52] Natali (1999, 511) suggests that it is the premise that has to do with the particular and with what to do. Broadie (2002, 379) suggests that Aristotle refers to the second premise of deliberation that deals with the particular situation that needs to be grasped by *nous*. Kenny (2016, 171) thinks that it is the major premise that contains the reference to the end.

[53] Kenny argues that what Aristotle says at 1246b14-15 regarding the incontinent person who has *nous* is in line with what he says at 1143b3, that *nous* is perception of the end. That is, the incontinent has *nous* insofar as this agent has a correct conception of the end (Kenny 2016, 173).

[54] *EE* VIII 1247a27-9.

nous, and some kind of divine protection.[55] The passage is part of a section of the *EE*—*EE* VIII.2—that has textual problems and that seem less revised and polished than other sections in the treatise. One may argue that in T5, Aristotle mentions *nous* in a broad sense that refers generically to thinking. However, at *EE* 1246b39, Aristotle refers to *eupragia* which suggests that the discussion concerns getting things right in the practical domain. And in *EE* VIII.2, Aristotle assigns to *nous* the same tasks that he assigns to *nous* as this virtue is described in *EE* V = *NE* VI.[56] At 1248a17–28, Aristotle investigates what the principle of movement in the soul is. And at 1248a28, he concludes that it is *to en hêmin theion*, which is *nous*.[57] Aristotle assigns to *nous* the same role of providing the starting points of practical thinking that he assigns to it in *EE* V = *NE* VI 1143a35–b6. This shows that *nous* fulfils tasks in the practical domain that are fundamental for *phronêsis*. To sum up, there is Ontological, Truth, and Functional Dependency between *nous* and *phronêsis*.

The other virtues of thinking on which *phronêsis* depends are good deliberation, comprehension, and consideration, which are discussed at 1142a33–43a23. They do not appear in the list of the virtues of thinking at 1139b16–7.[58] For this reason, they are often considered by scholars as 'minor' virtues of thinking.[59] In line with this consideration, they are less studied compared to the other

---

[55] This discussion is connected with what Aristotle says at *EE* I 1214a14–25, where he asks whether happiness is due to nature, study, exercise, divine protection, or fortune.

[56] In *EE* II, Aristotle explains that desiring the right thing is not due to one virtue or capacity, but rather it is due to many virtues, capacities, and states working together. Cf. Gabbe 2012, 358–79. On the idea that the role assigned to *nous* in *EE* VIII.2 is in line with the role of practical *nous* as described in *EE* V = *NE* VI, see Rowe 2021, 203–17.

[57] It is called *nous* at 1248a30.

[58] *Sunesis* is mentioned together with *phronêsis* and *sophia* as examples of virtues of thinking at *NE* 1103a4–6.

[59] This idea of 'minor virtues' can be found already in Tricot 1990, 298–302; see also Aubenque 2014, 149. Natali considers these virtues forms of *phronêsis*. He describes them as 'qualità' (qualities) that are the natural basis or *dunameis* from which *phronêsis* develops. Natali thinks that they are inferior forms of correctness that are not yet virtues. He argues that this list of minor virtues may have been originated from popular views (Natali 2017, 125). Cf. Grant 1874, 173; Stewart 1892, 78.

virtues of thinking. The set of virtues of thinking that we find in book V—not only the five virtues considered major virtues of thinking such as *epistêmê*, *technê*, *phronêsis*, *nous*, and *sophia*, but also good deliberation, *eustochia* (sagacity), *agchinoia* (quick mindedness), comprehension, and consideration—was already established before Aristotle.[60] The reduction of this set of virtues to five virtues is probably due to Xenocrates.[61] Aristotle says that *phronêsis*, *nous*, *technê*, *sophia*, and *epistêmê* are the virtues of thinking that aim at the truth and that cannot err. Good deliberation, comprehension, and consideration are not included in this list of five virtues that cannot err. One hypothesis to explain why they are missing from the list is that these virtues have a different epistemic and ethical outlook from the other five virtues that do appear in the list. While the virtues that appear in the list cannot err, good deliberation, comprehension, and consideration are states of truth as the other virtues of thinking, but they lack the infallibility of the five virtues in the list. Aristotle says that they are not forms of *epistêmai* or *doxai*, but they are forms of correctness (*orthotês*). What is more, the five virtues in the list are excellences that can be used for the good or for the bad with the exception of *phronêsis*: *phronêsis* and the virtues of thinking on which it depends—good deliberation, comprehension, and consideration, as well as practical *nous* when it is possessed together with *phronêsis*—cannot be used for the bad.[62]

While Plato connects comprehension and consideration to theoretical thinking and to contemplation, Aristotle refers to these virtues according to their use in common language.[63] According

---

[60] See Gauthier and Jolif 1959, 508; *Definitions* 413d; *On virtues and vices* 1250a30–9 (quoted by Aubenque 2014, 150).
[61] See Aubenque 2014, 150.
[62] At 1142b21–2, Aristotle specifies that *euboulia* is always for something good. At 1143a8, he says that *sunesis* has the same object as *phronêsis*: in this sense, it cannot be for the bad. And at 1143a22, Aristotle says that *gnôme* and *suggnôme* are proper of the decent person (*epieikês*), which suggests that they are for the good. At 1143a23, he specifies that *suggnôme* is about what is decent.
[63] Plato, *Cratylus*, 412a–b, 476 d, 411. See Aubenque 2014, 150.

to this use, good deliberation is the virtue of the good politician; it is the virtue that we need in the assembly to make decisions. In this light, it is no surprise that the *phronimos* is characterized as the good deliberator in Aristotle's ethics.[64] As I explained, scholars often consider good deliberation a part of *phronêsis*.[65] But at the time of Aristotle and before Aristotle, good deliberation was considered a virtue in its own right.[66] In the *Iliad*, and in Thucydides' works, good deliberation is the virtue that one exercises in the assembly when decisions are made.[67] In the tragedies, it often appears together with comprehension and consideration as the virtue that we use in situations where competing values need to be assessed.[68] For Isocrates and Xenophon, good deliberation is the virtue of the skilful military leader.[69] Before Aristotle, good deliberation, comprehension, and consideration occur often in close connection with *phronêsis*.[70] In this light, it is plausible that Aristotle inherited the idea that good deliberation, comprehension, and consideration occur together, have some relation with *phronêsis*, and are the virtues exercised in the assemblies when people need to reach a common decision.

At 1142a33, Aristotle asks whether good deliberation is a form of *epistêmê*, *doxa*, sagacity, or another genus.[71] This starting point of the discussion of good deliberation stresses the connection with

---

[64] This privileged relation between *phronêsis* and *euboulia* is evident at 1142b33. In English, *euboulia* is sometimes translated as 'deliberative excellence' or 'correctness in deliberation'.

[65] See Taylor (2016), Dahl (1984), Kenny (2016, 173). Broadie argues that *euboulia* is the virtue of seeking the truth, while practical wisdom is the virtue of having the truth. Cf. Broadie 2002, 376.

[66] Natali 1999; Schofield 1986, 6–31.

[67] Thucydides, *The History of the Peloponnesian War*, 1.78, 3.42–4, 2.97.

[68] Sophocles, *Antigone*, 1099, 1050–5; Euripides, *Iphigenia in Aulis*, 385–90; Euripides, *Phoenicians*, 721, 746.

[69] Isocrates, *Evagoras*, 46; Euripides, *Phoenicians*, 721, 746; Xenophon, *Agesilaus*, XI, 9 (all quoted by Aubenque 2014, 118).

[70] Sophocles, *Antigone*, 1050–1. For *euboulia* and *sunesis*, see Isocrates *Ad Demonicum*, 1.34. On the relation between *euboulia* and *phronêsis*, cf. *De virtutibus et vitiis*, 1250 a 29–39.

[71] Cf. *EE* VIII 1.

phronêsis, which is introduced by a similar question of whether it is a form of *epistêmê* or of *doxa*.[72] Good deliberation is not a form of *epistêmê* because it is a form of correctness, and *epistêmê* is not a form of correctness as it cannot err (hence, it does not make sense to speak of correctness). Good deliberation is not a form of *doxa* because correct *doxa* is truth, or so Aristotle argues.[73] Good deliberation is characterized by investigating (*zêtein*) and calculating (*logizetai*). This suggests that good deliberation is a form neither of *epistêmê* nor of *doxa* because it is about the process that leads to the truth. Aristotle concludes that good deliberation is a type of correctness in thinking.[74]

Aristotle contrasts the person with good deliberation with the incontinent (*akratês*) and the vicious (*phaulos*): the incontinent and the vicious reach the conclusion of practical thinking with correct *logismos*—reasoning—and yet, the result of this process is not a good action. These are cases of correct, but not virtuous, deliberation. Conversely, good deliberation is correct deliberation that ends in good action. Aristotle discusses four cases: (i) the case of correct deliberation with a bad end; (ii) the case of correct deliberation with a good end; (iii) the case of incorrect deliberation with a good end; (iv) the case of incorrect deliberation with a bad end. Aristotle says that in (iii), the agent grasps what she has to do, but she does not understand why. This seems to be the case

---

[72] This question relates to a discussion between philosophers in the Academy and rhetors. Aristotle engages with this in the *Protrepticus*. In the *Antidosis* (258–69), Isocrates criticizes philosophers in the Academy for teaching useless *epistêmê*. He argues that in practical matters we should rely on *doxa*. In the *Protrepticus* (VI 37.16–22), Aristotle replies to this critique by saying that the *epistêmê* taught in the Academy is useful for practical matters. In light of this debate we can understand the reference to *epistêmê* and *doxa* that opens the discussions of *phronêsis*, *euboulia*, and *sunesis* in the *EE* V = *NE* VI. Namely, for Aristotle it is important to establish whether *phronêsis*, *euboulia*, and *sunesis* are *epistêmai* or *doxai*.
[73] *EE* V = *NE* VI 1142b10–1.
[74] *Dianoia* refers to thinking. Aubenque (2014, 116) notices that *euboulia* retains its popular sense of ability to choose the mean rather than correctness with regard to intention (see Gauthier and Jolif 1959, 509–10). As Aristotle points out at 1142a22, deliberation can be correct or incorrect, while *euboulia* is correct deliberation.

of a syllogism that has false premises described in *Prior Analytics* 53b4–10. From false premises, one can derive true statements, but one cannot understand the relation between premises and conclusion. This point clarifies that good deliberation as *phronêsis* is about a process of thinking that must be correct and must have a good aim. Aristotle says that good deliberation (*eu bebouleusthai*) can be without qualification (*haplôs*) or in relation to something (*pros ti*).[75] Good deliberation without qualification is deliberation with regard to (*pros*) the end: this end without qualification is happiness. The following passage clarifies the connection between good deliberation and *phronêsis*:

> (T6) To deliberate well (*eu beboulesthai*) is a mark of practically wise people, then good deliberation would be correctness about what is beneficial with regard to the end, (*hou*) of which practical wisdom is true grasp (*hupolêpsis*).[76]

This sentence has been at the centre of scholarly debates. It is not clear what *hou* ('of which') refers to.[77] Some scholars argue that it refers to the end—*phronêsis* is true grasp of the end—other scholars argue that it refers to what is advantageous for the end—*phronêsis* is true grasp of what is advantageous for the end. Either *telos* or *sumpheron* can be the antecedents of the relative pronoun *hou*.[78] According to this second possibility, practical wisdom would not be true apprehension of the end. It would be true apprehension of what is advantageous for the end. In other words, it would be about

---

[75] *EE* V = *NE* VI 1142b29.
[76] *EE* V = *NE* VI 1142b31–3.
[77] See Natali (2017 and 1999, 510) for a summary of the main views. For Taylor (2016), *phronêsis* is a true conception of the end and not of what conduces to the end. Taylor summarizes the debate on this issue.
[78] Aubenque (2014, 118) thinks that the antecedent of *hou* is *sumpheron* against what Gauthier and Jolif propose (1959, 518). Aubenque argues that *phronêsis* is about means rather than ends. The end is provided by the virtues of character in conjunction with practical wisdom.

what leads to the end.[79] Scholars discuss whether the end has to be understood in light of the distinction at 1142b28–30 between end without qualification and particular end. What matters for present purposes is that Aristotle establishes a clear relation between *euboulia* and *phronêsis*. That is, *euboulia* is the virtue responsible for the process that leads to the end of deliberation.[80] The idea that *phronêsis* is a grasp of something achieved by good deliberation suggests that *phronêsis* depends on good deliberation. *Phronêsis* 'takes up' (*hupolambanô*) what good deliberation has achieved and integrates it in the whole, the same whole to which other virtues contribute. In this sense, the task of *phronêsis* depends on the task of good deliberation (Functional Dependency). What is more, *phronêsis* depends on good deliberation for its truth: as I showed, good deliberation is a form of correctness that contributes to the truth of the whole (Truth Dependency). That is, *phronêsis* cannot be about the truth unless it takes up the correct result of what good deliberation achieves.

Comprehension (*sunesis*) is as good deliberation a form of correctness. Its distinctive feature is that it is about judgement (*kritikê*). In Plato's *Philebus*, comprehension is a form of *phronêsis*. In the *Cratylus* (412ab), comprehension is knowledge (*epistêmê*). For Aristotle, comprehension is not a form of knowledge (*epistêmê*): he specifies that it does not concern things that are eternal but is about deliberation.[81] As in the cases of *phronêsis* and of good deliberation,

---

[79] For this last interpretation, see Moss 2011, 204–61; Burnet 1900, 227–8. Stewart (1982, 87) and Gauthier and Jolif (1959, 519) interpret it as referring to 'the end'. Some scholars interpret it as referring to the distinction between an end without qualification and an end with qualifications, whereas other scholars interpret it as referring to the entire chapter (cf. Aubenque 2014, ch. 10; Dirlmeier 1984, 462). All quoted by Natali 1999, 510.

[80] Segvic (2011, 160–86) writes: 'The specification that *euboulia* is a tendency to achieve the end is more demanding than in 1141b12 where *euboulia* is only responsible to aim at the end. Making correct inferences is necessary for correct deliberation but *euboulia* is not an inferential skill.'

[81] *EE* V = *NE* VI 1143a4–6, quoted by Aubenque 2014, 151. Aubenque stresses that Aristotle refers to the pre-Platonic popular sense of *sunesis* as the capacity of the agent to analyse practical situations.

Aristotle points out that comprehension and *eusunesia* (good comprehension) are neither forms of knowledge (*epistêmai*) nor forms of belief (*doxai*).[82] The relation between comprehension and good comprehension is not clear.[83] At 1143a17, Aristotle says that it is according to comprehension that we are said to be good at comprehending. He adds that comprehension and good comprehension are the same thing: why does Aristotle introduce a new term for something that is identical with comprehension? An hypothesis is that Aristotle stresses that, as in the case of good deliberation, we are dealing not only with correct deliberation, but with correct deliberation that aims at a good end, good comprehension is not only the virtue of good comprehension, but is good comprehension that aims at a good end. These three virtues of thinking on which *phronêsis* depends—good deliberation, comprehension, and consideration—are about correct cognitive processes, but are also about aiming at the good. In this sense, they are forms of correctness that contribute to the ways in which *phronêsis* is about the truth. Comprehension is about the same things *phronêsis* is about, that is, it is about what we puzzle over (*aporêsein*) and what we deliberate about, but whereas *phronêsis* is prescriptive, comprehension is about judging.[84]

(T7) Comprehension (*sunesis*) is not a matter of having or acquiring practical wisdom. But just as learning is said to be comprehending when it uses understanding, so too when we use belief to judge what someone else says about the things that practical wisdom is about it is said to be fine judgment (*krinein*) (good judgment is the same as fine judgment). And

---

[82] *Eusunesia* is a conjecture by Stephanus and Spengel. All the manuscripts have *asunesia*, which seems not plausible given the context.

[83] The term appears very rarely in ancient Greek: cf. Democritus fr. 119 DK.

[84] *EE* V = *NE* VI 1143a8–10. At 1143a12, Aristotle specifies that *sunesis* is not like medicine or geometry, which are *epistêmai* that concern particular fields. At 1143a14, Aristotle says that comprehending (*sunienai*) is using opinion (*doxa*).

the term 'comprehension', in virtue of which people are good at comprehending, is derived from comprehension in the case of learning, since we often say that learning is comprehending.[85]

Comprehension is a form of learning: Aristotle says that comprehending (*sunienai*) is learning (*manthanein*).[86] The verb for learning (*manthanein*) is the same that Aristotle uses for theoretical knowledge. This verb suggests that the learning involved in comprehension shares aspect with the learning proper of theoretical sciences.[87] Comprehension is at work when we 'put together'—as the word suggests—different pieces of information and we judge a situation that does not directly concern how we should act. Comprehension concerns, for example, what people say to us, as 1143a15 suggests.[88] Insofar as it does not concern how we should act, but what others say to us, it lacks the dimension of desire proper of practical wisdom.[89] In line with this, the end of comprehension is not decision and action, but rather judgement.[90] Comprehension and good comprehension are forms of correctness that contribute to the truth of *phronêsis*. What is more, qua judging capacities they are fundamental for the tasks of *phronêsis*. In this sense, there are three forms of dependency—Ontological, Truth, and Functional—between *phronêsis* and comprehension.

---

[85] *EE* V = *NE* VI 1143a11–18.
[86] Frede (2020, 696) points out that *sunesis* can be both the act of *sunienai* and the capacity as it is customary for all the noun in -sis. In the passage, Aristotle specifies that he refers to the capacity. Frede explains that *sunesis* is most of all 'Wissen'. This is clear from the occurrences of *sunesis* at *NE* 1161b26; 1181a18.
[87] Cf. Broadie 2002, 377. In *DA* 401b3, Aristotle says that *sunesis* is the opposite of ignorance (*agnoia*). Simon (2017, 79–90) argues that *sunesis* is some sort of 'grasping' and 'understanding'. Aubenque notices that in the *Philebus*, *sunesis* is the same thing as *phronêsis* which is theoretical. In the *Cratylus*, *sunesis* is *epistêmê*. Aristotle may have retained some aspects of this Platonic notion of *sunesis* (cf. Aubenque 2014, 149).
[88] Simon argues that it is other-regarding (Simon 2017, 79–90). He ultimately concludes that it is ethical discernment and that it differs from *phronêsis* because it is about actions in which we are not directly involved.
[89] This is defended by Natali (2014, 192). Reported also by Simon (2017, 79–90) who agrees with Natali.
[90] Louden (1997, 112); Greenwood (1909, 68).

Consideration (*gnôme*) as comprehension is about judgement.[91] In Plato's *Republic* (476d), *gnôme* is some sort of *epistêmê*.[92] For Aristotle, consideration is a form of correctness: Aristotle says that it is right judgement proper of the good agent. As Aristotle explains, *suggnôme* (sympathy) is *gnôme* about what is good or decent.[93]

(T8) What is called consideration (*gnôme*) is that in virtue of which we say that people are forgiving and are considerate; it is correct judgment about what is decent. Here is an indication of this. We say that a decent person is most likely to be forgiving; decency is being forgiving about some matters and forgiveness is a form of consideration based on a correct judgment about what is decent. And the correct judgment is the one that arrives at the truth.[94]

Consideration is proper of the decent person who aims at the good and who knows when someone deserves sympathy.[95] *Suggnôme* has both a cognitive and an emotional component and is other-regarding as *sunesis*.[96] If consideration is proper of the decent person (*epieikês*) and if it is correct judgement about what is decent, the *phronimos* cannot lack it. This virtue is fundamental to judge and to deliberate well. In this sense, consideration is essential for the tasks of *phronêsis* and qua correct state, contributes to

---

[91] See also the account in *Rhetoric* 1394a21–5. *Suggnôme* as *sunesis* is composed by the root of a verb of cognition: in the case of *suggnôme* the verb is *suggignôskô*. In the Classical period *suggnôme* is forgiveness. As Aristotle explains in the *NE*, we grant forgiveness to people who did something bad due to external forces or due to ignorance. *NE* 1109b18–11a2. Cf. Dover 1991, 173–82. Nussbaum 2006, 3–43.
[92] Cf. In early Greek philosophy, *gnôsis* is theoretical, or so Snell argues: see Heraclitus fr. 56, Philolaus fr. 6, Plato *Theaetetus* 193d (Snell 2011, 155).
[93] Aubenque (2014, 151) argues that *epieikeia* substitutes a geometrical and too abstract idea of what is good in the sense of what is just.
[94] *EE* V = *NE* VI 1143a19–24.
[95] *EE* V = *NE* VI 1143a21. The connection between *suggnôme* and the *epieikês* can be found also in the *Rhetoric*. Cf. Nussbaum 2006, 3–43.
[96] Segvic (2011, 160–86) argues that the good deliberator must have *sunesis* and *suggnômê*. She believes that *phronêsis* is excellence in learning.

the truth of *phronêsis*. Also in the case of consideration, there are three forms of dependency—Ontological, Truth, and Functional—between *phronêsis* and this virtue.

Aristotle mentions two other states that are connected to *phronêsis*: *eustochia* (sagacity) and *agchinoia* (quick mindedness). *Eustochia* and *agchinoia* are not virtues on which *phronêsis* depends even though the *phronimos* may possess these states. Namely, these states do not fulfil tasks that are fundamental for *phronêsis*, and *phronêsis* does not depend on them ontologically, for its truth, or for its function. Aristotle says that sagacity is quick and does not require reason.[97] Even before Aristotle, *phronêsis* and *stochasmos* were associated as qualities of good politicians.[98] Quick mindedness is a sort of sagacity.[99] In *Prior Analytics* 89b10–14, it is described as the capacity to grasp the middle term in a syllogism in a very short time. Aristotle points out that quick mindedness is not *euboulia*. Experience (*empeiria*) is required for *phronêsis* even though is not a virtue on which *phronêsis* depends. That is, the agent cannot develop *phronêsis* unless she has an adequate experience of life. In this sense, having experience is a condition for *phronêsis*. In 1142a11–19, Aristotle says that young people can be good at mathematics and geometry, but cannot be *phronimoi*. What Aristotle suggests is that for certain fields of knowledge such as mathematics, we derive the principles from abstraction, whereas for *phronêsis*, we need experience. At 1143b11–17, Aristotle adds that we should listen to experts and to old sages because they have a special eye that derives from experience.[100] From all this, it is clear that *phronêsis* needs time to come about. This is in line with the

---

[97] *EE* V = *NE* VI 1142b2–3.
[98] We find them associated in Isocrates, *Antidosis* 231–6. Cf. Poulakos 2004, 44–66. *Eustochia* occurs only in Aristotle and Euripides.
[99] *EE* V = *NE* VI 1142b5–6.
[100] Aristotle often compares *phronêsis* with eyes and sight. Cf. *EE* V = *NE* VI 1144a30. In 1144b11, the person who does not have *nous* is compared to a heavy body with no eyes. Cf. *NE* 1096b29. Cf. *Protrepticus* X 55.24–56.12.

idea that it is a dependent virtue: all the virtues on which *phronêsis* depends need to be in place for *phronêsis* to come about.

2.5 The emerging tasks of *phronêsis*

As I argued, some of the tasks of *phronêsis* are tasks of the virtues on which it depends. However, there are three tasks that are not tasks of the virtues on which *phronêsis* depends. These are what I call emerging tasks and they are in line with the idea of Additive Functionality that I develop throughout this book. That is, they are tasks that emerge from the interactions and co-functioning of the virtues on which *phronêsis* depends. These are:

(i) the commanding task;
(ii) the fulfilment task;
(iii) the capacity of grasping the good as a whole.

At *EE* V = *NE* VI 1143a8 as well as at *EE* VIII 1249b15–6, Aristotle says that *phronêsis* commands. There are at least two ways in which *phronêsis* commands and these two ways are connected. First, it commands for the sake of *sophia* (I develop this idea in chapter 5).[101] Second, *phronêsis* commands the virtues on which it depends: the interactions and co-functioning of the virtues on which *phronêsis* depends create a harmony. This harmony is functional to bring about theoretical activity: that is, when there is harmony in the soul we are in the best conditions for theoretical activity insofar as we are not distracted by the needs and desires of the non-rational part of the soul.

As the passage at 1143a8 suggests, *phronêsis* commands that a given action should be done. Kenny argues that this is some kind of self-addressed command.[102] Differently from Kenny, I understand

---

[101] *EE* VIII 1249b15–16.
[102] Kenny 2016, 171.

this command as directed toward the virtues on which *phronêsis* depends. That is, the very nature of *phronêsis* qua dependent virtue presupposes that all the virtues on which it depends should be in place and interact in the right ways. At 1220a10, Aristotle assigns the commanding function to the entire rational part of the soul: this part commands the non-rational part of the soul, which listens and obeys. Ultimately, it is *phronêsis* as the virtue of the calculative part of the rational part of the soul that does the commanding insofar as *sophia*, the virtue of the scientific part of the soul, is not about what is contingent and transient. What is more, the activity of *sophia* is the aim of the commands of *phronêsis*.

Phronêsis does not only command the virtues on which it depends, but brings also these virtues to fulfilment. In 1143b6–7, Aristotle says that while no one is *sophos* by nature, consideration, comprehension, and practical *nous* are by nature. They are by nature in the sense that we develop them naturally with age. The passage does not mention *phronêsis*, but *phronêsis* seems to work like *sophia*. That is, these virtues that depend on other virtues or in the case of *sophia*, that have other virtues qua parts cannot come about by nature. Conversely, some of the virtues on which they depend come in two forms: natural virtues and proper virtues. In their natural form, we develop these virtues in the same way in which we develop grey hair with age. As I showed, consideration, comprehension, and *nous* in their natural forms are by nature. However, only when these virtues are possessed with *phronêsis* they fulfil their full potential. That is, these virtues acquire additional tasks when they interact with other virtues. Together with *phronêsis*, they become proper virtues as opposed to natural virtues. *Phronêsis* forms a unity with other virtues: this provides stability to the virtues that are possessed together with *phronêsis* and to *phronêsis* itself. That is, the virtues on which *phronêsis* depends as well as *phronêsis* are stable states: once we acquire them, it is difficult to lose them. The interactions among the virtues guarantee that all the virtues on which *phronêsis* depends are constantly 'at work'. In this sense, all the virtues on which *phronêsis* depends, including the virtues of character, are necessary for acting virtuously.[103]

The most important emerging task of *phronêsis* is that qua virtue that is part of a unity of virtues, *phronêsis* grasps the good as a whole. The virtues on which *phronêsis* depends grasp the good part by part. At 1140a28, Aristotle points out that *phronêsis* is a state able to deliberate about things that are good and advantageous not part by part (*kata meros*) as it is the case when we deliberate regarding, for example, health and bodily strength, but regarding things good and advantageous for a good life as a whole (*holôs*). Namely, other virtues may be concerned with the good of parts, but *phronêsis* is concerned with the good of the whole.

2.6 Conclusions

In this chapter, I showed that *phronêsis* is a dependent virtue and that practical intelligence, good deliberation, comprehension, and consideration, as well as the virtues of character that I discuss in chapter 3, are the virtues on which *phronêsis* depends. I argued that there are three forms of dependency—Ontological Dependency, Truth Dependency, and Functional Dependency—between *phronêsis* and the virtues of thinking on which it depends. The idea that *phronêsis* is a dependent virtue is suggested by the tasks of *phronêsis* which are the tasks of the virtues of thinking on which it depends except for what I called the emerging tasks. I examined each virtue of thinking on which *phronêsis* depends, and I showed

---

[103] Cf. Louden 1997, 103-18. Louden quotes Ryle and Gadamer. Ryle and Gadamer say that we cannot forget how to distinguish right from wrong once we have acquired this ability (Ryle 1958; Gadamer 1979). This is in line with my interpretation: if all the virtues that form a unity with *phronêsis* are exercised when we act virtuously, we cannot lose the virtues that form a unity with *phronêsis*.

in which ways *phronêsis* depends on them. I concluded with a discussion of the emerging tasks of *phronêsis*. *Phronêsis*, practical intelligence, good deliberation, comprehension, consideration, and the virtues of character form what I call the practical unity of the virtues.

3
The interdependence between the character virtues and *phronêsis*

The ideas that all the virtues of character form a unity and that they need to be possessed together with *phronêsis* are fairly uncontroversial among scholars of Aristotle's ethics.[1] This latter idea has also been referred to as reciprocity of the virtues or mutual entailment to distinguish Aristotle's version of this thesis from Socrates' unity of virtue.[2] A comparison between the theory of mutual entailment in the *EE* and in the *NE* shows that there is almost no reference to the so-called mutual entailment in the undisputed Nicomachean books.[3] Conversely, there are references to mutual entailment in the undisputed Eudemian books.[4] This does not show that Aristotle changed his mind with regard to the theory of mutual entailment. However, if we combine the treatment

---

[1] *EE* V = *NE* VI 1144b33–45a2: this is the standard reference for mutual entailment and for the unity of the virtues (UoV) understood as unity of practical wisdom and the character virtues, and it occurs in the so-called common books. See Dahl 1984; Irwin 1988a, 71–8; Natali 1989; Badhwar 1996; Halper 1999; Kent 1999; Gardiner 2005; Russell 2009; Annas 2011, 83–100; Russell 2014.

[2] Irwin 1988a, 71–8. Gottlieb 2009, 92. Gottlieb argues that we should talk about reciprocation of the virtues to distinguish Aristotle's view from Socrates' view that she refers to as unity of the virtues.

[3] One exception is *NE* 1103b32, where Aristotle says that we should act in conformity with right principle and that this will be explained later. Similarly, in *NE* 1107a1–2, he says that virtue is observance of the mean determined by right principle. And in *NE* 1178a16–19, Aristotle seems to suggest that there is a unity of practical wisdom and character virtues. These three passages hint towards mutual entailment, but they do not clearly and indisputably refer to it. For a different view according to which the definition of virtue at *NE* 1106b36–7a2 already anticipates the discussion of mutual entailment in the common book, see Nielsen 2020, 294.

[4] *EE* III 1234a25–35, *EE* VIII 1246b10–4.

of mutual entailment in the *EE* with an analysis of how Aristotle conceives of the virtues of character and of *phronêsis* in this treatise, what emerges is that the relation between *phronêsis* and the virtues of character can be described in terms of interdependency. I rely on the definitions of Ontological Dependency and of Functional Dependency that I offer in chapter 2: I show that there is Ontological Interdependency and Functional Interdependency between *phronêsis* and the virtues of character. In preliminary and schematic terms, I conceive of the relation between the character virtues, the virtues of practical thinking as I define them in chapter 2 (i.e. practical intelligence, good deliberation, comprehension, and consideration), and *phronêsis* as follows. The virtues of character are not genuinely virtues of character when they are possessed without *phronêsis*. On its turn, *phronêsis* comes about only when agents possess the virtues of character, practical *nous*, good deliberation, comprehension, and consideration because it depends on these virtues.[5] This means that the virtues of character must be possessed always together with the virtues of practical thinking. In this sense, there is a unity of the practical virtues: this unity is constituted by the character virtues, *phronêsis*, practical *nous*, good deliberation, comprehension, and consideration. The 'natural' counterparts of the virtues of character that do not require *phronêsis* and the virtues of practical thinking are the so-called natural virtues.

In this chapter, I sketch different routes that scholars have taken to explain why the virtues of character must be possessed all together and show that Plato and Aristotle share an interest in the UoV (section 3.1). I clarify the distinction between natural virtues

---

[5] In chapter 2, I argued that *phronêsis* must be possessed together with practical *nous*, good deliberation, comprehension, and consideration. For brevity, throughout the chapter, I write that the character virtues must be possessed with *phronêsis*, but insofar as *phronêsis* depends on practical *nous*, good deliberation, comprehension, and consideration, the character virtues must be possessed with *phronêsis*, as well as with practical *nous*, good deliberation, comprehension, and consideration.

and character virtues. I show that agents can possess one or some natural virtues without possessing them all while agents must possess all the character virtues together (section 3.2). I discuss the interdependency between the character virtues and *phronêsis* (section 3.3). By way of conclusion, I address some challenges that have been raised (or that may be raised) to the unity of the character virtues (section 3.4).

3.1 The unity of the character virtues

The unity of the character virtues has been construed in a number of ways. For present purposes, I offer a non-exhaustive and preliminary list of scholarly reconstructions of the unity of the character virtues, put forward either with respect to the *NE* or, more generally, with respect to Aristotle's ethics. Further nuance will be added as my argument proceeds.

> Situational affective responses: agents need all the virtues insofar as they need proper affective responses to all situations in order to act virtuously. According to this view, the virtues are individuated by different emotions and activities.[6]
> Grasping the good: in order to act virtuously we need to grasp the good as a whole and for this task, we need all the virtues.[7]
> Aiming at the *kalon*: in order to grasp the *kalon*, the virtues of character must be unified.[8]
> Integration of the soul: agents need an integrated soul to act virtuously, and hence, they need all the virtues.[9]

---

[6] Halper 1999, 115–43.
[7] In *EE* V = *NE* VI 1140a28, Aristotle says that *phronêsis* calculates well (*kalôs*) not part by part, but for good living conceived as a whole. Frede (2014, 83–103) proposes a version of this thesis according to which the virtues are unified via the notion of the good life.
[8] Lear 2006, 123–47. Cf. *EE* III 1230a30–1.
[9] Gottlieb 2009, ch. 5.

Practical wisdom: the virtues of character are unified through practical wisdom insofar as all virtuous actions are also practically wise.[10]

In addition, consider a schematic overview of how the virtues are conceived in Plato's *Laches, Meno,* and *Protagoras*:

Parts of *phronêsis*: courage is considered a part of *phronêsis* which is a whole (*Laches*).[11]
Virtues as parts of virtue: the virtues are parts of a whole (*Meno*).[12]
Parts of a face or parts of gold: Socrates asks Protagoras whether the virtues are like the parts of a face or whether they are like parts of gold (*Protagoras*).[13]

None of these views will be examined in detail in this chapter. I mention them, however, in order to prepare the ground for how I understand the relation between *phronêsis* and the virtues of character in the *EE*. Plato shows an interest in the unity of *phronêsis* and the other virtues. Of course, there are differences between how Plato and Aristotle conceive of *phronêsis* and of its relation to the other virtues. For example, according to the Socratic/Platonic proposal, all the virtues are versions of one virtue, which is knowledge.

---

[10] Penner 1973, reprinted in 1992, 35–68; Irwin 1977, 134–5. Cf. Russell 2009. The doctrine of the mean has also been invoked to explain the unity of the virtues of character. Cf. Ackrill 1973.
[11] *Laches* 190c–d, 199d–e; Devereux 1992, 765–89.
[12] *Meno* 73e–74d; 78d–79e. For a different interpretation see Irwin 1977, 304–5.
[13] Cf. *Protagoras* 329d. In the dialogue, the option that virtues are parts of a whole is discussed in greater detail, though scholars disagree on their readings of relevant passages. The virtues are like the parts in a face if they differ from one another and if they are properly speaking virtues only when they are part of the whole and when they perform their function (e.g. an eye is properly speaking an eye if it can perform its function of seeing, which happens only if it is part of a face). Conversely, they are like parts of gold when they are all identical and perform the same function. In the case of gold, if the whole misses a part, this will not affect the function of the individual parts. Cf. Vlastos 1973, 221–69.

For Aristotle, the virtues of character are distinct and yet, they must be possessed together and in conjunction with *phronêsis*. In my brief overview of Plato's view, the relation among the virtues is conceived in terms of part/whole. On my reconstruction of Aristotle's view of the relation between *phronêsis* and the character virtues, I characterize this relation in terms of interdependency. *Phronêsis* depends on the character virtues to come about and for its tasks, and the virtues of character depend on *phronêsis* to come about and for their tasks (Ontological and Functional Interdependency). To show that the virtues of character must be possessed all together, I start with the distinction between natural virtues—which do not need to be possessed all together—and the virtues of character.

3.2 Natural virtues and character virtues

In order to understand why agents can have one or some natural virtues without possessing them all, we need to establish what natural virtues are and how they differ from the virtues of character. Scholars disagree on what natural virtues are.[14] Depending on one's interpretation, one may think of them as the positive traits that individuals have simply by being born with a certain temperament,

---

[14] Curzer argues that natural virtues become virtues proper when there is also practical wisdom (Curzer 2012). Lennox shows that natural virtues are innate dispositions that become full virtues with habituation and with the virtues of thinking (Lennox 2015, 193–214). Rossi argues that natural virtues are emotional dispositions favourable to certain virtues (Rossi 2013, 155–81). Telfer explains that they are innate good qualities (Telfer 1989, 35–48). Gottlieb shows that they are sheer temperament (Gottlieb 2009, ch. 5). Viano (2007, 23–42) argues that natural virtues are first impulses towards the *kalon*. Lawrence explains that 'natural excellence is to be well disposed by the canons or norms of the species in question' (Lawrence 2011, 254). Recently Jimenez argues that we have a natural imperfect appreciation for the *kalon*, which is the basis for developing virtue. As I understand it, Jimenez conceives of this natural appreciation in terms of natural tendency or emotion rather than natural virtue (see Jimenez 2021, 6.2). In particular, she focuses on shame as the proto-virtue of the learner that is responsible for the learner's initial responsiveness to the *kalon*.

combined perhaps with the impact of living in a given location at a given time and in a given community.[15] In this sense, natural virtues are some sort of proto-character virtues.[16] At the other end of the spectrum of interpretations, one may argue that natural virtues are the character virtues as far as they can be possessed by themselves, without *phronêsis*.[17] Leunissen distinguishes natural character traits, which she interprets as rational capacities, from natural virtues.[18] They are rational capacities because they are capacities of ensouled beings as opposed to capacities of inanimate beings.[19] For Leunissen, natural character traits are present at birth; through habituation, they become natural virtues. However, insofar as natural character traits are rational capacities, they are capacities for opposites: that is, natural rational capacities (*dunameis*) are two-directional, as Leunissen argues.[20] They can be habituated into natural virtues as well as into their opposites, natural vices.

[15] Cf. Leunissen (2012, 507–30). Leunissen argues that being born in a certain place and having certain material conditions (blood, etc.) result in predispositions to be habituated to certain natural virtues and not to others. For Leunissen, the character virtues are perfections and stable dispositions that come about starting from the natural virtues, which are capacities of the perceptive soul. The idea that the virtues are perfections is in line with what Aristotle says in *NE* III 1103a23–6. Foot understands the virtues of character as correctives, which implies that they correct an incorrect natural disposition (Foot 1978). Gottlieb argues that the virtues of character are self-sustaining and that they promote themselves (Gottlieb 2009, 53). Her view is in opposition to Foot's view and to Korsgaard's view that the virtues of character have conditional value that depends on the unconditional value of contemplation (Korsgaard 1986, 494). Cf. Morel 2021.

[16] Cf. Annas 1993, 197–98. Pakaluk 2005, 231.

[17] Leunissen argues that natural virtues are 'dispositions that need to be acquired through virtuous activities that require choice or desire' (Leunissen 2017, 126). Leunissen translates *hexeis* as 'dispositions' (see Leunissen 2017, 14). In what follows, I translate *hexis* as 'state', while I translate *diathesis* as 'disposition'. Leunissen refers to *Physics* VII.2 and to *Metaphysics* IX.2 and IX.5 for a discussion of habituation outside the ethical treatises. In particular, in *Physics* VII 246b5–10, Aristotle says that each character exists because agents are disposed (*diatithêsi*) towards one's own affections in a good or bad way. He adds that one's own (*oikeia*) affections are those affections that by nature promote generation or corruption. This capacity of being disposed towards certain affections that corresponds to a character seems no other than natural virtue.

[18] Leunissen 2017, ch. 5. Natural non-rational capacities—e.g. a stone that moves only downward (*NE* 1103a19–21)—are one-directional. Cf. *Metaphysics* IX.2, IX.5.

[19] Cf. *Metaphysics* IX.2.

[20] Cf. *Politics* 1332a40; *NE* 1109b1–7, 1103b24; *Metaphysics* IX 2, 5.

Leunissen explains that 'individual character virtues are the proper realisation of the natural character traits that humans have from birth'.[21] I do not distinguish between natural character traits and natural virtues.[22] As I conceive of them, natural virtues differ from character virtues. In my view, agents can possess one or some natural virtues without possessing them all insofar as natural virtues (i) are capacities to experience affections in a certain way and these capacities are by nature, (ii) they do not involve decision (*prohairesis*), (iii) they correspond to natural vices; agents can possess one or some natural vices without possessing them all together.

With regard to (i), in the *EE*, natural virtues are conceived as capacities (*dunameis*) to experience affections in a certain way, to be distinguished from character virtues, which are states (*hexeis*).[23] Aristotle offers a definition of virtue at the beginning of book II that fits both the natural virtues and the virtues of character:

> (T1) Let it be assumed further: concerning virtue, that it is the best disposition (*diathesis*) or state (*hexis*) or capacity (*dunamis*) of each of the things that have some use or function. This is clear from induction, since we consider things to be this way in all cases.[24]

With this definition, Aristotle does not specify whether virtue is a disposition, a state, or a capacity.[25] It is a definition derived from induction by observing things that have functions and virtues. As Aristotle progresses in his analysis, virtues of character are referred

---

[21] Leunissen 2017, ch. 5.
[22] Leunissen interprets the reference to natural virtues at *EE* V = *NE* VI 1144b33–45a2 as a reference to natural character traits.
[23] Sauvé Meyer (forthcoming) explains that Aristotle rejects the idea that virtues of character are *dunameis* only after the doctrine of the mean illustrated at *EE* II.3. Up to *EE* II.3, he considers the option that virtues of character may be *dunameis*.
[24] *EE* II 1218b38–19a3.
[25] The idea that virtue is a *hexis* is a standard one in all of Aristotle's ethical writings.

to as states (*hexeis*) and dispositions (*diatheseis*).[26] Natural virtues are referred to as capacities and dispositions.[27] The term *diathesis* (disposition) seems to be used interchangeably for virtues of character as well as for natural virtues.[28] Aristotle calls dispositions natural virtues and natural vices, as well as character virtues and proper vices.[29] In *EE* II, Aristotle explains what he means with affections (*pathê*), capacities (*dunameis*), and states (*hexeis*):[30]

(T2) By affections I mean things like anger, fear, shame, appetite, and in general things that are for the most part accompanied by perceptible pleasure and pain in their own right. According to these a person is not of a certain sort, but is merely affected. According to capacities there is quality. By capacities I mean those in relation to which people are described as actively experiencing affections—for example, being irascible, stolid, passionate, bashful, shameless. States are the cause of these affections being

---

[26] In *EE* II 1222a11, virtues of character are called *mesotêta*. In the final definition of virtue offered at 1227b9, virtue is a state (*hexis*). Cf. 1220b29, 1222a6. In *Categories* 8b27, Aristotle says that *hexeis* are also *diatheseis*, but not vice versa. Cf. Sauvé Meyer (forthcoming).

[27] In *NE* 1106a7-10, Aristotle explains that proper virtues and vices are not capacities because capacities are by nature. In the *EE*, Aristotle does not offer a similar explanation, but on my reading, from how he uses the terms 'capacities' and 'states', we can infer that also in this text, proper virtues and vices are not considered capacities because they are not by nature, and are with reason (and in particular with decision).

[28] Cf. *Categories* 8b.

[29] At *EE* III 1233a5, *megalopsychia* is called a *diathesis*. But as the discussion of this virtue suggests, *megalopsychia* is understood as a virtue of character and not merely as a natural virtue. Similarly, in *EE* III, courage is called *hexis* at 1228a37, and *diathesis* at 1228b3. In *EE* II 1220a30, Aristotle refers to virtues as *diatheseis*. The context of the passage at 1220a30 suggests that Aristotle refers to the virtues of character, which are announced at 1220a14 as the topic of the discussion that follows the passage. Cf. Sauvé Meyer (forthcoming).

[30] In 1220b10-12, Aristotle refers to a distinction of these three concepts—*pathê*, *dunameis*, and *hexeis*—done elsewhere in his writings: this reference is probably to *Topics* 125b20-7, where he distinguishes *hexis* from *dunamis*. In the *Topics*, *dunamis* is defined as the capacity associated with a certain state. Some examples are mildness as the state associated with the capacity to control anger; courage as the state associated with the capacity to control fears; justice as the state associated with control gains.

either in accordance with or contrary to reason—for example, courage, temperance, cowardice, indiscipline.[31]

Affections are accompanied by perceptive (*aisthetikê*) pleasure and pain in their own right (*kat'hauta*).[32] Capacities are defined as those in relation to which people are described as actively experiencing affections. That is, while affections are passive, capacities are active. This means that capacities to experience affections are important steps in the training to experience affections in certain ways. In this sense, natural virtues are an important advantage to develop the virtues of character.[33] However, they are not a requirement for developing the virtues of character. Aristotle offers examples of affections, capacities, and states. Being irascible, stolid, passionate, bashful, and shameless are Aristotle's examples of capacities.[34] States are different from capacities insofar as they are with reason or contrary to reason. Courage, temperance, cowardice, indiscipline are Aristotle's examples of states. All these examples occur in the list that we find at *EE* II 1220b38-21a12. However, in this list, the virtues have been most likely added by a later commentator.[35] As

---

[31] *EE* II 1220b12-20. At b15, I read with Rowe ποιός τις ἀλλὰ πάσχει.
[32] On perceptible pleasure and pain, cf. Woods 1992, 101-2. Woods stresses the connection with *Physics* VII, 246b20-247a19, where the virtues of character are defined as the right dispositions towards bodily pleasures and pains. Bodily pleasures and pains are described as changes that result from something acting on the perceiving part of the soul. Woods explains that for Aristotle, affections are accompanied rather than followed by pleasure and pain. He argues that for the most part species of the genus affection are accompanied by pleasure and pain, but there may be instances of any species that are not accompanied by pleasure and pain. For an alternative view, see Leighton 1984, 135-8. Leighton argues that Aristotle's specification that affections are for the most part accompanied by pleasure and pain is meant to stress that certain species of affections are without pleasure and pain.
[33] This point is discussed by Lawrence (2011, 233-84). Cf. *EE* VI = *NE* VII 1151a15-17.
[34] Being irascible (*orgilos*) is the only example that occurs also in the parallel passage in the *NE* at 1105b24-5 (see *orgisthênai*). The examples listed in the parallel passage in *NE* 1105b22 are different from the ones that we find in the *EE*.
[35] Rowe (2023b) argues that the disposition in columns is not Aristotelian and that the items in the third column are probably a later addition (he puts the third column in round brackets; cf. Rowe 2023a). Allan (1966, 138-49) proposes to delete the third column. In *EE* II 1221a12, *phronêsis* appears as the mean between knavery (*panourgia*)

I explain further on in the chapter, this list is a list of natural vices. And yet, cowardice and indiscipline, which may be considered proper vices as opposed to mere natural vices, figure in the list. An analysis of Aristotle's usage of state (*hexis*) and capacity (*dunamis*) suggests that individual virtues or vices are not classified as either states or capacities. Rather, individual virtues or vices can occur in two forms: they can be states (virtues of characters or proper vices) or capacities (natural virtues or natural vices).[36] It is plausible that agents have by nature some capacities to experience affections in certain ways and that these capacities are not all possessed together: for example, agents may have the natural virtue of courage and lack generosity or vice versa. Having the natural virtue does not mean possessing the virtue of courage or generosity as stable states accompanied by *prohairesis* and acquired by habituation.

With regard to (ii), Aristotle says that states are characterized by decision (*prohairesis*). As the definition at *EE* II 1220b18-20 shows, virtues and vices qua states are causes (*aitiai*). That is, they are causes of having certain affections according to reason.[37] In *EE* III 1234a25-31, Aristotle explains this point:

(T3) Though all these mean points (*mesotêtes*) are praiseworthy, they are not virtues, nor are their opposites vices, since they are

---

and silliness (*euêtheia*). It is listed in the third column so it is plausible that it is a later interpolation (cf. Spengel, Frietzsche, Susemihl, Woods, Rapp). Some scholars understand 1220b38-21a12 as a genuine list of virtues of character and of vices: Dirlmeier 1984, 246; Rowe 1971, 41; Woods 1992, 105-6; Donini 1999, 205. The idea of natural vices as distinct from proper vices, which are *hexeis prohairetikai*, has been defended convincingly by Nielsen (2017, 1-25).

[36] See footnotes 26 and 29. In *EE* V = *NE* VI 1144b8-9, Aristotle speaks of *phusikai hexeis*, which may seem a paradox if states are distinguished from capacities because they are not by nature. This is the only occurrence of this expression and the context suggests that Aristotle uses states to refer to all those states that belong by nature to children and beasts as well as to adult human beings. Cf. *HA* 588a18-b3; Burnet 1900, 285.

[37] Capacities are also causes, but not in the same sense as states. That is, capacities are not causes of experiencing a certain affection according to reason. Cf. *Metaphysics* 1049b5.

without decision (*aneu prohaireseôs*). They all fall under the classification of affections, since each of them is a certain affection (*pathos*). But because they are natural they are grouped together in the natural virtues. As will be discussed in what follows, each virtue in a way exists both naturally and in another form with practical wisdom.[38]

The mean points mentioned in T3 are natural virtues and natural vices insofar as they do not involve *prohairesis*.[39] Some scholars argue that the mean points mentioned in T3 are all the virtues and vices discussed in *EE* III.[40] Others argue that these mean points are only the ones discussed in *EE* III.7.[41] Among the virtues and vices that Aristotle discusses in *EE* III, there are examples of virtues and vices that cannot be simply mean points: for example, courage and *megalopsychia*. Of course, one may argue that these virtues can be possessed as natural virtues or as character virtues. However, as they are discussed in *EE* III, courage and *megalopsychia* are clearly virtues of character and not mere natural virtues. Hence, it seems plausible that in this passage, Aristotle refers only to the mean points discussed in *EE* III.7. Aristotle calls natural vices affections because they are capacities to experience affections in certain ways.[42] And some of the items discussed are indeed affections as the

---

[38] *EE* III 1234a25–31.

[39] Aubenque (2014, 121) says that *prohairesis* is what we are praised for, while we cannot be praised for natural virtues. The idea that *prohairesis* is fundamental for the transformation of natural virtues into proper virtues is stressed by Nielsen (2020, 291–318). Nielsen argues that also proper vice requires decision. She argues that the vicious person acts on principle. Scholars debate on how to understand vice in Aristotle's ethics and whether the vicious agent is conflicted and does not have a principle or whether this agent has a principle that is not correct. According to Nielsen's view, vice is ignorance in the decision (*NE* 1110b31). She points out that it is not possible for vices as well as for virtues to be affections (see *NE* 2.5). In her view, to be vicious is 'to have adopted a false view of what is fine and worthy of pursuit, and to act on the basis of this conception'. See Nielsen 2017, 19. Müller proposes a different view according to which the vicious does not have a principle and he is conflicted (Müller 2015, 459–77).

[40] Müller 2004, 18–53.

[41] Cf. Stewart 1892; Donini 1999; Simpson 2013b, 651–9; Inwood and Woolf 2013.

[42] Aristotle calls natural vices affections at *EE* II 1221b10.

example of shame (*aidôs*) at 1233b27 suggests.⁴³ In this sense, the mean points mentioned in T3 refer both to natural vices and virtues and to affections that are natural and can be grouped together with the natural vices and virtues, as the case of shame suggests. The idea explored in T3 that the natural virtues and vices do not involve decision (*prohairesis*) is another element that explains why agents can possess only some natural virtues or vices without possessing them all. That is, natural virtues and vices lack a rational component—decision—that unifies the virtues of character and makes them part of a unified state of the soul: the state of the soul of the virtuous person.⁴⁴

With regard to (iii), natural virtues correspond to natural vices. As agents can possess one or some natural vices without possessing them all, it is also plausible that agents can possess one or some natural virtues without possessing them all. Lawrence argues that a natural vice is the natural capacity to take pleasure in things that we should not enjoy.⁴⁵ In the *EE*, as there are proper vices that correspond to character virtues, there are natural vices that correspond to natural virtues. Aristotle provides a list of natural vices at *EE* II 1220b38–21a12. The idea that it is a list of natural vices as opposed to a list of natural vices and virtues is suggested by the discussion that follows the list, which is a discussion of vices and not of vices and virtues.⁴⁶ It seems plausible that at 1221b10, Aristotle refers

---

⁴³ *Aidôs* is not considered a virtue in the corresponding passage in *NE* III.15, but it is considered an affection. For a discussion of the mixed nature of shame, see Jimenez 2021.

⁴⁴ In the *EE*, Aristotle uses the singular more often than the plural when he refers to the virtues of character: that is, he talks about virtue instead of virtues. Virtue occurs in the singular at 1219a33, 1219b9, 1219b28, 1220a30, a39, 1222a6, 1227b2, 6, 9, 24, 39. The plural occurs at 1222b9. Cf. also 1144b32. At *EE* II 1220a14–5, Aristotle says: 'we need to examine ethical virtue, what it is and what its parts are.' The use of the singular supports the idea that the virtues of character are part of a unified state of the soul.

⁴⁵ Lawrence 2011, 233–84. At *EE* VI = *NE* VII 1148b19–49a24, Aristotle speaks of natural bestiality. He says that there are things that are pleasant by nature: some of these things are truly pleasant, others are pleasant even if they should not be pleasant. In the latter case, nature is one of the causes of these things being pleasant for someone even if they should not be pleasant.

⁴⁶ The division in columns that we find in modern editions is not Aristotelian and it does not appear in the manuscripts. Cf. Rowe 2023a; 2023b, 32–3. At 1221a13, I read

to the list that occurs at *EE* II 1220b38–21a12. He specifies that these affections, and things similar to affections, that is, as I read it, natural vices, can be further divided into species according to the time, intensity, and circumstances in which we feel affections. This suggests that natural vices and their counterparts—natural virtues—are ways to respond to situations rather than aspects of a unified state of mind as the character virtues are. At 1231b8–9, Aristotle says that irascibility, fierceness, and savagery fall all under the same disposition (*diathesis*).[47] That is, they are species of the same natural vice. While character virtues are the exact mean between excess and deficiency, natural virtues and natural vices are organized in a continuum. Each character virtue is a mean that corresponds to two vices, excess and defect, that form a triad.[48] Natural vices as well as natural virtues are characterized by the lack of this triadic structure. Irascibility, fierceness, and savagery, which are three vices, correspond to two defects rather than to three.[49] The defects are being servile and being meek, as Aristotle says at 1231b10. The list of natural vices that occurs at *EE* II 1220b38–21a12 may suggest that there are two natural vices—one excess and one defect—that correspond to one virtue. However, the examples of irascibility, fierceness, and savagery at 1231b9–10 clarify that

---

with Rowe τὰ μὲν πάθη ταῦτα καὶ τὰ τοιαῦτα συμβαίνει ταῖς ψυχαῖς. Reading τὰ before τοιαῦτα suggests that the list that appears before 1221a13 is not a list of affections, but of things that are somehow similar to affections, that is, natural vices. Cf. Rowe 2023b, 33.

[47] In this passage, he refers to a distinction of these vices, which is probably the list of natural vices at *EE* II 1220b38–21a12. Aristotle may also refer to the discussion of affections and natural vices at 1221a13–17 or to the discussion of these particular vices at 1221b10–7. Cf. Donini 1999, fn. 155. The backward reference is not precise: these three dispositions (irascibility, fierceness, and savagery) do not occur in the list of the natural vices at *EE* II 1220b38–21a12 with the only exception of *orgilos/orgilotês*. Similarly, the discussion at 1221b10–7 is not precisely about the vices mentioned at 1231b8–9: at 1221b10–7, the discussion is about being choleric (*oxuthumos*), which is related to irascibility (*orgilos/orgilotês*). In a way, being choleric can be considered a species of irascibility.

[48] Gottlieb (2009, 32–6) stresses the importance of the triadic structure for Aristotle's understanding of the virtues.

[49] *EE* III 1231b9–10.

there can be three excesses that correspond to two defects. All this suggests that natural virtues and vices are organized in a continuum that goes from excess to deficiency and that may include species of the same vice.[50]

(i)-(iii) show that natural virtues differ from character virtues in fundamental ways and in ways that make it plausible for agents to possess one or some natural virtues without possessing them all. Conversely, possessing all the virtues of character is an essential requirement for possessing each virtue of character. Natural virtues are not a necessary prerequisite to develop the virtues of character: they are an advantage, but we can develop the virtues of character without having the corresponding natural virtues.[51]

3.3 The interdependency between the character virtues and *phronêsis*

For Aristotle, agents must possess the virtues of character together with *phronêsis*. As I mention in the introduction, this relation between the virtues of character and *phronêsis* has been referred to as mutual entailment or reciprocity of the virtues. In what follows, I refer to it as interdependency as I wish to stress that *phronêsis* cannot come about and fulfil its tasks unless there are the character virtues. Correspondingly, the character virtues cannot come about and fulfil their tasks unless there is *phronêsis*. I call these two kinds of interdependency Ontological Interdependency and Functional Interdependency.

---

[50] Brown (2014, 64-80) argues against the idea that there is a continuum between excess, virtue, and defect. I agree with this view as I think that there is a continuum only in the case of natural virtues and natural vices. Brown argues that in agreement with Plato's view in *Republic* 444c, vices can have many forms while virtue has only one.

[51] For a different interpretation, see Kenny who argues that the union of *phronêsis* and the character virtues depends on the possession of natural virtues (Kenny 2016, 163).

(T4) In this way the argument could be refuted, the argument that someone may use dialectically to show that the virtues can be separated from each other given that the same person is not best suited by nature for them all, with the result that he will have already acquired one virtue but not yet acquired another. This is possible, in fact, for the natural virtues but it is not possible for the virtues with reference to which one is said to be good without qualification. Together with practical wisdom that is one and that belongs to the agent, all the virtues belong to him.[52]

T4 shows that practical wisdom is one: that is, it is not the case that we have one form of practical wisdom for each virtue of character. In the passage, Aristotle refers to a dialectical argument that shows that agents can possess some virtues without possessing them all. The reference to this argument is puzzling insofar as several philosophical theories in antiquity, as far as we know, agreed—at least in outline—on the UoV.[53] That is, though they disagree on the specifics, they agree on the idea that all the virtues must be possessed together. With this reference to a dialectical argument, Aristotle may refer to an argument based on our intuitions that not everyone is by nature provided with the same virtues, as we see people who are more prone to courage, others who are more prone to temperance, and so forth. This argument is compatible with the idea that agents may possess one or some natural virtues without possessing them all. However, it is not possible to be good without qualification (*haplôs agathos*) and lack one or more virtues of character. That is, we should distinguish two states: the state of being good with qualification, that is, the state of having some natural virtues, from the state of being good without qualification. This second state comes about only when one has all the character virtues together with *phronêsis*.

---

[52] *EE* V = *NE* VI 1144b33–45a2.
[53] Cf. Introduction, footnote 1.

Aristotle specifies that someone cannot have *phronêsis* and be incontinent: that is, if one has *phronêsis* one has also the virtues of character.[54] The *phronimos* knows what is right and does what is right. However, one can have cleverness (*deinotês*) and be incontinent.[55] Aristotle compares the relation between natural virtues and the character virtues to the relation between cleverness and *phronêsis*.[56] He presents cleverness as one species (*eidos*) of the calculative part of the soul.[57] Of course, this remark should be read in the context of the analogy between *phronêsis* and cleverness: that is, insofar as cleverness does not involve *prohairesis*, it cannot be a virtue of thinking.[58] Cleverness is a capacity to lead us to the aim (*skopos*) that we want to reach regardless of whether the aim is good or bad. However, this capacity is not always good for the agent who possesses it. It is a natural rational capacity: namely, it is a capacity for opposites that can lead us to the good or to the bad, and that we develop by nature.[59] And it can be harmful.[60] Even though the tasks that cleverness and *phronêsis* fulfil may seem similar, cleverness functions as a natural virtue of thinking that is not anchored in right affections and good starting points, which are provided, respectively, by the virtues of character and by practical *nous*.[61]

---

[54] *EE* VI = *NE* VII 1152a10–4.
[55] *EE* V = *NE* VI 1144b15. *Deinotês* can be considered a natural virtue of thinking. See *Historia Animalium* 588a24 for evidence of virtues of thinking that are natural and that can be possessed also by animals.
[56] *EE* V = *NE* VI 1144b14–7. As Gottlieb notes, the analogy is the wrong way round as *deinotês* should be the analogue of natural virtue and not of virtue proper, as Aristotle puts it. Cf. Gottlieb 2009, 108.
[57] *Deinotês* is mentioned in this section of the common books, in 1152a11–2, and in *MM* 1197b19–37.
[58] Cf. *EE* VI = *NE* VII 1152a12.
[59] Cf. Leunissen 2017, ch. 5.
[60] In the passage, Aristotle speaks of states, but the reference is clearly to capacities—that is, natural virtues—rather than to proper virtues of thinking and virtues of character.
[61] *Nous* has a fundamental role in guaranteeing that natural capacities are not harmful. Cf. *EE* V = *NE* VI 1144b6–17. Some scholars think that at *EE* V = *NE* VI 1144b9, Aristotle is not referring to *nous* as the virtue discussed in *EE* V = *NE* VI, but he is referring to thinking broadly understood. However, the role that he assigns to *nous* in this passage is in line with how Aristotle conceives of *nous*, in particular practical *nous*, in other passages in the *EE*. Natali (1999, 513, fn. 658) argues that at 1144b9, *nous* has a generic sense and it does not refer to the virtue of thinking described in *EE* V. In this passage,

In EE V = NE VI 1144b17–32, Aristotle rejects Socrates' view according to which the virtues of character are forms of *phronêsis* (*phronêseis*). Aristotle points out that everyone agrees that virtue is a state (*hexis*) and that it is a state according to right reason (*kata ton orthon logon*). However, Aristotle explains that the view that the virtues are according to right reason, which he says is a view held by everyone, is not precise. We should say that the virtues are with right reason (*meta tou orthou logou*).[62] In 1144b28, he specifies that right reason is *phronêsis*. This idea that the virtues are *with* right reason needs to be clarified. Gottlieb translates the Greek expression *meta logou* as 'involving right reason'.[63] According to Gottlieb, the expression is in contrast with 'being in accordance (*kata*) with right reason'. She explains that when the virtues of character involve right reason, the agent's soul is an integrated harmony of emotions and reason.[64] According to her view, this means that practical wisdom is fully integrated in the virtues of character and it does not run parallel to them. Gottlieb's analysis focuses primarily on the *NE*; however, the distinction between being in accordance with right reason vs involving or being with right reason is

---

Aristotle speaks of *phusikai hexeis*, but the context clarifies that he is not talking about stable states that require *prohairesis*. One possible explanation of why he talks about *hexeis* as opposed to *dunameis* is that he includes in these capacities also *deinotês*, which is a virtue of thinking that occurs by nature. Lawrence explains the passage by saying that the virtues discussed in this passage are natural virtues and that they are not proper virtues of character. Cf. Lawrence 2011, 233–84.

[62] *EE* V = *NE* VI 1144b27.
[63] Gottlieb 2009, 94.
[64] Hardie, Irwin, Broadie, and Rowe believe that involving (*meta*) right reason is weaker than being in accordance (*kata*) with right reason. Cf. Hardie 1968, 236–9; Irwin 1985, 349; and Broadie and Rowe 2002, 188. Ross, Crisp, and Lawrence agree with Gottlieb. See Ross 1925; Crisp 2000, 117–8; Lawrence 2011, 233–84. Morel defends the view that the virtues of character are rational insofar as they are *hexeis prohairetikai*. Cf. Morel 2017, 141–53. Sorabji offers an argument in favour of the view that the virtues of character are 'moral dispositions', as he calls them. As he interprets them, the virtues of character are directed by practical wisdom. He stresses the role of intellect (with intellect, he seems to refer to the rational part of the soul in general) in the virtues of character by focusing on *prohairesis*, practical wisdom, and moral disposition, see Sorabji 1980, 201–19.

prominent also in the *EE*. The passage on which Gottlieb focuses is in the common books. In the undisputed books of the *EE*, Aristotle says that the virtues of character are with *phronêsis*.[65] The idea of being 'with *phronêsis*' shows that the virtues of character form a unity with practical wisdom.[66] With *phronêsis*, natural virtues are transformed into character virtues. On its turn, practical wisdom cannot come about without the character virtues. That is, practical wisdom must be possessed always with the character virtues. In this sense, there is Ontological Interdependency between *phronêsis* and the character virtues.

Evidence in favour of the idea that the virtues of character form a unity with *phronêsis* and depend ontologically on *phronêsis* and vice versa is provided by the distinction between states (i.e. the virtues of character) that are with reason and with *prohairesis* vs capacities (i.e. natural virtues) that are without reason as I discussed in section 3.2. It is clear from the definition of states that the relation between the virtues of character and practical wisdom is more than a mere occurring together: that is, reason (in the sense of practical wisdom) is a defining element of the character virtues. The interdependency between the virtues of character and *phronêsis* guarantees that agents experience the right affections according to reason in the relevant situations and feel pleasure and pain in what they ought. A clear example of this is temperance. In *EE* V = *NE* VI 1140b11–6, Aristotle explains that temperance is what saves *phronêsis*. That is, temperance saves the kind of apprehension (*hupolêpsis*) that is *phronêsis*.[67] Aristotle clarifies that pleasure and pain do not corrupt all kinds of apprehensions but only practical apprehension. For this reason, *phronêsis* needs temperance—and the other virtues of character insofar as all the

---

[65] *EE* III 1234a31.
[66] On *meta phronêseôs*, cf. *Euthydemus* 278e3–282e5; *Phaedo* 69b3; *Meno* 87e5–89a5; *Republic* 591b5–7, 621c5; *Theaetetus* 176b2. Cf. Sedley 2014, 65–91.
[67] *EE* V = *NE* VI 1142b33.

virtues of character must be possessed together—in order not to be corrupted by pleasure and pain.

Scholars debate on whether the character virtues are about the means or the end of deliberation, or whether these tasks—i.e. providing the means and the end of deliberation—are fulfilled by *phronêsis*. That is, it seems that the character virtues and *phronêsis* contribute to the same tasks. As I argue in chapter 2, one option to explain why two or more virtues contribute to the same tasks—let's think about *phronêsis* and good deliberation as I discuss them in chapter 2—is to conceive of these virtues as depending on one another.[68] That is, there is Functional Interdependency between the character virtues and *phronêsis*: that is, the character virtues and *phronêsis* cooperate to fulfil the same tasks concerning the means and the end of deliberation.

The paradigmatic example of courage can elucidate how the virtues of character and *phronêsis* interdepend. Aristotle characterizes courage as something that follows or obeys reason.[69] On the view that I defend, courage follows or obeys reason insofar as it depends on reason/*phronêsis* ontologically and for its function. Aristotle explains that reason commands that we choose the *kalon*. This relation between courage and reason is in line with Aristotle's characterization of each character virtue as capable of decision (*prohairetikê*): each virtue makes us choose everything for the sake of the *kalon* insofar as it obeys reason.[70] In *EE* VIII, Aristotle offers some further elucidation regarding the relation between *phronêsis* and the virtues of character. He explains that

---

[68] This is compatible with the idea that *phronêsis* has tasks that are not tasks of the virtues of character. I argue in favour of the idea that *phronêsis* has emerging tasks in chapter 2.

[69] *EE* III 1229a2: ἡ γὰρ ἀνδρεία ἀκολούθησις τῷ λόγῳ ἐστίν. The same term occurs in the description of *megalopsychia*, which is said to accompany (*akolouthei*) all the virtues (*EE* III 1232a31). Cf. Plato, *Laws* 631c–d. In this passage, all the virtues are said to follow (*sunakolouthei*) *phronêsis*. Cf. Sedley 2014, 65–91.

[70] *EE* III 1230a29. For a teleological conception of *prohairesis* cf. Nielsen 2022, 93.

phronêsis uses virtue.[71] And he says that at the same time we are *phronimoi* and the states of our irrational soul are good.[72] These remarks that occur at the end of the *EE* reinforce the idea that *phronêsis* and the virtues of character must be possessed together and depend on one another.

The last piece of evidence that I discuss in favour of the idea that there is interdependency and unity between the virtues of character and *phronêsis* concerns the limit (*horos*). Aristotle refers to the limit in two parallel passages, respectively at *EE* V = *NE* VI 1138b21–34 (A) and at *EE* VIII.3 1249a23–b27 (B). In A, the limit is explicitly called the limit of mean points, while in B, it is a limit of *kalokagathia*, which is relevant for the natural goods and for the virtues of character. As I show in what follows, with regard to the virtues of character, the limit is established by *phronêsis* and guides the character virtues. In the *EE*, Aristotle speaks of a limit in the singular rather than of limits (*horoi*) in the plural as he does, for example, in the *Protrepticus*. The use of the singular instead of the plural suggests that there is one limit for all the virtues of character, which brings evidence in favour of the unity of the practical virtues.

With regard to B, some scholars think that the limit is not a limit of action, but instead is a limit for the choice of natural goods.[73] Other scholars think that the limit does indeed concern actions.[74] Natural goods are good by nature for human beings: examples of natural goods as they are listed by Aristotle at 1248b29–30 are honour, wealth, bodily excellences, pieces of good fortune, and capacities.[75] On the view that I defend, in both passages—A and B—the limit is relevant for the virtues of character. Kenny explains that practical wisdom sets the mean for the virtues of character and

---

[71] *EE* VIII 1246b12. Cf. 1248a30, where Aristotle says that virtue is an instrument of *nous*.
[72] *EE* VIII 1246b35–6.
[73] Monan 1968, 129–31; Rowe 1971, 110; Cooper 1975, 137–41.
[74] Kenny 1992, 182–3; Gosling and Taylor 1982, 342–4.
[75] I discuss natural goods in Bonasio 2021, 123–42.

for the sake of the contemplation of the divine.[76] For Kenny, the limit is a limit of perfect virtue. A similar interpretation is defended by Gosling and Taylor. According to Gosling and Taylor, the limit concerns actions and not only natural goods.[77] The reading defended by Kenny, and by Gosling and Taylor, presupposes that the limit is a limit of the soul and of *kalokagathia*, and not only of natural goods. According to this reading, in B, Aristotle refers to the same limit throughout the entire passage. Broadie argues that there are at least two limits: the limit of natural goods and the limit of *kalokagathia* discussed in *EE* VIII.3. She argues that *kalokagathia* is the limit of natural goods and that *theôria* is the limit of *kalokagathia*.[78] Broadie interprets *horos* as 'moral safeguard': virtue allows the agent to choose and acquire natural goods with a view to what would contribute to a good life. Walker focuses on the *EE* as well as on the *Protrepticus*: he argues that there are limits that are boundary makers of the virtues and that are provided by *theôria*.[79] Wolt argues that in A, the limit concerns the mean in action, while in B, it concerns natural goods.[80] I agree that in A, the limit is about the mean, and that in B, it is relevant for the natural goods. In A, Aristotle says that there is a limit for the mean states and that the mean should be as right reason indicates. He then compares this notion of the mean, which is according to right reason, to the situation of someone who has been told to do everything that 'medicine and the doctor prescribe'.[81] This guideline is not clear and the agent would not know what to do to promote her health. In a similar way, saying that the mean is according to right reason is not clear. Aristotle concludes that we should explain what right reason is. And he proceeds with an analysis of the virtues of thinking that occupies

---

[76] Kenny 1992, 100.
[77] Gosling and Taylor 1982, 343.
[78] Broadie 1993, 385.
[79] Walker 2018.
[80] Wolt 2022, 1–23.
[81] *EE* V = *NE* VI 1138b, 31–2.

the entire book (*EE* V = *NE* VI): in this analysis, practical wisdom has a prominent place.[82] As I explained, practical wisdom is right reason.[83] Either as virtues on which practical wisdom depends or as that for the sake of which practical wisdom prescribes—which is theoretical contemplation that is the activity of *sophia*—all the virtues of thinking are involved in the mean and in the limit.[84]

In B, Aristotle says that there is a limit that is comparable to the limit that the doctor has to establish whether a body is healthy. This time the limit is the limit of possession, choice, and use of natural goods.[85] Aristotle repeats that it is a limit for choosing and possessing natural goods.[86] These clarifications stress the idea that choosing natural goods is important, at least as much as possessing them. Choosing the right natural goods and in the right amount is already an indication that the agent has the character virtues. In *EE* VIII 1249b1, Aristotle specifies that these natural goods that are relevant for the limit are not goods that are praiseworthy (*epaineta*). Virtues are good and beautiful and are praiseworthy.[87] Aristotle contrasts temperance and justice, which are praiseworthy, with health and vigorous action, which are good but not praiseworthy. This shows that the natural goods mentioned at 1249b1 are not the virtues, but they are health, wealth, and so forth. However, this limit is important for the virtues of character for at least two reasons. First, the person who has the character virtues must apply the limit correctly insofar as this agent chooses and acquires natural goods in the right way. Second, Aristotle says explicitly that we should live according to the commanding element in the soul and that this is the state according to the activity of what commands.[88] One cannot

---

[82] Natali (2017, 121) goes as far as interpreting the entire book V as an effort of clarifying what *orthos logos* is, which is *phronêsis*.
[83] *EE* V = *NE* VI 1144b22–4.
[84] I discuss the relation between practical wisdom and *sophia* in chapter 5.
[85] *EE* VIII 1249b1–2.
[86] *EE* VIII 1249b18–9.
[87] *EE* VIII 1248b22–38.
[88] *EE* VIII 1249b7–8.

be in the state according to the activity of what commands unless the agent has all the virtues of character and *phronêsis*.

For present purposes, establishing whether the limit is about the mean or about natural goods does not ultimately make a difference. That is, the mean as well as natural goods are all directly relevant for the virtues of character. Namely, the virtues of character are about the mean and require natural goods. What is more, the person who has the virtues of character chooses the right amount of the right natural goods. In both passages, the limit is established by practical wisdom. This shows that the interaction between practical wisdom and the character virtues is structured in such a way that practical wisdom commands the character virtues by providing the limit.[89] This relation between practical wisdom and the virtues of character is compatible with the idea that there is interdependency between the virtues of character and *phronêsis*. That is, even though *phronêsis* depends on the character virtues both to come about and for its function, it is superior to the character virtues in the sense that it commands them. In a similar way, a general needs soldiers to fully be a general and to fulfil her function, but at the same time, she commands the soldiers. All this shows that there is not only Ontological but also Functional Interdependency between the character virtues and *phronêsis*.

3.4 Challenges related to the unity of the character virtues

As I showed, while agents can possess one or some natural virtues, character virtues must be possessed all together. Scholars and philosophers already in the Middle Ages raised objections to this unity of the character virtues: for example, they argued that given

---

[89] Rowe (1971) argues that *EE* VIII.3 narrows down the application of *horos* that was introduced in book V.

this unity, it is not possible to distinguish one virtue of character from another. At *EE* III 1232a20-2, Aristotle himself admits that the virtues are close to each other in scope and ways of functioning to such an extent that it is difficult to distinguish the individual virtues. Scholars have proposed different ways for individuating or distinguishing the virtues of character. These discussions focus mostly on how the virtues of character are presented in the *NE*. Some scholars argue that the virtues are individuated by characteristic emotions.[90] Others explain that they are individuated by their activity.[91] Other scholars propose a combination of these two proposals.[92] Some scholars argue that the virtues of character are distinguished by the object and circumstances of the desire associated with the virtues.[93] Other scholars distinguish the virtues on the basis of the reasons for acting in a certain way.[94]

On the view that I defend, the virtues of character are individuated on the basis of the emotions involved and by the types of pleasures and pains.[95] Each virtue of character involves certain emotions and certain types of pleasures and pains. And each virtue of character is individuated by the fact of being a mean between two vices.[96] Gottlieb argues that for each virtue of character,

---

[90] Urmson (1980, 157-70) shows that there is a correlation between virtues and emotions. Gottlieb (2009, 93) explains that the virtues are exercised in a particular sphere and associated with particular emotions.
[91] Nussbaum (1988b, 32-53) individuates the virtues based on their sphere of activity. West (2016, 877-97) shows that multiple virtues are involved in the same sphere of activity and that the same virtue can be involved in many spheres of activity. According to Walker (1993, 44-62), virtues are individuated by their exercise in action.
[92] Frede (2014, 83-103) argues that each virtue of character is confined to one type of action and one affection.
[93] Deslauriers (2002, 101-26) argues that the virtues of character are numerically one but many in being. According to Deslauriers, the virtues are differentiated by the object of desire and the circumstances in which this desire arises. On her view, the virtues are the same *hexis* qualified by different properties.
[94] Russell (2009) argues that the virtues are distinguished based on their characteristic reasons. Cooper (1999a, 212-36) argues that virtues are individuated by the reasons according to which we decide to act in a certain way.
[95] *EE* II 1222b5-12.
[96] Cf. Gottlieb 2009, ch. 1.

there is a triad formed by two vices and one virtue.[97] She explains that each virtue of character is a state of equilibrium and there are many ways to be in equilibrium between two vices. However, this approach seems to generate a multiplication of the virtues of character beyond those that Aristotle discusses in the *EE*. In *EE* II–III–IV, Aristotle describes the virtues of character and the corresponding vices. As I see it, there seems to be no reason to suppose that there are other virtues of character or vices in addition to the ones discussed in these books. As I explained in section 3.2, whereas natural virtues and natural vices constitute a continuum with species, virtues of character and proper vices do not constitute a continuum. That is, there are no intermediate states in-between a given virtue of character and the two corresponding vices. This is necessary to individuate the virtues of character and to posit that they are a unity rather than species of the same virtue.

A further objection to the unity of the virtues arises if we consider large-scale virtues such as magnanimity (*megalopsychia*) and magnificence (*megaloprepeia*). Magnanimity requires suitable conditions for the agent to acquire honour and to have political roles. Magnificence requires the possession of wealth.[98] According to the unity of the virtues of character, if agents lack wealth or if they do not live in a political situation suitable for them to acquire honour, they would not be able to have any virtue of character.[99] Different solutions have been proposed to solve this problem and to explain why the virtues of character need to be possessed

---

[97] Gottlieb 2009, ch. 1; Brown 2014, 64–80. Brown argues that virtue is a *mesotês* because it achieves the *meson* in feelings and actions. The case of justice is somehow difficult to situate: some scholars think that justice has one opposite—injustice—but it is not a mean between two vices (cf. Lee 2022, 101–21). As an alternative interpretation, justice may be considered the virtue of wanting our proper due that corresponds to two vices: *pleonexia* as a greedy desire for more than one deserves and desiring less than what we deserve. Against this interpretation, see Broadie (2002, 35–36) who argues that particular justice has a single opposite: injustice.

[98] Irwin 1988a, 71–8; Gottlieb 2009, 28.

[99] Aquinas already discussed this problem: these large-scale virtues require exceptional natural goods to be exercised. Not everyone has these goods. Cf. Aquinas, section 405.

all together.[100] Gardiner proposes to restrict the unity of the virtues of character to those virtues that are not magnificence and magnanimity.[101]

One may argue that whereas it seems plausible for us to have one or some virtues of character without having them all, this option is not in line with how Aristotle conceives of the virtues of character. The virtues of character are stable states to act aiming at the *kalon* in all possible situations. They are individuated on the basis of the emotions and on the basis of the kind of pleasure and pain that we experience, and they can be distinguished from one another because each virtue is a mean between two vices. However, as we can distinguish and individuate the parts of the soul with the scope of analysing them, we cannot truly separate them; in the same way we can distinguish the virtues of character, but we cannot separate them. They are aspects of the same state of the soul. In this sense, one cannot lack one virtue of character, but one may not perform one or more virtuous actions (e.g. a magnificent action) due to a particular situation (e.g. the lack of external goods such as wealth). This approach is in line with Aristotle's claim that when agents possess the virtues of character, they act according to them. That is, even when fully virtuous agents cannot perform a magnificent action due to lack of wealth, they still possess the virtue of magnificence and in a way, they exercise it. They exercise the state of the soul that results from the possession of all the virtues of character when they evaluate the situation, decide that they should perform the virtuous action, and are aware that they lack the necessary wealth to perform it. In this process of deliberation all the virtues of character as well as *phronêsis* and the virtues on which *phronêsis* depends are involved.

---

[100] Cf. Walker 1993, 44–62; Lemos 1993, 85–106; Cooper 1999a, 212–36; Wolf 2007, 145–67; Russell 2009, ch. 8. For an overview of the debate, see Wilson 2021, 9835–54. I discuss this in more detail in the conclusion of the book.
[101] Gardiner 2001, 261–96.

3.5 Conclusions

In this chapter, I argued that agents can have one or some natural virtues without having them all because natural virtues are mere capacities to experience affections in a certain way, they do not involve *prohairesis*, and they correspond to natural vices. The virtues of character are states that require *phronêsis*, they are developed by habituation, and they are not organized in a continuum as the natural virtues. Agents must possess all the virtues of character together. What is more, agents do not need to possess the natural virtues in order to develop the character virtues. In the chapter, I conceived the relation between the character virtues and *phronêsis* in terms of Ontological and Functional Interdependence. Namely, I explained that the character virtues need *phronêsis* to come about and to fulfil their function. In a similar way, *phronêsis* needs the character virtues to come about and to fulfil its function. I argued that even though they must be possessed all together, it is possible to individuate and distinguish the virtues of character. This chapter is a fundamental step towards an account of the full UoV that I defend in this book insofar as it shows that within the full UoV as parts of *kalokagathia* there is a less comprehensive unity that comprises all the character virtues as well as *phronêsis*, practical intelligence, good deliberation, comprehension, and consideration: the unity of the practical virtues.

4
Epistêmê is said in many ways

In the *EE*, *epistêmê* is said in many ways. *Epistêmê* qua knowledge fulfils fundamental tasks in the practical domain and co-functions with *phronêsis*. It has a double role in the Functional Unity of the Virtues: in the theoretical domain, it is a part of *sophia*, and in the practical domain, it co-functions with *phronêsis*.[1] With this proposal, which I defend throughout the chapter, I contribute to long-standing debates: on the distinction between scientific understanding and knowledge of a more ordinary kind and on the distinction between practical and theoretical wisdom, to name just two especially prominent themes. I borrow Aristotle's 'said in many ways'-locution to show that the many ways in which *epistêmê* can be said become evident if we draw distinctions along several dimensions of Aristotle's work. I start by clarifying the terms that Aristotle uses to refer to knowledge and to having knowledge (section 4.1). I then turn to a distinction between what I call the Understanding Account (UA) of *epistêmê*, according to which *epistêmê* proceeds via demonstration and is about what is necessary and eternal, and the Knowledge Account (KA) of *epistêmê*, according to which *epistêmê* is explanatory knowledge that may proceed by demonstration or not, and has contingent objects. With the KA I aim to capture all the many ways in which *epistêmê* is said that do not fall under the UA (section 4.2). I explain that there are many ways of having knowledge and of failing to use it

---

[1] For brevity, I write that a virtue co-functions with *phronêsis*, but I mean that it co-functions with *phronêsis*, as well as with the virtues on which *phronêsis* depends (the virtues of character, *euboulia*, *sunesis*, *gnôme*, and practical *nous*). In chapters 2 and 3, I argued that *phronêsis* is a dependent virtue and I explained on which virtues it depends.

(section 4.3). I develop four criteria for acquiring, possessing, and using *epistêmê* (section 4.4). According to the KA, I argue that *epistêmê* fulfils important roles not only in the theoretical domain, but also in the practical one. Nonetheless, *epistêmê* is distinct from *phronêsis*. I show that the four criteria for acquiring, possessing, and using *epistêmê* do not apply to how *phronêsis* functions and to how we use and acquire it (section 4.5). And I conclude with a discussion of the different ways in which *phronêsis* and *epistêmê* relate to the truth (section 4.6). Given these considerations on the many ways in which *epistêmê* is said, I tend to leave *epistêmê* untranslated. I do so even though the standard translation—knowledge— is not necessarily misleading. In fact, I use knowledge as a general term.[2] It hides, however, some of the differences that matter to my reconstruction of the many ways in which *epistêmê* figures in Aristotle's *EE*.

Even though my focus is the *EE*, in my analysis, I must refer to how Aristotle understands *epistêmê* outside the *EE* insofar as the scholarly debate on *epistêmê* concerns in particular how *epistêmê* is discussed in the *Prior* and *Posterior Analytics*, and in the *Metaphysics*.

4.1 *Epistasthai kai eidenai*

In order to clarify the many ways in which Aristotle understands *epistêmê* in the *EE*, I start from a distinction between *epistasthai* without qualification (*haplôs*) and qualified *epistasthai* that Aristotle makes in the *Posterior Analytics*. In this text, Aristotle says

---

[2] I remain sceptical about the possibility of rendering in modern languages the distinction between *epistasthai*, *eidenai*, and *gignôskein*. When I refer to UA, I translate *epistasthai* as 'understanding'. I translate qualified *epistasthai* (*epistasthai* that is not *haplôs*) as 'to know'. When I refer to KA, I use 'knowledge' (*epistêmê*) and 'having knowledge' (*eidenai*, *gignôskein*). However, I use 'understanding' and 'knowledge' interchangeably to translate *gignôskein*. Cf. Burnyeat 2011, 3–29; 1981, 97–139; Cohoe 2022, 1–13.

that *epistasthai* is understanding (*gignôskein*) the cause through demonstration.

(T1) We believe that we understand (*epistasthai*) each thing without qualification (*haplôs*), but not by accident according to the sophistical way, when we think that we know the cause through which that thing is, that is the cause of that thing, and that it cannot be otherwise.[3]

In the passage, Aristotle says that we have understanding—*epistasthai*—when we know the cause of something, and this thing is necessary. Aristotle speaks of *epistasthai haplôs* to stress the distinction with *epistasthai* with a qualification. This already shows that there are many ways of knowing, and that not all kinds of *epistasthai* are without qualification.[4] Aristotle admits that not all *epistêmê* is demonstrative.[5] *Epistasthai haplôs* refers to demonstrative understanding of what is necessary, which is in line with the description of *epistêmê* that we find in *EE* V = *NE* VI 1139b18–36.[6] But there is another kind of *epistasthai*—*epistasthai* with a qualification. Aristotle does not say this explicitly, but it seems plausible that this *epistasthai* with a qualification concerns knowledge that may or may not be demonstrative and that is not about necessary causes. *Epistasthai* with a qualification proceeds in a different way from *epistasthai haplôs*. Correspondingly, qualified *epistêmê* (and qualified *epistasthai*) is not about necessary objects known by demonstration.[7] This provides preliminary evidence in

---

[3] *Posterior Analytics* 71b9–12, my translation.
[4] *Posterior Analytics* 71b16; 72b18–20.
[5] *Posterior Analytics* 72b18–20; at 87b24–5, Aristotle admits that there is *epistêmê* of what is for the most part. Cf. Barnes 1994, 91. Barnes points out that Aristotle uses *epistêmê* in ways that do not correspond to the account given in T1. Cf. 99b16–17 on knowledge of first principles which cannot be demonstrative.
[6] At *Posterior Analytics* 73a23, Aristotle says that a demonstration is a syllogism that proceeds from what is necessary.
[7] Gartner argues that *epistêmê* is not always understanding/scientific knowledge of what is necessary and eternal (Gartner 2019, 125–45). Gartner distinguishes *epistêmê haplôs* from qualified *epistêmê*. She considers the idea that unqualified *epistêmê* may be

favour of the idea that *epistasthai* and *epistêmê* are said in at least two ways: *epistasthai/epistêmê* without qualification and qualified *epistasthai/epistêmê*.

Scholars debate on how to understand three verbs—and their correlative nouns—that Aristotle uses to refer to knowledge: *epistasthai/epistêmê*, *eidenai/eidêsis* (very rare), and *gignôskein/gnôsis*. Since Ryle, scholars tried to find a correspondence between these ancient Greek terms and what Burnyeat calls the epistemic troika, namely knowledge that, knowledge how, and knowledge by acquaintance.[8] Despite the many attempts to find a correspondence between the ancient Greek verbs for knowledge and the epistemic troika, the results are not clear. There seems to be a consensus on the distinction between *epistêmê/epistasthai* and *eidenai/gnôsis*. *Eidenai/gnôsis* refer to a less demanding and more general notion of knowledge.

Burnyeat argues persuasively that it is methodologically flawed to impose on Aristotle's epistemology a modern distinction such as the distinction among knowledge that, knowledge how, and knowledge by acquaintance. Aside from modern parallels, Burnyeat agrees with Barnes' initial intuition that there is a contrast between *eidenai/gignôskein* (knowing) and *epistasthai* (understanding).[9] Burnyeat argues that the epistemic verbs *eidenai*, *gignôskein*, and *epistasthai* express two ideas: (i) explanatory knowledge, and (ii) plain knowledge. This shows that there is no one-to-one correlation

---

impossible in ethics since the object of this *epistêmê* is contingent rather than necessary and eternal. As Gartner points out, unqualified *epistêmê* is a demonstrative state. She shows that in *Posterior Analytics* 1.30, Aristotle hints toward the possibility of ethical demonstrations that hold for the most part. Gartner concludes that there must be some theoretical ethical understanding that informs practical thinking. Lorenz shows that we can distinguish full understanding (*epistêmê*) from understanding of particulars (Lorenz 2014, 242–62). This second type of understanding is referred to as perceptual understanding.

[8] See Burnyeat 2011, 4.
[9] Barnes 2007, 7–30. Barnes later changed his mind and is now sceptical about any possible way of disentangling the relation among the three verbs of the epistemic troika.

between Greek verb and kind of knowledge that the verb expresses. For Burnyeat, *epistêmê* is correlated with *epistasthai* and should be translated as understanding (or scientific knowledge). *Epistêmê* and *epistasthai* refer to explanatory knowledge. *Gnôsis* is correlated with *gignôskô* which is plain knowledge as opposed to explanatory knowledge.[10] *Eidenai* is more general than *epistasthai* and *gignôskein*.[11]

Fine and Bronstein agree with Burnyeat that *eidenai* is more general than *epistasthai*. Fine argues that Aristotle has a broad notion of knowledge and that *epistêmê* is just one kind of knowledge. As she explains, the notion of *epistêmê* that we find in *Posterior Analytics* I.2 is very demanding, but is not exhaustive of all the ways in which agents can have knowledge. Aristotle makes room for a lower form of knowledge that does not require an explanation. For Fine, *gnôsis* is weaker than *epistêmê*, but is still genuine knowledge.[12] Bronstein agrees that *gnôsis* is a lower form of knowledge if compared with *epistêmê* which is demonstrative. He explains that *eidenai* is a place holder for any term of *gnôsis*. What emerges from these debates is a consensus that *eidenai* and *gnôsis* are more general and less demanding than *epistasthai* and *epistêmê*.

Scholars who focus on the ethical treatises recognize that in these works, *epistêmê/epistasthai* are not always used to refer to demonstrative understanding. They agree that *epistêmê/epistasthai* do not always refer to the very demanding notion of understanding described in *Posterior Analytics* I.2.[13] Pace Burnyeat, in the ethical treatises, *epistêmê* does not seem to be always correlated to

---

[10] See Burnyeat 2011, 3–29 and 1981, 97–139. Cf. Lyons 1963, quoted by Burnyeat 2011. I do not think that in the ethical treatises, *epistêmê* is always correlated with *epistasthai*. This approach is not a unicum in Aristotle since scholars defend the idea that *theôria* has a technical meaning in Aristotle that the verb *theôrein* lacks (see Nightingale 2004).
[11] As Burnyeat (2011, 3–29) points out, this reading is in line with what Lyons (1963) argues.
[12] This is compatible with occurrences where Aristotle uses *gnôsis* for something broader than knowledge (e.g. perception), or so Fine argues. Cf. Fine 2021, 221–42.
[13] Gartner 2019, 125–45.

epistasthai, even though *epistêmê* and *epistasthai* are correlated in *EE* VI = *NE* VII.3.[14] These findings are confirmed by my analysis of these terms in the *EE*: as I show, in this treatise, Aristotle uses *epistêmê* and *gnôsis* to refer to knowledge. Borrowing Burnyeat's terminology, *epistêmê* can be understood as demonstrative understanding, but also as plain knowledge. *Gnôsis* is used as a broad term that refers to a factive cognitive state.[15] As *EE* 1246b38 shows, *phronêsis* is characterized as a form of cognition (*gnôsis*) which confirms the idea that *gnôsis* is more general and less demanding than *epistêmê*.

Epistasthai and *eidenai* figure prominently in a key passage of the *Eudemian Ethics*, where Aristotle explains that we should distinguish between having knowledge and using it.

(T2) Understanding (*epistasthai*) and knowing (*eidenai*) have two senses: one is possessing, the other using knowledge. A person who possesses knowledge but does not use it might in some circumstances be said to be justifiably (*dikaiôs*) ignorant, in others unjustifiably, for example, if he failed to use it due to lack of care (*ameleian*). Similarly one who did not even possess it might be blamed, if the knowledge that is lacking was easy or necessary and the lack was due to lack of care or pleasure or pain.[16]

Aristotle explains that *epistasthai* and *eidenai* can refer to two things—namely, they can refer to having knowledge and they can refer to using the knowledge that one possesses. In the ethical treatises, *epistasthai* occurs very rarely.[17] In line with T1, it seems plausible that *epistasthai* as it occurs in T2 is not *epistasthai*

---

[14] Cf. Lorenz 2014, 242–62. Burnyeat (2011, 24) argues that in *EE* VI = *NE* VII.3, in the discussion of akrasia, '*epistêmê* and *epistasthai* are treated on a par'.

[15] With factive state, I understand a mental state that allows agents to grasp the truth. Cf. Nagel 2017, 525–44.

[16] *EE* II 1225b12–17.

[17] In addition to this occurrence, it is mentioned at *EE* VI = *NE* VII 1146b31, 1146b33, and 1147b11–12.

haplôs.[18] That is, in the passage, Aristotle refers to knowledge that matters in practice rather than demonstrative knowledge of what is necessary. T2 stresses that there is a normative dimension related to having knowledge. Namely, Aristotle says that we are blamed if we do not possess the knowledge that we should possess. He qualifies this knowledge as easy to acquire or necessary for action: namely, we would not blame someone who does not possess knowledge difficult to acquire or not necessary for action. But we would blame someone who did not acquire knowledge that was easy to acquire and necessary for action. T2 occurs in a section where Aristotle discusses what is voluntary and involuntary with regard to what is according to thinking (*dianoia*). At 1225b2-3, Aristotle specifies that what is voluntary is defined as acting with understanding (*eidota*) of the person, the mean, and the end. He uses the example of someone who knows (*oida*) that that particular person is his father. These occurrences provide preliminary evidence in favour of two ideas: first, knowledge has a role in voluntary action; second, Aristotle favours *eidenai* to refer to knowledge that matters for action rather than *epistasthai*.[19]

In T2, Aristotle explains the paradoxical case of agents who have *epistêmê* and can be considered ignorant because they do not use the *epistêmê* that they possess. They can justifiably be considered ignorant when they have only partial or potential knowledge, or when the knowledge is superficial and has not been fully grasped. The case of someone who should not be justifiably considered ignorant is the case of someone asleep, drunk, overcome by emotions, or mad (as Aristotle describes it in *EE* VI = *NE* VII 1147a10-17). In this case, the cognizer cannot use the knowledge that she possesses due to lack of care (*ameleian*), as Aristotle says. Namely, the agent

---

[18] I translate it 'understanding', which is the translation that I use for *epistasthai* without qualification, not because I think that here Aristotle refers to understanding without qualification, but in order to distinguish it from *eidenai*.

[19] At *EE* II 1225b12, there is the only occurrence of *epistasthai* in the undisputed books of the *EE*.

cannot use knowledge because her affective, cognitive, and desiderative attitudes are not in line with her reasoning capacity. In all the other cases, when agents have knowledge, they should be able to use the knowledge that they possess. This is compatible with cases when agents decide to use the knowledge that they possess against nature and in a distorted way. I discuss these cases in section 4.3 of this chapter. Evidence that *eidenai* refers to a broader notion of knowledge than *epistasthai* is provided by this passage in the *Physics*:

> (T3) In all investigations (*methodous*) that are concerned with principles or causes or elements, it is acquaintance with these that constitutes knowledge and understanding (*to eidenai kai to epistasthai*). For we think that we know a thing when we are acquainted with its ultimate causes and first principles, and have got down to its elements. Obviously, then, in the study of nature too, our first object must be to establish principles.[20]

As the passage shows, *eidenai kai epistasthai* refers to knowledge of principles (*archai*), causes (*aitia*), and elements (*stoicheia*). The difference among principles, causes, and elements, as these terms occur in the passage, is not clear. In antiquity, while commenting this passage, Alexander points out that *epistasthai kai eidenai* is not a pleonasm: Simplicius reports that Alexander explains that *eidenai* refers to knowledge through perception and belief (*doxa*), and to knowledge of the immediate premises, while *epistasthai* refers to understanding through demonstrations.[21] For Alexander, *eidenai* is more generic than *epistasthai*. In disagreement with Alexander, Simplicius argues that while *eidenai* and *epistasthai* are not synonymous in Aristotle, they are synonymous in the

---

[20] *Physics* 184a10–16, my translation.
[21] Simplicius, *On Aristotle Physics* 12.14–13.13. Reported and discussed by Burnyeat 2011, 3–29.

passage at *Physics* 184a10–16.[22] Burnyeat showed that Alexander's interpretation better captures Aristotle's usage of the verbs in the *Physics* than Simplicius' and is in line with what we find in *Posterior Analytics* I.2. For Burnyeat, *epistasthai* does not apply to first principles or to contingent things. *Gignôskein* applies to these things. Burnyeat thinks that for Aristotle, *epistêmê* is coordinated with *epistasthai haplôs*.[23] For Burnyeat, we should reject Simplicius' idea that *eidêsis*—which is very rare in Aristotle—and *gnôsis* are equated and that *eidenai* and *gignôskein* are also equated. We should rather agree with Alexander that *eidenai* is the genus of *epistasthai*. One possible objection to the analysis of *eidenai kai epistasthai* that I develop so far comes from the common books:

(T4) Knowing (*epistasthai*) is used in two senses. A man who has knowledge (*epistêmê*) but is not using it is said to understand, and so is a man who is actually using his knowledge. It will make a difference whether a man does wrong having the knowledge that it is wrong but not actively thinking (*theôrounta*) of his knowledge, or having knowledge and actively thinking of his knowledge (*theôrounta*). The latter would be felt to be surprising; but it is not if he is not actively thinking of his knowledge (*theôrôn*).[24]

The passage occurs in a section where Aristotle examines different ways of having knowledge and not using it. Aristotle explains that it does not matter whether it is *epistêmê* or true *doxa* against which the akratic agent acts. At 1146b9 and at 1147b18–19, the question under examination is whether the akratic agent has knowledge (*eidenai*) or not. Hence, the context suggests that the knowledge that Aristotle refers to is knowledge relevant for ethics. Since in T4, he discusses knowledge relevant for ethics, we may expect to find

---
[22] Simplicius, *On Aristotle Physics* 12.14–13.13.
[23] *Posterior Analytics* I.2, 71b9–16.
[24] *EE* VI = *NE* VII 1146b31–5.

eidenai rather than *epistasthai*. *Eidenai* occurs in the discussion that follows T4: at 1147a8–10, Aristotle distinguishes two cases of *eidenai*: one in which the knowledge is in actuality and one in which it is not.[25] At 1147a21, Aristotle says that those who have just learned how to put together discourses do not yet know them (*isasi*). It is evident that the knowledge mentioned in the passage is not demonstrative understanding of what is necessary and eternal. *Epistasthai* is used in a qualified way and in the passage, it is synonymous with *eidenai*. What is more, in T4, *epistasthai* stresses the continuity with the previous passage where Aristotle points out that it does not matter whether one has *epistêmê* or true *doxa*. Namely, in this specific passage, the choice of *epistasthai* rather than *eidenai* highlights the continuity with this discussion of *epistêmê*.[26] If read in this light, this occurrence does not provide evidence in favour of an objection to the idea that *epistasthai* usually refers to demonstrative understanding while *eidenai* refers to knowledge that is not demonstrative understanding of what is necessary and eternal.

4.2 The Understanding Account and the Knowledge Account in the *EE*

Epistêmê figures in the discussion of the virtues of thinking that Aristotle offers in *EE* V = *NE* VI: it is indeed the first virtue that Aristotle discusses.[27] In this discussion, *epistêmê* is characterized

---

[25] *EE* VI = *NE* VII 1145b22–3: we find a reference to *epistêmê/epistamenon*. However, I think that in using these terms, Aristotle is adopting Socrates' terminology to explain his position.

[26] Fine suggests that knowledge in the sense of *eidenai*, which according to her interpretation is a weaker form of knowledge as compared to *epistasthai*, can be *eidenai hoti* without being *eidenai dioti*. In this sense, she argues that *eidenai hoti* is justified true belief and the justification can be a good argument, but does not need to be a deductive argument or a demonstration (which are required for *epistasthai*). Cf. Fine 2021, 234. Ackrill (1981, 359–84) and Lorenz (2014) disagree: Ackrill argues that *eidenai hoti* requires that one must grasp the explanation. Lorenz shows that *epistasthai* is knowledge of the explanation. Cf. Bronstein 2016, 16–21, 77–8.

[27] *EE* V = *NE* VI 1139b18–36.

by its object—what is necessary and eternal—and by its way of proceeding—via demonstrations.[28] *Epistêmê* conceived in this way is a part of *sophia*: that is, it is necessary for theoretical wisdom. However, this account of *epistêmê* does not capture all the ways in which Aristotle conceives of *epistêmê* in the *EE*. I distinguish what I call the UA and the KA. Admittedly, the KA is an umbrella account that captures all the ways in which *epistêmê* is said that do not fall under the UA. *Epistêmê* can refer to a systematic field of understanding, to borrow Gartner's expression, as well as to the state/activity of the cognizer.[29] To have *epistêmê* of something is to be able to give an account of something. (i) According to what I call the UA, *epistêmê* is demonstrative understanding of what is necessary and eternal and is acquired through learning. (ii) According to what I call the KA, *epistêmê* is explanatory knowledge, it can be demonstrative as well as non-demonstrative, and its objects are contingent. A distinction between the UA and the KA clarifies that while we do not need theoretical knowledge of the good to act as the good person acts, and relatedly, we do not need demonstrative understanding of the good, explanatory knowledge plays a fundamental role in the practical domain. We need this knowledge for actions and choices.

Evidence that in the *EE*, *epistêmê* is conceived according to UA is provided by the description of *epistêmê* at *EE* V = *NE* VI 1139b18–36: in this description, *epistêmê* refers to 'a holistic grasp of the structure of a domain'.[30] KA speaks to a growing consensus in the literature. Scholars move away from the traditional idea that *epistêmê* is always of what is necessary, proceeds by demonstration, and has nothing to do with ethics.[31] Preliminary evidence in favour of KA

---

[28] For a discussion of *epistêmê* and *epistasthai*, see Burnyeat 2011, 3–29; Burnyeat 1981, 96; Cohoe 2022, 1–13; see also Morison 2011; and Frede 2019, 84–116. *Epistêmê* refers to a whole body of knowledge in Plato: cf. *Theaetetus* and *Philebus* 18c–d.
[29] For the reference to a systematic field of knowledge, see Gartner 2019, 125–45.
[30] See Morison 2011, 29–57.
[31] Cf. Gartner 2019, 127. Gartner reports that both Reeve (2012) and Nielsen (2015, 29–49) admit that there is some sort of *epistêmê* of ethics insofar as there are principles of ethics that are necessary and unchanging. Reeve argues that there are ethical universals,

is provided by Aristotle's claim that there are many *epistêmai*. In the *EE*, he divides *epistêmai* in theoretical and productive.[32] Examples of theoretical *epistêmai* are astronomy, the science of nature, and geometry.[33] Examples of productive *epistêmai* are medicine and politics.[34] These examples show that under the category of productive *epistêmai*, Aristotle includes also practical *epistêmai*. What matters for present purposes is that Aristotle distinguishes these *epistêmai* on the basis of their object as well as their aims: the aims of theoretical *epistêmai* are to know (*gnôrisai*) and to think theoretically (*theôrêsai*) about objects; the aim of productive *epistêmai* is something different from understanding (*epistêmê*)—conceived according to UA—and knowledge (*gnôseôs*).[35] And yet, Aristotle says that even for productive *epistêmai*, knowledge has a fundamental role. He refutes Socrates' ideas that virtue is knowledge and that it is enough to know what virtue is in order to be virtuous. But he explains that we need to know (*gignôskein*) how to bring virtue about. In this sense, there is a kind of knowledge that plays a fundamental role in the practical domain.[36]

Knowledge has a prominent role in voluntary actions. Aristotle defines voluntary actions as actions that are performed with understanding of the person, the intermediate, and the end.[37] While working his way toward the definition of the virtues of character

whatever they are; Nielsen argues that practical wisdom requires understanding of the human good.

[32] In *EE* I 1217b35–6, Aristotle says that there is not a unique *epistêmê* of being and of the good. Cf. *EE* II 1221b5, where Aristotle speaks of *epistêmai* that are theoretical (*theôrêtikai*) and productive (*poiêtikai*).
[33] *EE* I 1216b12–13.
[34] *EE* I 1216b18–19.
[35] A similar distinction between theoretical and productive, as opposed to the distinction that we find in the *NE* between theoretical and practical, can be found in *Protrepticus* VII.
[36] See also the following passages: at *EE* II 1226a36–7, Aristotle says that doctors have *epistêmê* of things about which they deliberate. Similarly, at 1227a26–7, Aristotle speaks of *epistêmê* of sickness and of healing. What is more, at *EE* VIII 1247b14, he suggests that there are *epistêmai* that are acquired by experience (*empeiria*).
[37] *EE* II 1225b3: τὸ εἰδότα ἢ ὂν ἢ ᾧ ἢ οὗ ἕνεκα.

and of voluntary actions, Aristotle divides actions in epistemic (*epistêmonikê*) and non-epistemic (*anepistêmonikê*), expert (*technikê*) and non-expert (*atechnô*).[38] And he says that the intermediate is determined by what *epistêmê* and *logos* order. It is not clear what epistemic actions are. Donini takes epistemic actions to be actions that stem from *technê*. But this idea seems to be ruled out by Aristotle's explicit reference to the distinction between expert versus non-expert actions that occurs right after the distinction between epistemic versus non-epistemic.[39] Insofar as the passage leads to the definition of the virtues of character and of voluntary action, it seems plausible that epistemic actions are actions in which knowledge has a fundamental role: that is, voluntary actions that are performed with knowledge of the person, the intermediate, and the end. In this sense, an action is epistemic if it is informed by knowledge. In a related way, the intermediate is established by *epistêmê* and *logos* in the sense that some knowledge is involved. This is compatible with the idea that *phronêsis* together with the virtues of character establishes the intermediate. This last point is suggested by the reference to *logos* and is clarified at *EE* V = *NE* VI 1138b25.[40]

Further evidence in favour of the role of *epistêmê* in the practical domain is provided by the practical syllogism.[41] It is clear that in order to arrive at the conclusion of the syllogism and to act accordingly, one needs *phronêsis*, the character virtues, and the virtues of

---

[38] *EE* II 1220b25–6.
[39] Donini 1999, 204, footnote 63. Donini observes that commentators do not comment on this idea except Dirlmeier (Dirlmeier 1984, 245) who explains that these are actions that are based on a particular knowledge. Donini says that in the passage in question, Aristotle uses *epistêmê* in a broader sense that includes also *technê*.
[40] For the reference to *logos*, see *EE* II 1220b28–9. Cf. *EE* I 1214a27–9, where Aristotle says that all processes that come from thought can be grouped together with those that come from *epistêmê*. The sentence is not clear and the context does not clarify what Aristotle means. We may hypothesize that actions are some kind of processes: in this sense, actions qua processes may come from *epistêmê* if they are done with full knowledge of the person, the mean, the end, and the possible consequences of the action. They 'come from' (*apo*) *epistêmê* in the sense that they are informed and guided by knowledge.
[41] *EE* VI = *NE* VII 1146b31–5.

thinking on which *phronêsis* depends.[42] But one cannot grasp all the individual steps of the syllogism without *epistêmê*. I turn to the role of *epistêmê* in the practical syllogism in section 4.3, when I discuss the cases of failing to use knowledge. For the moment, it is sufficient to establish that all these passages show that in order to act virtuously, some form of *epistêmê* is involved.[43] This kind of knowledge must be understood according to the KA and is different from the demonstrative *epistêmê* whose objects are necessary and eternal that is described in *EE* V = *NE* VI and that is captured by the UA.

4.3 Failing to use knowledge

Aristotle explains that for actions, it matters not only that we possess knowledge, but that we use the knowledge that we possess.[44] Aristotle speaks of *chrêstai epistêmê*: 'to use *epistêmê*'.[45] We use *epistêmê*, for example, when *epistêmê* informs our choices and actions, when it guides the process of deliberation, and when it co-functions and interacts with other virtues. As Aristotle says in T2, someone may not use *epistêmê* because she does not possess it—in this case, the agent is rightly called ignorant—or because there is a lack of care. This lack of care seems to be the same phenomenon described at *EE* VI = *NE* VII 1146b33–5. In this passage, Aristotle says that it would be strange if someone acted contrary to how she thinks she should act when knowledge of how she should act is in actuality (*theôrounta*). But it is not strange if she does this when knowledge is not in actuality. To express that knowledge is in actuality Aristotle uses the Greek verb *theôrein*: this is a standard way

---

[42] As I argue in chapter 2, the virtues of thinking on which *phronêsis* depends are *euboulia, sunesis, gnôme*, and practical *nous*.
[43] For an argument that knowledge of the human good is required for virtuous action, see Nielsen 2015, 24–49.
[44] Cf. T2.
[45] *EE* II 1225b13.

for Aristotle to refer to knowledge that is put to use.[46] Knowledge is in potentiality as opposed to actuality when we possess it and do not use it.[47] In *EE* VI = *NE* VII, Aristotle outlines different ways in which agents may fail to use the knowledge that they possess:

1. One may have knowledge only in potentiality as opposed to having knowledge in actuality (1146b 33–5);[48]
2. One may not employ the minor premise of the practical syllogism. That is, one may have only universal knowledge of the conclusion of the syllogism, but not particular knowledge (1146b35–1147a10);[49]
3. One may not use the knowledge that one possesses because one is asleep, mad, drunk, or driven by emotions (1147a10–18);
4. One may have just acquired some knowledge that one is not able to use because the knowledge has not been fully grasped (1147a 21–4).[50]

---

[46] Cf. Lorenz 2014, 242–62.

[47] In *Posterior Analytics* 99b25–6, Aristotle engages with the possibility of having the state (*hexis*) responsible for knowing the principles (*archai*) of *epistêmê* without actually being aware (*lelêthasin*) of having this state. Scholars discuss whether Aristotle may consider this plausible. In agreement with Adamson (2010, 1–19), I do not think that Aristotle considers this plausible. That is, we cannot have the state responsible for knowing the principles without being aware of possessing this state. In evoking this possibility, Aristotle seems to refer to Plato's theory of recollection. That is, for Plato we have knowledge before birth and we need to recollect it. Both for Plato and for Aristotle, if cognizers have knowledge, they are aware of it and they should be able to give an account of what they know (*Phaedo* 76b). Hence, it is not possible to have knowledge and not be aware of it. Connectedly, we cannot be unaware that we have the state responsible for a certain type of knowledge if indeed we are aware of that certain type of knowledge. This is compatible with the idea that for Aristotle, we may have knowledge only in potentiality. Cf. Barnes 1994. See also *Phaedo* 73a; *Meno* 85c.

[48] Lorenz (2014, 242–62) argues that *theôrounta* does not refer to the idea of attending to knowledge, but rather to the contrast between occurrent (*theôrounta*) as opposed to dispositional cases of grasping the truth. The idea of having *epistêmê* and not attending to it (*mê theôrôn*)—that is, having *epistêmê* in potentiality but not in actuality—occurs also in *Physics* 255b2–3. Aristotle uses the term *theôrounta* to explain knowledge in actuality. Cf. Gauthier and Jolif 1959, 605. The two cases of agents who possess and not use knowledge correspond to the two cases described by Plato in *Theaetetus* 198d.

[49] Cf. Morison 2011, 50.

[50] In *EE* VI = *NE* VII 1147a22, the verb *sumphuênai* suggests that people have fully grasped the knowledge that they acquired.

According to (1), Aristotle contrasts having knowledge in actuality (*theôrounta*) with having knowledge only in potentiality.[51] He adds that it is surprising when agents do what they know is wrong and have knowledge in actuality. However, it is not surprising that agents act against what they know when their knowledge is only in potentiality. As I explained, knowledge in potentiality is not knowledge that is ready and available to be used in practice. As Aristotle explains in (2), agents may not use knowledge because they have incomplete or partial knowledge of the practical syllogism. Scholars debate whether this is the case of someone who knows only the universal premise of the syllogism, or whether it is the case of someone who knows only the particular premise. Morison argues persuasively that at 1147a1–10, Aristotle is not referring to the akratic agent, but rather to two ways of knowing a proposition: universal and particular (or *simpliciter*, as Morison calls it).[52] These two ways are outlined in *Prior Analytics* 67a16–20: as Aristotle explains in this text, we may have universal knowledge that the sum of the angles of a triangle is two right angles, but at the same time we may not know that a particular triangle C exists. In this sense, we have universal knowledge of the proposition 'C has two right angles', but we do not have particular knowledge of this proposition because we do not know that C exists.[53] Morison shows that having particular knowledge is the proper way of having knowledge.[54] The agent described at 1147a1–10 does not have particular knowledge of the conclusion of the syllogism, but she has only universal knowledge of the conclusion of the syllogism. This agent does not employ the minor premise of the syllogism in conjunction with the major premise. As a result, the agent has

---

[51] Lorenz (2014, 242–62) argues that in this passage, *theôrein* refers to the 'activity that comes about when understanding is put to use'.
[52] Morison 2011, 30–57.
[53] *Prior Analytics* 67a18–19: τὸ μὲν τῷ τὴν καθόλου ἔχειν ἐπιστήμην τὸ δὲ τὴν καθ' ἕκαστον.
[54] Morison 2011, 30–57; cf. *Prior Analytics* 67a27.

universal knowledge of the conclusion, but not particular knowledge of the conclusion. And this is not enough to make the agent act according to the conclusion of the syllogism. This case is different from the case of the akratic agent: the akratic agent cannot exercise her knowledge due to the state in which she is. The state of the akratic agent is captured by (3): this state can be compared to the state of someone who has knowledge but is asleep, mad, drunk, or overcome by emotions. In all these cases, one may have knowledge of the particulars, but she cannot connect her knowledge to her broader epistemic and ethical views: for this reason, the agent cannot act on the knowledge that she has.[55] At 1147a12, Aristotle says that we see that a state (*hexis*) presents differences with regard to possessing and not using it.[56] According to Burnyeat, it is significant that Aristotle does not speak of *gnôsis* in (3) insofar as acting against *epistêmê* (*para tên epistêmên*) means acting contrary to an entire body of knowledge, that is, everything that one knows that is ethically good. Lorenz and Morison argue that the akratic agent has knowledge, but she cannot access this knowledge because even if she grasps the particulars, she cannot connect them to her general ethical view. In this sense, the akratic agent has perceptual knowledge because she grasps the particulars, but she cannot grasp the conclusion of the syllogism. As Lorenz argues, the akratic agent has knowledge in a loose sense: this agent does not have full or proper knowledge. Aristotle calls the akratic agent an *epistêmôn* (1147b6), but he is using *epistêmôn* in a loose sense. That is, this agent does not have proper *epistêmê* (*kuria*). She has some kind of perceptual (*aisthêtikês*) *epistêmê*.[57]

---

[55] See Lorenz 2014, 242–62.
[56] Cf. also NE 1098b33–99a1; *Physics* 255b2–4. As Aristotle explains in *Categories* 8b27, *epistemai* are *hexeis*: they are lasting states and are hard to change. *Hexeis* are *diatheseis*, but not vice versa.
[57] This provides a way to reconcile Aristotle's claim in *EE* VI = *NE* VII 3—that there is perceptual *epistêmê*—with the idea outlined in *Posterior Analytics* 1.31—that there is no *epistasthai* through perception. Lorenz (2014, 242–62) interprets this as understanding of particulars.

The last way of having and not using *epistêmê* (4) is the case of someone who has just acquired knowledge but she cannot use it because this knowledge is only superficial and has not been fully grasped. In many ways, this is not truly a case of having knowledge.

All these cases of failing to have knowledge show that knowledge has a fundamental role in the practical syllogism and more generally in the practical domain, in actions and choices. They provide evidence that *epistêmê* according to KA must not only be possessed, but also used in order to be relevant in the practical domain. And they support my thesis that *epistêmê* interacts and co-functions with *phronêsis* as well as with other virtues in the practical domain.

4.4 Criteria for acquiring, possessing, and using *epistêmê*

Epistêmê can be used in many ways. In the *EE*, it is possible to distinguish four criteria for acquiring, possessing, and using *epistêmê*: what I call the Use Criterion, the Nature Criterion, the Distortion Criterion, and the Teaching Criterion.[58] These four criteria do not need to occur together. They capture different ways in which *epistêmê* can be acquired, possessed, and used. So far I explored the Use Criterion, namely that *epistêmê* can be possessed and not used. Let me move to the Nature Criterion.

According to the Nature Criterion, *epistêmê* can be used according to nature or contrary to nature.[59] At *EE* II 1227a24–5,

---

[58] I call these 'criteria' because later on, in section 4.5, I use these criteria to show that *epistêmê* and *phronêsis* are different and have different roles in the practical domain.
[59] At *EE* IV = *NE* V 1129a13–14, Aristotle stresses that *epistêmai* are of contraries and that there are *epistêmai* that are not good. At *EE* VI = *NE* VII 1153b8–9, Aristotle speaks of some *epistêmê* of what is bad (*phaulon*). Natali notices that for Aristotle, there cannot be bad *epistêmai* (Natali 1999, footnote 805). Burnet (1900, 337, reported by Natali) argues that this is an attack against the Platonists. Natali observes that here *epistêmê* may have a looser sense of 'body of knowledge' similar to the occurrence in *MM* 1205 a32. On the view that I defend, there are *epistêmai* that can be used for a bad end.

Aristotle says that certain things can be used only for their natural purpose as, for example, sight that can be used only for seeing. Other things can be used for purposes that are not their natural ones: this is the case of *epistêmê* that can be used for what is not *epistêmê*.[60] For example, *epistêmê* of health is the same as *epistêmê* of sickness. *Epistêmê* of health is according to nature (*kata phusin*), while *epistêmê* of sickness is contrary to nature (*para phusin*).[61] As it is clear from the example, in this case, *epistêmê* is not demonstrative understanding of what is necessary and eternal. In the *Metaphysics*, Aristotle explains the idea that *epistêmai* are of contraries. At 1046b2-3, productive forms of knowledge (*poiêtikai epistêmai*) and expertise (*technai*) are considered capacities (*dunameis*). Rational *dunameis* are of contraries, while irrational ones are not of contraries. This happens because *epistêmê* qua rational capacity is *logos* that is about a fact (*pragma*) as well as its privation (*sterêsin*).[62] In this sense, medicine qua *epistêmê/technê* produces its end according to nature—health—as well as its privation—sickness.[63]

Admittedly, Aristotle explains that *epistêmê* that is against nature is by accident (*kata sumbebêkos*).[64] This is in line with the account that Aristotle offers in *EE* VIII.1. In *EE* VIII.1, Aristotle distinguishes between a simple (1246b8)/natural (1246a28) use of knowledge from a use that is not simple/natural and that is by accident (1246a29). Aristotle illustrates this with the example of the eye: the eye can be used for a purpose that is not its natural one. For example, the eye can be used against nature to see double.[65]

---

[60] *EE* II 1227a27.

[61] In *Metaphysics* 1046b7-9, Aristotle explains that rational capacities (*dunameis*) explain the positive form and its privation because they are *logoi*.

[62] *Metaphysics* 1046b7-9. Aristotle defines privation at *Metaphysics* 1046a32-3: he explains that privation occurs when something that by nature should have a property in fact does not have it.

[63] Cf. *Metaphysics* 1071a9-10; 1032b2-5; 1046b4-15 quoted in Baker 2021, 411-49.

[64] *Metaphysics* 1046b13.

[65] This is compatible with *EE* II 1227a25 insofar as in *EE* VIII.1, the subject is 'the eye', and not 'seeing': the eye can be used to see double.

Similarly, *epistêmê* can be used for a purpose that is not natural. At *EE* VIII 1246b2-4, Aristotle clarifies the idea of using knowledge according to nature as well as against nature: he explains that it is possible to commit errors on the basis of knowledge (*apo epistêmês*).[66] Aristotle uses two examples: knowledge of how to write that can be used to write in an incorrect way; and knowledge that dancers possess of how to move their hands and feet that can be used to move hands as if they were feet and vice versa.[67] Both examples refer to expertises or productive forms of knowledge, as they are called in *Metaphysics* Θ II.

According to the Distortion Criterion, *epistêmê* can be used in a distorted way. At 1246b10, Aristotle considers the case of something above *epistêmê* that produces a distortion of *epistêmê*. He does not offer clarifications of how this may work. The idea seems to be that what is superior or above *epistêmê* can cause *epistêmê* to be used in a distorted way.[68] In the *Metaphysics*, we find a reference to a form of *epistêmê* that is the most dominant or sovereign: this form of *epistêmê* is the *epistêmê* of the highest good that is that for the sake of which we do everything else.[69] This passage in the *Metaphysics* suggests that *epistêmai* are organized in a hierarchy and superior forms of *epistêmai* use the inferior ones. They may use them for a good or for a bad end. Superior forms of *epistêmai*, or whatever is above *epistêmê* as in the passage in the *EE*, may also distort the inferior ones. The Use, Nature, and Distortion Criteria show that when *epistêmê* is possessed without *phronêsis* and the

---

[66] Cf. *EE* VI = *NE* VII 1146b31-3 on having knowledge and not using it.

[67] Dirlmeier (1984, 473) suggests that Aristotle refers to *technai* and not to theoretical forms of knowledge. He notices that the first example can be found in Xenophon's *Memorabilia* IV 2.20, and in *Lysis* 209 b. The second example can be found in Xenophon's *Symposium* VII.3.

[68] The occurrence of *nous* at 1246b12 is probably a later addition (cf. Rowe 2023b). Dirlmeier (1984, 475) points out that in this passage, Aristotle refers to the architectonic type of *phronêsis*, that is, political *phronêsis*, and not to *phronêsis* as both theoretical and practical, as we find in Plato. I think that the passage is part of a continuous argument about the nature of *phronêsis* and how it differs from *epistêmê*.

[69] *Metaphysics* 982b4-5.

virtues of character, it can be used contrary to nature and can be distorted, or it may not be used at all.

Finally, according to the Teaching Criterion, *epistêmê* can be taught. That is, we can acquire *epistêmê* via teaching: we do not need to develop it via habituation or practice. This last criterion is best illustrated via a contrast between *epistêmê* and *phronêsis*.[70] Namely, *phronêsis* needs to be acquired through practice and habituation (in addition to teaching), while *epistêmê* can be taught with no need for practice and habituation.

4.5 *Epistêmê* and *phronêsis*

Despite the difference in how we acquire these virtues and given the role that I assigned to *epistêmê* in the practical domain, one may ask whether *epistêmê* is any different from *phronêsis* and whether Aristotle refers to *epistêmê* in a way that is interchangeable with *phronêsis*.[71] To show that these two virtues are indeed different and have different roles in the practical domain, the criteria that I individuated are particularly useful. Scholars debate whether *phronêsis* involves some form of knowledge or whether it is informed by knowledge.[72] The idea that *phronêsis* is a form of knowledge is not foreign to Aristotle's scholars even though most scholars conceive of *phronêsis* in terms of wisdom rather than knowledge.[73]

---

[70] Murgier's argument that in developing his notion of *phronêsis*, Aristotle answers Plato's question in the *Meno* of whether virtue can be taught seems plausible. Cf. Murgier 2014, ch. 5.

[71] For Plato, *phronêsis* can refer to practical as well as to theoretical wisdom and to knowledge (*Protagoras* 330b4, *Phaedrus* 247d7, *Theaetetus* 145d7–e7). Cf. Sedley 2014, 65–91. For a discussion of the difference between *epistêmê* and *phronêsis*, see Reeve 2021, 294–9.

[72] Cf. Reeve 2012, 148–50, 157; Nielsen 2015, 32. Both reported by Gartner 2019, 133.

[73] Gauthier (1958, 83) argues that *phronêsis* is a virtue whose act is knowledge. Monan (1968) calls it moral knowledge.

As I showed, some knowledge is necessary to act virtuously and to deliberate well.[74]

The relation between *epistêmê* and *phronêsis* has been conceived in terms of part and whole by Karbowski who argues that *epistêmê* is part of legislative *phronêsis*.[75] Karbowski argues that '*phronêsis* is a unified epistemic state that integrates *epistêmê* of ethical kinds or universals with an experience-based capacity for reading situations and processing all the factors that impact how we ought to act'.[76] Karbowski conceives of *phronêsis* as a unified state with parts. He characterizes it as an epistemic state in the sense that it is about the truth.

On the view that I propose, *epistêmê* is not a part of *phronêsis*. However, as I argued in section 4.2, *epistêmê* fulfils tasks that are fundamental in the practical domain. In this sense, when *phronêsis* is possessed together with *epistêmê*, it benefits from the tasks fulfilled by this virtue. The two virtues interact and co-function. Insofar as *epistêmê* can be used contrary to nature and can be distorted, it must be possessed together with *phronêsis* to aim at the good. In this sense, the good or best agent of the *EE* needs to have *epistêmê* as well as *phronêsis*.

At first sight, *EE* V = *NE* VI 1141b14–22 seems to downplay the role of knowledge in the practical domain: Aristotle says that *phronêsis* is concerned not only with universals (*katholou*), but must know (*gnôrizein*) also the particulars (*ta kath'hekasta*). He explains that people who do not have knowledge (*ouk eidotes*), but have experience, are more successful in action than people with knowledge and without experience. Aristotle uses an example from medicine and diet to illustrate his point: people who know that light meats are healthy, but do not know which kind of meat

---

[74] Wolf, who engages with Aristotle's unity of the virtues from a contemporary perspective, stresses that we need some form of unified knowledge to act virtuously. Cf. Wolf 2007, 145–67.
[75] Karbowski 2019, 159.
[76] Karbowski 2019, 15.

is light would not produce health. By contrast, the person who wishes to eat a healthy meal and knows that chicken is a light meat and that light meat is healthy, can eat chicken. Aristotle concludes that insofar as *phronêsis* is practical, knowledge of the particulars is more important than universal knowledge even though both kinds of knowledge are necessary. The passage is controversial for a number of reasons: first of all, it refers to the practical syllogism and as I explained, there are different views on how to interpret the practical syllogism. In line with the case of failing to have knowledge that I discussed above (1145a1–10), I interpret this passage as referring to the idea that particular knowledge (e.g. 'this chicken meat is healthy') is immediately relevant for action (e.g. eating a healthy meal) rather than universal knowledge alone (e.g. 'light meat is healthy'). Second, the passage is controversial insofar as Aristotle uses an example from medicine and diet instead of an example about virtuous versus vicious actions.[77] While for the purpose of health, particular knowledge may be enough, it seems that universal knowledge of what is good for human beings has a role in virtuous practice. This is suggested by the reference to the good for human beings at 1141b13 and by Aristotle's remark at *EE* VIII 1249b6–7 that it is not clear what we mean when we say that someone should follow what the *orthos logos* says. Namely, we cannot simply follow commands, in order to be virtuous, we need also to grasp the reasons and the universal perspective from which these commands stem. Third, the passage is controversial insofar as Aristotle says that particular knowledge is more immediately relevant for actions, but he concludes that both kinds of knowledge—universal and particular—are necessary. We may explain this as follows: it is not enough to have universal knowledge in order to produce the relevant action. But at the same time, if we have particular knowledge we automatically have also universal knowledge.[78]

---

[77] Cf. Frede 2020, 683.
[78] Cf. Morison 2011, 35.

What matters for present purposes is that Aristotle's claim that *phronêsis* needs to know the particulars is compatible with the idea that *phronêsis* is not *epistêmê* of universals and of particulars, but co-functions with *epistêmê*.

In *EE* VIII.1, Aristotle offers an argument that shows that *phronêsis* is not an *epistêmê* because it does not function as *epistêmê*.[79] As I see it, the Use, Nature, Distortion, and Teaching criteria that characterize different ways of acquiring, possessing, and using *epistêmê* do not apply to *phronêsis*. *Phronêsis* does not meet the Use Criterion: that is, it cannot be possessed and not used. When one has *phronêsis*, one acts in a practically wise way.[80] This is compatible with the idea that agents may not use *phronêsis* if there are external impediments. *Phronêsis* cannot be possessed partially. Of course, this allows cases of agents that have *phronêsis*, and are asleep or seriously ill. In these cases, agents do not act like the *phronimos*. Cases such as the one of children who do not have *phronêsis*, but may develop it in the future, are also compatible with these considerations. Let me move to the Nature Criterion.

Phronêsis cannot be used against nature. If virtue was knowledge—as Aristotle reports that Socrates thought—we would be able to use justice as if it was injustice.[81] Namely, we would be able to use it to do unjust actions in the same way in which we can make mistakes on the basis of *epistêmê*. In a similar way, we would be able to act and think in an unwise way on the basis of *phronêsis*. But *phronêsis* must be possessed always with the virtues of character, and both the virtues of character and *phronêsis* cannot be used against nature: that is, they cannot be used for acting viciously

---

[79] In the *Topics*, Aristotle seems to understand *phronêsis* as knowledge. In *Topics* 137a15, Aristotle argues that *phronêsis* is related in the same way to the good and to the bad and it is knowledge of both. Von Arnim (1927) argues that in the *Topics*, Aristotle has still not formulated the idea of the virtues of thinking. In particular, according to Von Arnim, for the Aristotle of the *Topics*, *phronêsis* is both practical and theoretical. For a discussion of *phronêsis* in the *Topics*, see Natali 2001, 3; Reeve 2021, 294–9.

[80] For a different view according to which the *enkrates* has *phronêsis*, see Callard 2017, 31–63.

[81] *EE* VIII 1246a36–7.

and for thinking in an unwise way.[82] *Phronêsis* and the virtues of character always aim at the good.

Differently from *epistêmê*, *phronêsis* cannot be distorted by a superior *epistêmê* or by something above it. In the case of *phronêsis*, there is no superior form of knowledge that distorts it.[83] At *EE* VIII.1 1246b10–11, Aristotle says that *phronêsis* cannot be distorted because it is the master (*kuria*) of all the other forms of *phronêsis*.[84] The reference may be to the division of forms of *phronêsis* that occurs at 1141b32–3. Namely, there is *phronêsis* of the universal that is legislative, and *phronêseis* of particulars such as *phronêsis* of the good for the individual, of the household, and so forth.[85] *Phronêsis* has its own structure that is the structure of a genus with species characterized by *diaphora* (1141b34), rather than a hierarchical structure of superior and inferior *epistêmai*.

Finally, *phronêsis* cannot be acquired solely by teaching. For Aristotle, *phronêsis* is developed through practice, habituation, and experience: we need to look at the *phronimos* to learn how to act in a practically wise way. Aristotle says that the *phronimos* is *kanon kai metron* of how we should act.[86] *Phronêsis* cannot be acquired solely by teaching because it must be possessed always with the character virtues which are acquired by habituation and by practising virtuous actions.

While the agent who has *phronêsis* acts always like the *phronimos*, *epistêmê* is somehow ethically neutral. This means that the akratic agent may have *epistêmê*. What is more, the vicious may have *epistêmê*: if someone is vicious, *epistêmê* can be used for

---

[82] This is in line with what Aristotle says in *EE* IV = *NE* V 1129a11–17, where Aristotle explains that capacities and forms of knowledge are of contraries, while states are not of contraries.

[83] Cf. *EE* VIII 1246b10–11. On the hierarchy of forms of knowledge cf. *Metaphysics* 982b4–5.

[84] At *EE* VIII 1246b11, I read with Rowe: αὐτῆς δὲ τῆς πασῶν κυρίας τίς. Robinson adds κυρία after τίς. Rowe (2023b, 184) writes that κυρία has to be implied, but that 'in any case with no need for it to be spelled out'.

[85] See Gauthier and Jolif 1959, 500.

[86] *NE* 1113a33.

a bad end. And as I showed, *epistêmê* can be distorted by something above it. Conversely, *phronêsis* functions together with the character virtues: it always aims at the good. Insofar as it functions together with all the virtues of character, the akratic agent cannot have *phronêsis*.[87] Hence, Aristotle concludes that *phronêsis* is not an *epistêmê*, but is a form of *gnôsis*.[88] This means that it must occur with true *logos*, but is not an *epistêmê*. In light of the distinctions that I outlined in section 4.1, now it is clear that Aristotle's characterization of *phronêsis* as *gnôsis* is meant to further differentiate it from *epistêmê*.

4.6 *Epistêmê, phronêsis*, and the truth

The last step in my argument that shows that *epistêmê* and *phronêsis* are different virtues, but interact and co-function when they are possessed together as part of the Functional Unity of the Virtues, concerns the relation of these virtues to the truth: *epistêmê* and *phronêsis* relate in different ways to the truth. As Aristotle says at *EE* II 1221b30, all the virtues of thinking are about the truth. However, not all the virtues of thinking are about the truth in the same way. Aristotle says that the truth is the *ergon* of both parts of the rational soul (practical and theoretical).[89] He explains that each part of the soul is in the truth (*alêtheusei*) according to the virtues.[90] This way of expressing the relation among the parts of the soul, the virtues, and the truth is relevant: namely, Aristotle says that the soul or its parts are in the truth. He refrains from saying that all the virtues of thinking directly grasp the truth or are in the truth. This is confirmed by 1139b15, where the soul—rather than individual

---

[87] For a different view, see Callard 2017, 31–63.
[88] *EE* VIII 1246b38. Cf. *EE* V = *NE* VI 1141b34.
[89] *EE* V = *NE* VI 1139b12.
[90] *EE* V = *NE* VI 1139b13.

virtues—is said to be in the truth (*alêtheusei*).[91] This suggests that whereas the rational part of the soul as a whole grasps the truth, the virtues are about the truth and they occur with true *logos*, but only some of them grasp the truth directly. At one end of the spectrum, there are virtues such as *epistêmê* and *nous* that directly grasp the truth—the former grasps the truth in demonstrative or non-demonstrative ways, the latter grasps the truth as some sort of intellectual perception—at the other end of the spectrum, there are *phronêsis* and *technê* which are states that occur with true *logos*.

Scholars distinguish practical from theoretical truth: *phronêsis* has to do with practical truth. *EE* V = *NE* VI 1139a17–31 is the fundamental reference for discussions about practical truth. This is the only passage where Aristotle explicitly mentions practical truth. For this reason, some scholars are sceptical about the idea that Aristotle distinguishes between practical and theoretical truth.[92] In a paper that shaped the debate on practical truth, Anscombe argues that practical truth is the fit between the agent's taking himself to be doing X and actually doing X.[93] Broadie develops this view by arguing that practical truth is not 'a semantic property of propositions, but a property that the mind has when it is in the best relation to objects'.[94] In a more recent contribution, Broadie explores this position further. She argues that practical truth is success of the intellect. As she explains, for practical truth we need good *prohairesis* which means true *logos* (assertorically true) and correct desire. On the view that she defends, correct desire is required for good *prohairesis* and for practical truth.[95] In this sense, truth attaches to *logos* but also to desire. Her interpretation rejects

---

[91] This way of speaking about the soul and its parts, and the virtues that belong to the parts, is in line with Aristotle's way of assigning the virtues to the parts of the soul in *EE* II. Cf. chapter 1 and Sauvé Meyer (forthcoming).

[92] This is the position that Kenny attributes to Barnes. Cf. Kenny 2011, 277–84.

[93] Anscombe 1965, 143–58; Anscombe 1993. Reprinted in 1999, 68–76, and Geach and Gormally 2005, 149–60.

[94] Broadie and Rowe 2002, 362. Cf. Broadie 2020, 249–71.

[95] Broadie (2020, 249–71) argues that this is necessary for keeping Aristotle's definition of happiness as virtuous rational activity stable.

Olfert's proposal that practical truth is definitive of the rational activity that is practical thinking.[96] Kenny argues that in practical reasoning, truth and goodness must be both preserved and that the aim of practical reasoning must be practical.[97] Whatever practical truth is, what matters for present purposes is that *phronêsis* does not relate to the truth in the same way as *epistêmê*. What is more, *epistêmê* is necessary for *phronêsis* to grasp the truth.

Aristotle calls *phronêsis* a true state (1140b5) and a state with true *logos* (1140b20–1).[98] It is not clear what a true state is: Aristotle uses this expression only at 1140b5. The idea that it is a state with true *logos* suggests some sort of partnership between *phronêsis* and *epistêmê*. Aristotle calls *phronêsis* a true *hupolêpsis* as opposed to a false *hupolêpsis*.[99] *Hupolêpsis* is a very general term: in *DA* 427b24–6, *hupolêpsis* is the genus of which *epistêmê*, *doxa*, and *phronêsis* are the species. Hence, saying that *phronêsis* is a *hupolêpsis* does not entail that *phronêsis* directly grasps the truth.

As I explained, the closer Aristotle gets to say that *phronêsis* grasps the truth is saying that *phronêsis* needs to know (*gnôrizein*) universals and particulars.[100] Universal and particular knowledge is necessary for the practical syllogism. And the *phronimos* grasps all the steps of the practical syllogism. But this does not show that *phronêsis* grasps the truth of universals and particulars. The claim is compatible with the idea that *phronêsis* integrates and uses the truth grasped by *nous* and by *epistêmê*.[101]

---

[96] Olfert 2014, 205–31.
[97] Kenny 2011, 277–84. Kenny argues that all accounts of practical inference are ultimately not satisfactory insofar as practical thought is defeasible. That is, the soundness of practical reasoning is different from the soundness of theoretical reasoning. For theoretical reasoning, 'a conclusion that follows from a set of premises will follow from any larger set that includes them. The same is not true of practical reasoning' (Kenny 2011, 284).
[98] The occurrence at 1140b5 is debated since it is not clear what a true state with *logos* is. Susemihl-Apelt correct *alêthê* in *alêthous*.
[99] *EE* V = *NE* VI 1142b33. As it is suggested at 1139b15, an *hupolêpsis* can be false.
[100] *EE* V = *NE* VI 1141b14–15.
[101] *Phronêsis* is not the only virtue of thinking that does not directly grasp the truth: *technê* is characterized in a similar way as a virtue that occurs with true *logos*. At

At 1141b33-4, Aristotle says that to know (*eidenai*) one's own interest or good is a form of cognition (*gnôseôs*?).[102] This claim is in line with *EE* VIII 1246b38, where Aristotle calls *phronêsis* another form of *gnôsis*. As I discussed earlier, *gnôsis* is not synonymous with *epistêmê*. Aristotle says that *phronêsis* has many differences (*diaphoran pollên*) presumably from other forms of *gnôsis*.[103] These differences seem to relate to the fact that *phronêsis* refers to what is proper of the individual as opposed to what is proper of the household or of the community. The *phronimos* is the one who knows (*eidôs*) what is good regarding oneself.[104] This account of *phronêsis* as a form of *gnôsis* is in line with the occurrence of *gignôskein* at 1143a34, where Aristotle says that the *phronimos* needs to know (*gignôskein*) practical and ultimate things, and with the occurrence at *EE* VIII 1246b38. All these occurrences show that the *phronimos* needs to have knowledge. However, *phronêsis* is not knowledge and does not grasp the truth directly. The best or good agent needs *epistêmê* in order to grasp the truth. For this reason, *epistêmê* must be regarded as a fundamental component of the Functional Unity of the Virtues.

DA 428a4, Aristotle says that *phantasia* is a *dunamis* or a *hexis* according to which we are in the truth or not. That is, he does not say that *phantasia* grasps the truth. Aristotle uses the same formulation that we find in the ethics: namely, that the soul or the agent *alêtheusei*—literally, they are in the truth—and that *phantasia* is that according to which (*kata*) we are in the truth. At 428a17, Aristotle says explicitly that *phantasia* is not like *nous* or *epistêmê* which are always true. That is, it is a fallible state, but nonetheless it contributes to the truth.

[102] Gauthier and Jolif (1959) read *to hautô* 'son intérêt à soi'. Dirlmeier (1984, 458) agrees with this reading, and he adds that it is in line with *ta peri hauton eidôs* (1142a1). In the manuscripts, there is no word that expresses what *phronêsis* is a form of: Spengel and Rackham adds *gnôseôs*, but another option could be *phronêseôs* following Eustrate. Gauthier and Jolif argue that it is a form of *gnôsis*, but they agree that it would be better to read *phronêseôs*. That is, Aristotle is differentiating among forms of *phronêsis*: some are about what is universal (legislative *phronêsis*) and others are about the individual (*phronêsis* that has to do with the family, household management and so forth). Stewart, Burnet, Greenwood, Ross, Rackham, and Dirlmeier agree with Gauthier and Jolif.
[103] *EE* V = *NE* VI 1141b34.
[104] *EE* V = *NE* VI 1142a1-2.

4.7 Conclusions

I argued that in the *EE*, *epistêmê* is said in many ways. It can be understood according to the UA as well as according to the KA. The KA includes all the ways in which *epistêmê* is said that are not captured by the UA. As I showed, in the *EE*, Aristotle uses *eidenai* and *gignôskein* (as well as the noun *gnôsis*) to refer to having knowledge in a broad sense. *Epistasthai* can refer to having demonstrative understanding of what is necessary and eternal, if it is used in an unqualified sense (*haplôs*). And it refers to explanatory knowledge of what is contingent if it is used in a qualified way. As I showed, in the *EE*, *epistêmê* is not always correlated to *epistasthai* which is very rare. As my analysis shows, knowledge plays a fundamental role in the practical domain: it co-functions with *phronêsis* to fulfil many different tasks. And there are many ways of having knowledge: qualified versus unqualified; particular versus universal; in actuality versus in potentiality. Even though *epistêmê* has an important role in the practical domain, it is a distinct virtue from *phronêsis*: *epistêmê* is not *phronêsis* and *phronêsis* is not a form of *epistêmê*. I individuated four criteria for acquiring, possessing, and using *epistêmê*—Use, Nature, Distortion, and Teaching—and I showed that these criteria do not apply to how *phronêsis* functions, and to how it is acquired and possessed. *Phronêsis* is a different virtue from *epistêmê*, but it functions together with *epistêmê* to fulfil some tasks and to relate to the truth. All this brings evidence in favour of the idea that *epistêmê* should be included in the Functional Unity of the Virtues. *Epistêmê* as it is conceived in the UA, must be included in the Functional Unity of the Virtues insofar as it is a part of *sophia* (I discuss this in more detail in chapter 5). *Epistêmê* as in the KA must be included in the Functional Unity of the Virtues insofar as explanatory knowledge fulfils important tasks in the practical domain and co-functions with *phronêsis*.

5
The virtues of theoretical thinking in the Functional Unity of the Virtues

Sophia and cognates appear only six times in the undisputed Eudemian books: 1215a24, 1220a7, 1220a12, 1243b33, 1243b34, and 1248a36. Rowe argues that in none of these occurrences does Aristotle refer to the virtue described in *EE* V = *NE* VI.[1] Rather, Aristotle uses *sophia* in a non-technical/ordinary sense. Earlier authors at times use *sophia* simply to refer to some kind of expertise. They use it in ways that Aristotle invokes in *Metaphysics* I.1–2, as the most highly revered cognitive achievement.[2] Given the rare occurrences of *sophia* in the *EE*, scholars have questioned the role of theoretical wisdom in this treatise: Jaeger famously argued that Aristotle assigns to *phronêsis* the role of the virtue of theoretical and practical contemplation.[3] However, if we consider the common books part of the *EE*, this option is ruled out: in *EE* V = *NE* VI, Aristotle contrasts *phronêsis* and *sophia* as, respectively, practical wisdom and theoretical wisdom. *Sophia* is not the only virtue of theoretical thinking: at *EE* V = *NE* VI 1141a18–19, Aristotle says that theoretical *nous* and *epistêmê* are parts of *sophia*. I have already shown that in the practical domain, *nous* and *epistêmê* co-function

---

[1] Rowe 2022, 122–36.
[2] This usage is supported by Kenny (see Rowe 2022, footnote 21) and Rowe (2022, 125). *Sophia* is used at *EE* V = *NE* VI 1141b4 in an ordinary sense. For a study of *sophia* in Greek literature up to Aeschylus, see Gladigow 1965. Gladigow argues that Xenophanes and Bacchylides use *sophia* in the sense of *aretê*. Pindar and Heraclitus seem to conceive of *sophia* as philosophical wisdom as well as wisdom with which we grasp the beauty of the cosmos. In Plato's *Theaetetus*, *sophia* is used as some sort of *epistêmê*.
[3] Jaeger 1948.

with *phronêsis* and with the virtues of character. I now turn to the role of these virtues in the theoretical domain.

Even though the occurrences of *sophia* in the *EE* are rare and some of these are not technical, I show that theoretical wisdom has an important role in this treatise. I base my analysis on Aristotle's references to theoretical capacity (*to theôrêtikon*), contemplation (*theôria*), and in particular to some references to the divine.[4] I show that these notions relate to the activities, capacities, objects, and characteristics proper of the virtues of theoretical thinking. In section 5.1, I lay out a key premise of my argument: I clarify and defend why I base my argument on occurrences of theoretical capacity, contemplation, and references to the divine. In section 5.2, I develop three arguments in favour of the idea that the virtues of theoretical thinking belong to the Functional Unity of the Virtues and interact with the other virtues. In section 5.3, I explain that when agents possess the virtues of theoretical thinking as part of the Functional Unity of the Virtues, these virtues acquire additional functions according to the principle of Additive Functionality. Namely, the virtues of theoretical thinking do not function in the same way when they are possessed outside the Functional Unity of the Virtues and when they belong to the Functional Unity of the Virtues.

5.1 *Theôria, theôrein,* and *theôrêtikon*

As they are described in *NE* X.7–8, the virtues of theoretical thinking seem to have no role at all in the Functional Unity of the Virtues. Scholars argue that for Aristotle, we do not need theoretical knowledge of the good to act as the good person acts.[5] They

---

[4] 'Divine' is my translation of *theos*. I prefer to translate *theos* as 'divine' instead of 'god' because Aristotle uses *theos* to refer to an external divine principle and more often in the *EE*, to an internal divine principle, that is, 'the divine in us'. My translation 'divine' aims to capture all these usages.

[5] See Achtenberg 2002, 90.

think that ethics does not concern causes or first principles which are the objects of theoretical knowledge.[6] Aristotle's perspective in the *NE* is often regarded as different from Plato's perspective insofar as Aristotle does not consider theoretical knowledge useful for practical purposes. This approach is in line with the distinction of happiness in two kinds or degrees that Aristotle offers at *NE* X.7–8. That is, Aristotle distinguishes a higher kind or degree of happiness which is the happiness of the contemplator from the happiness of the agent involved in politics and virtuous actions. How to understand these two kinds or degrees of happiness is contested: for example, it is not clear whether the life of the contemplator involves also excellence with regard to the virtues of practical thinking and the virtues of character. This division of happiness in two kinds or degrees is absent from the *EE*. This does not mean that in the *EE*, there is no distinction between practical and theoretical domains. That is, in the *EE*, Aristotle acknowledges that there are practical activities which are distinct from theoretical ones; there are practical and theoretical fields of knowledge; and there are virtues of practical and theoretical thinking.[7] But the absence of a division

---

[6] Cooper initially argued that the theoretical person does not need to be moral (Cooper 1975, ch. 3). But then, he changed his view and argued that the theoretical life is not separated from the moral life (Cooper 1999a, 216). Nightingale thinks that theoretical contemplation is amoral (Nightingale 2004, 222). Against these views, there is an increasing effort to unify the theoretical and the practical domain: Reeve 1992, 2012, 2013; Charles 1999; Lear 2006; Henry and Nielsen 2015. See the reconstruction of the debate in Gartner 2019, 125–45. Kraut defends the idea that contemplation has some kind of utility for our practical life and that the philosopher must be an ethically good person (Kraut 1989, 6). Walker thinks that through contemplation we derive boundary markers for virtuous actions. As he shows, we derive the ethical mean by figuring out our place between animals and the divine (Walker 2018, ch. 8). This position is similar to the one that scholars attribute to Plato: Bobonich argues that in Plato's *Statesman* and *Philebus*, as well as in Aristotle's *Protrepticus*, contemplation is useful to hit the mean (Bobonich 2007, 153–75).

[7] Aristotle refers to theoretical philosophy at *EE* I 1214a12. The division between political life and philosophical life at 1215b1 suggests a distinction between practical and theoretical activities. At 1215b13–14, Aristotle refers to a divine form of speculation which suggests that he distinguishes between theoretical knowledge and practical. At 1216b11 and at 1216b17, Aristotle distinguishes theoretical forms of knowledge from productive ones. The account of productive forms of knowledge suggests that practical forms of knowledge are included in the productive ones. Cf. Frede 2019, 101.

between two kinds of happiness suggests that the life of theoretical contemplation and the life of virtuous actions and political engagement are one and the same happy life. What is more, it suggests that there is a deeper interaction between the virtues of theoretical thinking and the virtues of practical thinking. Namely, all the virtues need to be possessed and interact in order for agents to live a happy life.

In the undisputed Eudemian books, Aristotle assigns a prominent role to theoretical activity in good human lives. This suggests that the virtues of theoretical thinking should have a role in the Functional Unity of the Virtues. References to the activity and to the virtues of contemplation are implicit in the so-called function argument in *EE* II, where Aristotle refers to complete virtue, which I interpret to be *kalokagathia*. *Kalokagathia* includes all the virtues comprising also the virtues of theoretical thinking, or so I argue.[8] In *EE* VII, theoretical activity is mentioned as a fundamental component of life and as an activity that we love to share with friends.[9] And in *EE* VIII, Aristotle explains that theoretical activity is the final end of a good human life and is ultimately that for the sake of which we do everything else.[10]

Aristotle refers to theoretical activity as the activity of *theôria*. As scholars have pointed out, the verb *theôrein* is more generic than the noun *theôria*. The verb may refer to thinking, but also to considering and even to the activity of seeing. In what follows, I focus on occurrences of *theôrein* where it is clear that *theôrein* is specifically directed toward divine objects or where there are other indications that specify that *theôrein* refers to the activity of the virtues of theoretical thinking.[11] An analysis of the occurrences of the verb

---

[8] *EE* II 1219a39–40. I argue in favour of this in chapter 6.
[9] *EE* VII 1245b5.
[10] *EE* VIII 1249b15–16, 22–3.
[11] Roochnik (2009, 69–82) offers an analysis of *theôria* in particular in the *NE*. He argues that in *DA*, *theôria* is the actualization of knowledge (cf. *DA* 412a10–11). He disagrees with Kraut (1989) and Nightingale (2004) who distinguish the noun *theôria* from the verb *theôrein*: they argue that there is a technical sense of *theôria*, while the

theôrein shows that other virtues of thinking—and not only the virtues of theoretical thinking—are able to engage in *theôrein*. This is especially clear at *EE* V = *NE* VI 1139a5–8, where Aristotle says that all the virtues of thinking engage in *theôrein*:

(T1) Now we should make a similar division with regard to the rational part, and let it be postulated that there are two rational parts, one by which we contemplate the kinds of existing things whose starting points cannot be otherwise and the other by which we contemplate things that admit of being otherwise.[12]

As the passage shows, there are two rational parts of the soul. They both engage in *theôrein*. In the passage, we have to supply the verb *theôroumen*—contemplate—in the second coordinated sentence. That is, the first rational part contemplates things whose starting points cannot be otherwise. In this case, the verb *theôroumen*—contemplate—is explicitly used. The second rational part contemplates—and we need to supply again *theôroumen*—things that can be otherwise. This is the central passage for the division of the rational part of the soul in scientific and calculative. What matters for present purposes is that Aristotle uses the verb *theôrein*

---

sense of *theôrein* is often non-technical. Kraut argues that *theôria* is activity that goes on when we bring truth to mind, it is the activation of theoretical wisdom. Broadie (2002) translates the verb *theôrein* in the *NE* as 'having regard', Inwood and Woolf (2013) translate it in the common books as 'focusing on what one knows'. Jirsa (2017, 210–38) argues that *theôria* can have different objects, not all of them are necessary and eternal.

[12] *EE* V = *NE* VI 1139a5–8. Cf. 1139a26; *EE* I 1217b37; at *EE* I 1214a8, Aristotle refers to *theôrêmata* which are objects that must be investigated for the sake of knowledge (*gnônai*) and for acquisition and action (*ktêseis kai praxeis*). Cf. *Metaphysics* 993b20. Cf. Roochnick 2009, 74. Eriksen (1976, 82–4) reviews discussions of this issue by Burnet, Düring, and Stenzel. He cites the following passages to support the idea that *theôria* is the actualization of knowledge: *NE* 1146b30, 1153a22; *Metaphysics* 1048a34, 1072b24; *Physics* 255a33-b5; *De Anima* 412a9–22; *Protrepticus* B87; *On the Generation of the Animals* 735a9. Burnet (1900, 258) argues that *theôrein* is 'the *energeia* of knowledge'. According to this picture, *theôria* is the actualization of *epistêmê* in potentiality. Cf. Hardie 1968, 339; Düring 1966, 472.

for both parts of the rational part of the soul, rather than using it only to describe the activity of the theoretical part of the soul.

There is further evidence in favour of the idea that *theôrein* is not limited to the activity of the virtues of theoretical thinking: at *EE* V = *NE* VI 1140b8–10, Aristotle says that Pericles is able to theorize (*theôrein*) about what is good for human beings. Nightingale and Kraut argue that this instance of the verb *theôrein* refers to the activity of considering or seeing something.[13] This is plausible insofar as the object of Pericles' theorizing—*theôrein*—is the human good. Additional evidence is provided by the participle *theôrôn* that is used at *EE* VI = *NE* V 1152a14–15 to refer to having knowledge in actuality as opposed to having knowledge only in potentiality.[14] The knowledge and the type of theorizing that Aristotle has in mind here is concerned with what is right. This is said explicitly. That is, theorizing has a practical aim: knowing what is right in order to do what is right. All this shows that *theôrein* may refer to the activity of the virtues of theoretical thinking, but may also refer to seeing or considering.

In the argument that I develop, I assign a central role to *theôrêtikon* and I argue that Aristotle uses this term to refer to the capacity of theoretical thinking and to the virtues of theoretical thinking which are related to this capacity. However, one particular occurrence of *theôrêtikon* could be considered evidence against my premise that *theôrêtikon* refers to the virtues of theoretical thinking, to their objects, and to their activities.[15] That is, at *EE* II 1226b26–7, Aristotle says that the deliberative capacity (*bouleutikon*) is the capacity of knowing (*theôrêtikon*) a certain cause (*aitias tinos*). The passage appears in the context of a discussion of what is voluntary

---

[13] Kraut 1989, 73; and Nightingale 2004, 238.
[14] Cf. *EE* V = *NE* VI 1146b33–4. Broadie (2002, 389) notes that theorizing is the Academic example of using knowledge as opposed to having it and not using it.
[15] Cf. *DA* 415a12; *Metaphysics* 1061b11.

and of *prohairesis*: in this sense, the capacity of *theôrêtikon* that is a capacity of knowing the cause has a practical role. As Aristotle specifies in the discussion that follows *EE* II 1226b26–7, the cause referred to is a final cause—it is that for the sake of which (*hou heneka*) we do something and it is the reason why we do something (*dia ti*). Aristotle discusses the following example: collecting one's money is the final cause of walking if we walk in order to collect our money. The final cause is that for the sake of which we walk. The passage shows some parallelism with a passage that is central in my argument and that occurs at *EE* VIII 1249b13–16. There, Aristotle says that everyone should live with reference to one's own commanding principle and this is according to the *theôrêtikon*. Aristotle explains that *phronêsis* commands for the sake of the divine and this is that for the sake of which (*hou heneka*) it commands. He adds that 'that for the sake of which' can be understood in two ways and that this has been explained elsewhere. The final cause can be understood as the beneficiary and as the final aim.[16] One example of these two possible ways of understanding *hou heneka* is the discussion at *EE* II 1226b26–7, where *hou heneka* is the final cause of a process of deliberation that has a practical aim. This shows that *theôrêtikon* can refer to a general capacity of knowing the causes that serves a practical purpose, as in *EE* II 1226b26–7, but it can refer also to a theoretical capacity that grasps the divine as in *EE* VIII 1249b14. On the view that I defend, the reference to the divine is what suggests that we are in the domain of the virtues of theoretical thinking.

The idea that *theon* and *theos* may refer to the object of the virtues of theoretical thinking, as well as to a cosmic divine principle, and

---

[16] On *hou heneka* as a way to refer to the final cause: cf. *Physics* 194a35–6; *De Anima* 415b2–3, b22; *Metaphysics* 1072b1–2. Cf. Leunissen 2010, ch. 3; Johnson 2005, ch. 3. As I discuss in section 5.2, the final cause can be understood as the beneficiary or the final aim.

that they are attributed to what is determined, ordered, and rationally graspable via standards and patterns is attested not only in the *EE*, but also in other Aristotelian works, in particular in the *Metaphysics* and in the *Protrepticus*.[17] In *Metaphysics* 1026a15–20, Aristotle says that first philosophy is about what is separated and immutable, and that the causes of divine objects are eternal. Aristotle adds that if there is something divine, it must belong to first philosophy as the highest form of theoretical philosophy (other forms of theoretical philosophy are physics and mathematics). In *Protrepticus* VIII 48.9–13, Aristotle says that *nous* and *phronêsis* are what is divine and blessed (*makarion*) in us. *Phronêsis* is here understood as the knowledge of the philosopher rather than the virtue of practical wisdom. In *Protrepticus* X 55.26–56.2, Aristotle explains that the philosopher looks at the divine. And in V 35.14–18, he says that human beings would be like gods if they were fully rational and if they lived following *nous*. All this suggests a connection between the divine and the virtues of theoretical thinking.[18]

In light of this analysis not every occurrence of *theôrein* and of *theôrêtikon* points in the direction of the virtues of theoretical thinking. However, occurrences of these terms in conjunction with references to the divine especially in the case of activities that have the divine as their object—in particular, contemplation and cultivation of the divine, as Aristotle calls them—are reliable indicators that Aristotle refers to the virtues of theoretical thinking. This is the methodological approach that I adopt in the argument I develop in the rest of the chapter.

---

[17] In addition, see also *Phyiscs* 196a33; *De Caelo* 290a32. Quoted by Eriksen 1977, 90. Cf. Grant 1874. See also *NE* 1177b28–31, where *nous* is called divine.

[18] This connection is, of course, evident in many passages in *NE* X.

5.2 The virtues of theoretical thinking in the Functional Unity: three arguments

In what follows, I develop three arguments that show that the virtues of theoretical thinking must be included in the Functional Unity of the Virtues:

1. The Inclusion Argument (IA): in order to achieve happiness, we need not only the virtues of character and the virtues of practical thinking, but also the virtues of theoretical thinking.
2. The Cooperation Argument (CA): *phronêsis* and the virtues on which it depends (the character virtues, practical *nous*, *euboulia*, *sunesis*, and *gnôme*—from now on, I call these virtues VPD: 'virtues on which *phronêsis* depends') accomplish tasks that are fundamental for the virtues of theoretical thinking to fulfil their full potential. That is, when agents have these virtues, their souls are in the best conditions for theoretical activity.
3. The Teleological Argument (TA): virtues of theoretical thinking and their activities are the final cause of the activities of all the other virtues and their activities. The virtues of theoretical thinking and their activities move everything in the soul qua final cause; they are the aim and the beneficiary of the activities of the other virtues.

The ideal conditions for human theoretical activity are met when agents possess *phronêsis* and VPD. As I discuss at the end of the chapter, this does not entail that agents need to have *phronêsis* and VPD in order to engage in some sort of theoretical activity. Similarly, the virtues of theoretical thinking are not required for having *phronêsis* and VPD. However, *phronêsis* and VPD prepare the ground for contemplation of divine objects. On their turn, the virtues of theoretical thinking provide the final cause of the activities of *phronêsis* and VPD. When agents have *phronêsis* and

VPD, the virtues of theoretical thinking acquire new tasks and co-function with these virtues. Similarly, when they function with the virtues of theoretical thinking, *phronêsis* and VPD acquire new tasks and co-functions with these virtues (what I call Additive Functionality). To sum up, when they are part of the Functional Unity of the Virtues, all the virtues function at their best.

5.2.1 The Inclusion Argument

According to the inclusive interpretation of happiness, happiness consists not only in contemplation, but also in the activities of all the virtues.[19] In what I call the Inclusion Argument, I explore this idea in relation to the unity of the virtues. The main evidence in favour of IA comes from Aristotle's definition of happiness in *EE* II. At *EE* II 1219a39–40, Aristotle specifies that happiness is activity according to complete virtue. I interpret this complete virtue as *kalokagathia*, which is explicitly mentioned only at the beginning of *EE* VIII.3. According to my interpretation, *kalokagathia* includes all the virtues comprising also the virtues of theoretical thinking.[20] In this sense, the virtues of theoretical thinking must be part of the unity of the virtues: we cannot engage in the activity of happiness,

---

[19] The distinction between a dominant and an inclusive interpretation is first proposed by Hardie 1968. Hardie explains that we can interpret happiness in the *NE*, given the two accounts of happiness—one in *NE* I and the other in *NE* X—according to an inclusive reading or according to a dominant reading. For Hardie, in the *NE*, Aristotle conceives of happiness in an inclusive way, namely as a final end composed of multiple independent goods. However, in book X, the best kind of happiness seems to consist exclusively in philosophical activity. Among others, Kenny 1992, Cooper 1975, and Kraut 1989 defend the dominant interpretation of happiness in the *NE*; Ackrill 1980 defend the inclusive interpretation. Lear (2006) argues that virtuous activity is an approximation to contemplative activity. Labarrière (2003) defends the dominant view against Destrée (2003) who defends an inclusive view. Cf. Austin 1967; McDowell 1980; Nagel 1972; Kraut 1989; Crisp 1993; Broadie 1994; Sherman 1998; Lännström 2006; Pakaluk and Pearson 2011; Reeve 2012; Destrée and Zingano 2014. Long (2011) summarizes the debate. Vogt (2017, 44) argues persuasively that even if we disagree on Aristotle's substantive proposal about the best life, we should preserve his realism regarding the idea that different lives may be best for different agents. For a history of happiness, see De Luise and Farinetti 2001.

[20] Cf. chapter 6.

that is, we cannot achieve the highest good for human beings, if we do not have the virtues of theoretical thinking. Throughout the *EE*, Aristotle develops his argument that happiness includes the activities of all the virtues. In the first book of the *EE*, Aristotle refers to happiness as something divine. At *EE* I.5, Aristotle focuses on what the philosophical life consists in. He reports the opinion of Anaxagoras, who thinks that a human being is blessed (*makarion*) if she takes part in some divine form of contemplation. Aristotle does not refute Anaxagoras' view, which suggests that he aligns himself with Anaxagoras in considering theoretical activity divine. The idea that happiness has to do with the divine insofar as theoretical activity is the final aim of a happy life becomes explicit at the end of *EE* VIII.[21] This idea is common in other Aristotelian works where Aristotle explains that the life of theoretical contemplation is a divine life.[22] He understands the divine as pure actuality and as continuous and self-sufficient activity of thinking.[23] In this sense, theoretical contemplation is the human activity that most closely resembles the divine and, therefore, is called divine. In *Metaphysics* 1072b22, Aristotle says that *nous* has something divine which is the capacity to grasp the *noêton* and the *ousia*. These considerations are in line with what we find in the *EE*. For present purposes, it is sufficient to point out that Aristotle calls theoretical contemplation divine. Happiness—in the particular case, blessedness—is divine insofar as it consists in theoretical activity (it consists in the activities of all the other virtues as well). Aristotle refers to the good life as divine at *EE* I 1215a12–20:

(T2) For if living well depends on things that come about by chance or by nature then many could not hope to achieve it, since

---

[21] *EE* VIII 1249b10–25.
[22] Cf. *NE* 1178b7–32; *Metaphysics* 1072b23–4. Cf. Jost 2014b, 287–313; Sedley 1997, 327–41.
[23] *Metaphysics* 1072b13–24. Cf. Beere 2009, ch. 13. Beere argues that divine's thinking is pure *energeia* without the exercise of a capacity. Namely, the divine engages in thinking without exercising the capacity of thinking. Non-eternal *energeiai* require the exercise of capacities.

its acquisition is not up to them through their engagement or effort. If on the other hand it depends on one having a certain quality and on the actions according to this quality, then the good (*to agathon*) would be more common and more divine, more common because more can share in it, more divine because happiness will be available to those who bring about certain qualities in themselves and in their actions.[24]

In the passage, Aristotle moves from talking about living beautifully (*to kalôs zên*), to the good (*to agathon*), to happiness (*eudaimonia*). It is clear that the three terms are connected. Happiness is living well and is the highest good for human beings. Aristotle explains that the good for human beings would be more common because more people could achieve it. He says that if the good life consists in being of a certain quality and in performing actions of a certain quality, more people can achieve it. That is, it is in our power to try to acquire a certain quality and to perform actions that possess this quality. Conversely, if the good life is due to luck or nature, it is not in our power to achieve it. Aristotle characterizes this good life as achievable by more people as divine. This life is divine because it has to do with having a certain quality and with performing actions of a certain quality. Aristotle does not explain what this quality is. But it is clear that this quality results from being completely virtuous. In this sense, it is clear that acquiring this quality and achieving happiness require the virtues of theoretical thinking.[25]

---

[24] *EE* II 1215a12–20. In agreement with Rowe (2023a), at 1215a19, I do not see the need to accept ἐν before τοῖς αὐτοὺς as Woods (1992) does. I read θειότερον δὲ τῷ κεῖσθαι τὴν εὐδαιμονίαν [ᾇ] τοῖς αὐτοὺς παρασκευάζουσι ποιούς τινας καὶ τὰς πράξεις.

[25] The idea that happiness is divine can be explained also in another way: namely, happiness is divine because those who are happy bring about qualities and actions as the divine is able to bring about things. I am grateful to an anonymous reviewer for suggesting this alternative reading of T2. I still find the interpretation that I propose more plausible insofar as Aristotle says that happiness, as opposed to those who are happy, is divine. Additional evidence of the connection between the theoretical virtues and the divine is

5.2.2 The Cooperation Argument

According to the CA, all the virtues cooperate. If CA is correct, the Functional Unity of the Virtues must include the virtues of theoretical thinking, which fulfil tasks that benefit the virtues of character and the virtues of practical thinking. On their turn, the tasks of the virtues of character and the virtues of practical thinking benefit the virtues of theoretical thinking. *EE* I 1216b38–9, where Aristotle says that for politicians it is useful to engage in *theôria*, provides preliminary evidence in favour of the idea that the virtues of theoretical thinking fulfil tasks that benefit other virtues and have an impact in the practical domain.[26]

> (T3) One should not, even for those who pursue politics, regard as superfluous the kind of theoretical study (*toiautê theôria*) that clarifies not only what something is but also its cause.[27]

In the passage, Aristotle says that *theôria* understood as the study of what something is and, most of all, of its cause is useful for good politicians. Politicians aim to bring about the good of the community; they do not aim to contemplate divine objects. If they benefit from *theôria*, this means that *theôria* has a role in the practical domain. Insofar as Aristotle uses the noun *theôria* as opposed to the more general verb *theôrein*, we should not dismiss this occurrence as an example of non-technical use of *theôria*. What is more, Aristotle says that *theôria* clarifies the cause of something, which suggests a technical meaning of *theôria* as investigation of the causes. That is, the term *theôria* is not used in the generic

provided by the passages that I refer to in footnote 22 as well as by Anaxagoras' view that I discuss above.

[26] Achtenberg (2002, 81–3) offers a different interpretation. She argues that the passage is not evidence that politicians benefit from a theoretical approach that considers the causes of things.
[27] *EE* I 1216b38–9.

sense of rational activity. This reading is further supported by the references before and after T3 to philosophical method: namely, Aristotle considers the theoretical study that clarifies the cause that is useful for politicians something that pertains to philosophical method. The passage shows that figures that are paradigmatically associated with the virtue of practical wisdom, such as politicians, benefit from theoretical activity.[28]

The cooperation of the virtues is prominent in two parallel passages which occur respectively in *EE* V = *NE* VI and in *EE* VIII.

(T4) (*Phronêsis*) is certainly not authoritative over theoretical wisdom (*sophia*) nor over the better part of the soul, in the same way that medicine is not authoritative over health, since it does not make use of it but rather sees to it that it should come to be. It *gives order for its sake* but does not give orders to it.[29]

(T5) Since human beings too are by nature composed of a commander and a commanded, each person would also have to live with reference to his own commanding principle. This has two aspects. For the art of medicine and health are commanding principles in different ways (the former is for the sake of the latter). This is how it is with regard to the theoretical capacity. The divine is not a commanding principle in the sense of giving orders but as *that for the sake of which practical wisdom (phronêsis) gives orders.*[30]

---

[28] Cf. Jirsa 2017, 210–38. Jirsa discusses occurrences that show that *theôrein* is attributed to practically wise agents (e.g. Pericles) and that *theôria* concerns not only eternal and necessary objects, but a variety of things.

[29] *EE* V = *NE* VI 1145a6–9: emphasis GB. The passage is controversial. Reeve (1992, 97) argues that *phronêsis* prescribes for the sake of *sophia* and aims to bring it about. Gauthier and Jolif (1959, 560–3) argue that the thesis according to which if a capacity governs another capacity, the capacity that governs is superior to the capacity governed, may be a platonic thesis. Sauvé Meyer (2011, 47–65) argues that practical wisdom does not give direction to *sophia* qua subordinate capacity. Conversely, it legislates on its behalf. Cf. Dahl 2011, 89. See also *EE* V = *NE* VI 1143a8, b33–5; *EE* VIII 1249a23–b6; *Politics* 1334b17–28; *MM* 1198b12–18; 1208a9–21. For a different view, see Jirsa (2017, 210–38), who argues that *sophia* is a formal cause of *eudaimonia* and that practical wisdom is also a formal cause that works for the sake of *sophia*.

[30] *EE* VIII 1249b10–16; emphasis GB.

T4 is part of the common books. T5 occurs at the end of *EE* VIII in the discussion of *kalokagathia*. In both passages, Aristotle says that *phronêsis* gives orders (*epitattei*) for the sake of something: in T4, it gives orders for the sake of *sophia*; in T5, it gives orders for the sake of the divine.[31] Scholars debate on how to understand the divine—*theos*—in T5. It is clear that the divine is in need of nothing, and hence, it cannot depend on *phronêsis*. I discuss some interpretative options below. For the moment, it is sufficient to say that if the divine refers to the same thing as the theoretical capacity (*to theôrêtikon*) mentioned at 1249b14, then we can plausibly argue that *phronêsis* gives orders for the sake of theoretical activity.[32] The theoretical activity mentioned in T6 can be understood as the activity of *sophia*, or more generally, as the activity of the virtues of theoretical thinking. One way to explain in which sense *phronêsis* gives orders is to refer to *phronêsis* as excellence in deliberation: for example, by deliberating well, agents succeed in organizing their lives so that they have time and energy for contemplation. On the view that I defend, *phronêsis* depends on practical *nous*, good deliberation, consideration, comprehension, and the virtues of character, and must be possessed together with VPD. In this sense, when agents have *phronêsis*, they have also the best dispositions toward pleasure and pain (which are co-constitutive for the character virtues), they are able to judge correctly (due to *sunesis* and *gnôme*), and they grasp the starting points of practical thinking correctly (thanks to practical *nous*). Namely, the soul is in the best condition for theoretical activity. For all these reasons, *phronêsis* and VPD

---

[31] Cf. In *Magna Moralia* 1198b12–18, Aristotle says that *phronêsis* is the steward (*epitropos*) of *sophia*. *Phronêsis* promotes leisure for the master.

[32] If this is the case, T5 brings further evidence in favour of my view that Aristotle's reference to the divine is often a reference to theoretical activity as I explained in section 5.1. Rowe seems to interpret it in a similar way: that is, *to theôrêtikon* is assimilated to *theos* and refers to our reasoning capacity. Cf. Rowe 2021, 203–17. Woods (1992) translates *to theôrêtikon* 'speculative (part)'; Inwood and Woolf (2013) translate 'contemplative'; Donini (1999) translates 'capacità speculativa'.

prepare the ground for theoretical activity.[33] And theoretical activity benefits from the activities of *phronêsis* and VPD.[34]

Further evidence in favour of the idea that *phronêsis* together with VPD offers the best conditions for the soul to engage in theoretical activity is provided by a passage in the so-called common books. In *EE* V = *NE* VI 1143b18-21, Aristotle says that *sophia* does not contemplate anything that leads to happiness (literally, 'anything from which'—*ex hôn*—happiness is brought about) because it does not concern processes. The passage suggests that *phronêsis* and *sophia* have different tasks: *phronêsis* focuses on what leads to human happiness (*ex hôn*), while *sophia* concerns that for the sake of which (*hou heneka*) *phronêsis* prescribes, as T5 suggests. *Sophia* is about contemplation and the cultivation of the divine. Aristotle refers to these two activities as the final cause of the choice and acquisition of natural goods at *EE* VIII 1249b22-3. *Sophia* and its activities are about the end and provide direction and guidance to *phronêsis*. In this light, *phronêsis* and *sophia* cooperate. All this brings evidence in favour of CA.

5.2.3 The Teleological Argument

In the TA, I distinguish three ways in which the virtues of theoretical thinking and their activities are the final cause of all the other virtues and their activities:[35]

---

[33] Cf. Rowe 2022, 122-37; Devereux (2014, 159-207). Spencer (2020, 93-114) supports a stronger interpretation according to which *sophia* relies on *phronêsis* to come into existence.

[34] A similar position has been defended by Lear (2014, 61-89). I agree with most of what Lear says, even though I do not characterize the relation between the virtues of theoretical thinking and the other virtues as a relation of approximation. Lear argues that we do everything for the sake of contemplation, but middle-level ends are still worth choosing for their own sake. Qua end, contemplation is a source of value for middle-level ends. Lear explains the relation between practical and theoretical virtues as one of analogy: on the view that I defend, these virtues cooperate and interact. On the idea that a thing's end is a source of value, see Lear (2014, 61-89).

[35] For a discussion of final cause, see Furley 1996, 59-81 and Gotthelf 2012.

- they move everything in the soul;
- they are the aim and the beneficiary of the activities of the other virtues;
- they benefit from the limit (*horos*) of actions and choices and, in particular, from the limit of choice and acquisition of natural goods.

The virtues of theoretical thinking move everything in the soul insofar as the activities of the virtues of thinking are the final cause of all the other activities in the soul.[36] The virtues of theoretical thinking and their activities are the aim and the beneficiary of the activities of the virtues of practical thinking and of the character virtues. They are the beneficiary not in the sense that they need *phronêsis* and VPD, but in the sense that theoretical thinking is supported by the tasks fulfilled by *phronêsis* and VPD. The virtues of theoretical thinking fulfil their full potential and work at their best when they work together with *phronêsis* and VPD.

At *EE* VIII.2 1248a28, Aristotle says that we search for the principle of movement in the soul which is 'the divine in us'.[37] He explains that in the cosmos, the divine moves everything.[38] In the soul, 'the divine in us' moves everything. Aristotle asks what could be superior to *epistêmê* if not the divine (*theos*).[39] In agreement with Dirlmeier, I think that at *EE* VIII 1248a27–30, Aristotle

---

[36] In the *Protrepticus*, Aristotle says that theoretical activity provides guidance and direction for ethical action. In X 54.5–56.12, Aristotle says that the philosopher looks at nature and at the divine and derives from them guidance on what is just and on how to act. Cf. Devereux 2014, 159–207. Bobonich (2007, 153–75) seems to suggest that the *Protrepticus* and the *EE* share the view that philosophical understanding is necessary for ethical and political judgements. Walker (2018, ch. 8) argues that *theôria* sets the boundary markers (*horoi*) for the virtues. Cf. Sherman (2002, 467–92) argues that contemplation of the human soul provides practical guidance.

[37] Cf. Kosman 2009, 101–107. The idea that *nous* is the 'the divine in us' was common in Greek thought. Kosman refers to Euripides: cf. Richard Kannicht, *Tragicorum Graecorum Fragmenta*, 5.2, 988: fr. 1018. See also Pindar, *Nemean Ode* VI. Cf. Dirlmeier 1984, 502. Cf. *NE* 1177b28–30.

[38] At 1248a27, I read καὶ πᾶν ἐκεῖ κινεῖ following Jackson and Rowe.

[39] *EE* VIII 1248a28.

refers to two things that he calls *theos*: on the one hand, he refers to a cosmic divine principle that moves everything in the universe, on the other hand, he refers to the divine in us which are the virtues of theoretical thinking and, more specifically, *nous*.[40] These virtues move everything insofar as the activity of these virtues is the ultimate end that we want to achieve and is the best activity for human beings. *Nous* is the best candidate for this role of principle of movement insofar as Aristotle says that it provides the starting points in the practical and in the theoretical domains, as Aristotle explains in *NE* VI = *EE* V.[41]

The virtues of theoretical thinking and, more precisely, the highest activity of these virtues which is contemplation of divine objects is the final cause. At *EE* VIII 1249b7–8, Aristotle says that we need to live subordinated to the state and activity of the commanding principle (*to archon*). Scholars debate how to interpret the relevant notion of the commanding principle.[42] Aristotle says that

[40] Dirlmeier 1984, 490.
[41] At *EE* VIII 1248a29–30, I read τί οὖν ἂν κρεῖττον καὶ ἐπιστήμης εἴη ποτε πλὴν θεός following Rowe 2023a. Spengel follows MSS BF and adds καὶ νοῦ. Rowe (2023b) explains that it makes little difference for what Aristotle is saying and that there is no evidence in the MSS that Aristotle wrote καὶ νοῦ, which is probably a gloss by someone else. For a different interpretation, see Gabbe (2012, 358–79) who argues that in *EE* VIII.2, the divine is the *archê* in the sense that it is the final cause of thoughts and desires: the divine explains the nature of the desiderative and rational faculties in human beings. In other words, god explains why we desire what we take to be good. I agree with Dirlmeier who argues that the divine in us mentioned at 1248a28 is intelligence. Cf. Dirlmeier 1984, 502; Rowe 2021, 203–17. For an alternative reading, see Verdenius 1971, 291.
[42] Cf. According to Gosling and Taylor (1982, 342–4), the commander is the divine. They argue that natural goods promote *theôria*, and in particular the contemplation of the divine. Kenny translates *to archon* as 'one's superior' and as 'raison d' être'. According to Kenny (1992, 95), it is possible to distinguish two parts of human reason that are related to one another as the superior to the inferior. On his view, the superior part is a 'broad intellectual faculty' (*theôrêtikon*) and the inferior part is practical wisdom (*phronêsis*). Kenny says that health is the raison d'être of medicine and both are *archai* (causes or principles). In the soul, there are two principles that resemble medicine and health. One can compare practical wisdom (*phronêsis*) to medicine; the 'speculative part of the soul'—as Kenny calls it—is its raison d'être. On similar grounds, as health is what medicine is for, the divine is what practical wisdom is for. There are two *archai*: the divine who does not issue commands, and practical wisdom that does issue commands. In this sense, the divine is not like a master with a slave (the soul). According to Kenny, practical wisdom is more suited to this analogy since it commands to the soul as a master commands to a slave.

each person must live according to *his* commanding principle.[43] The commanding principle seems to be the entire rational part of the soul which includes virtues of practical and of theoretical thinking.[44] This is in line with what Aristotle says at *EE* II 1219b30–2, where he explains that the entire rational part of the soul gives commands to the non-rational part of the soul that listens and obeys. *Phronêsis* is a commanding principle because it gives orders to the part of the soul that listens and obeys. And it gives orders for the sake of the virtues of theoretical thinking.[45] As I discussed in relation to T5, at 1249b15–16, Aristotle says that the divine is that for the sake of which (*hou heneka*) *phronêsis* prescribes. The expression *hou heneka* can be understood in two ways: *to hou heneka tinos* is the aim for which we do something; *to hou heneka tini* is the beneficiary of what we do.[46] Right before this passage, Aristotle proposes a comparison with health and medicine. As medicine is for the sake of health, practical wisdom is for the sake of the divine. The relation between *phronêsis* and the theoretical capacity (*to theôrêtikon*) is like the relation between medicine and health: that is, medicine prescribes for the sake of health. The comparison suggests that *phronêsis* prescribes for the sake of the theoretical capacity. If the divine mentioned at 1249b15 is the same thing as the *theôrêtikon* mentioned at 1249b14, then we can plausibly argue that

---

[43] At 1249b12, in manuscripts P, C, B, and L, we find ἑαυτῶν, Spengel reads αὐτοῦ.

[44] Von Arnim (1924), Needler (1926), Gauthier and Jolif (1959), Monan (1968), and Dirlmeier (1984) interpret θεός as νοῦς. For Dirlmeier (1984, 502), *phronêsis* is the inferior part of the soul and νοῦς is the superior part. In order to substantiate his reading, Dirlmeier points out that already in the fifth century the idea of νοῦς as the 'divine in us' was widespread. In *MM* 1198b7, *phronêsis* is called the steward of *nous*, and it procures leisure for the 'master'. Cf. Buddensiek (2014, 313–35) argues that *theos* refers to the best possible object of contemplation.

[45] This is compatible with the idea that the aims of *phronêsis* (together with the character virtues and the virtues on which *phronêsis* depends) are practical thinking and virtuous actions. Its final aim is to promote theoretical activity. On the idea that ends can be for their own sake and have contemplation as ultimate aim, see Lear 2014, 61–89.

[46] Cf. *Physics* 194a32–6; *De Anima* 415b2–3; *Metaphysics* 1072b1–4. Cf. Gastaldi 2003, 80. Cf. Baghadassarian 2024.

the activity of the virtues of theoretical thinking is the final cause of the activity of *phronêsis* (and VPD). Scholars debate how to interpret the reference to the divine at 1249b15.[47] The divine is the final cause insofar as it is called *hou heneka*. Qua final cause, it can be the aim or the beneficiary. But the divine is in need of nothing, so how can it be the beneficiary?[48] The idea of the divine as beneficiary may be supported by the reference to the cultivation of the divine (*ton theon therapeuein*) at 1249b22.[49] Aristotle does not explain what he means with cultivation of the divine.[50] As in the case of the reference to the divine at 1249b15, also in the case of the expression 'the cultivation of the divine', interpretations can be divided in two groups: those who argue that *theos* refers to god versus those who argue that it refers to *nous* or to some other theoretical virtue.[51] Dirlmeier argues that at 1249b15, the divine refers to some internal divine principle—on his view, it refers to *nous*. He shows that there is continuity between 1248a28, where *nous* refers to the divine in us, and the occurrence of *theos* at 1249b15. Dirlmeier refers to *Timaeus* 90c4 to support his interpretation that *theos* is the divine in us: he says that Aristotle is

---

[47] Von Arnim (1924, 28) thinks that *theos* is an interpolation of a Christian author. Walzer and Mingay seem to defend a similar position insofar as they read τὸ <ἐν ἡμῖν> θεῖον θεραπεύειν with Robinson.
[48] Cf. Leunissen 2010, ch. 3; Johnson 2005, ch. 3.
[49] This is the reading that we find in the MSS and that is reported by Rowe (2023a). Cf. τὸν νοῦν ἐνεργεῖν von Arnim; τὸ <ἐν ἡμῖν> θεῖον θεραπεύειν Robinson.
[50] Kenny points out that the passage has strong similarities with the notion of *therapeia* in *Euthyphro* 13b–d where it refers to the care that a slave has for his master (Kenny 1978, 178; 1992, 102). Baghadassarian (2024) argues that the cultivation of the divine is ultimately contemplation. Jost argues that *therapeia* refers to a way to attend to our human nature; it is a way to improve ourselves (Jost 2014b, 287–313).
[51] Cf. Woods 1992, 180–4; Verdenius 1971, 288–93; Rowe 1971, 68; Kenny 1978, 174–8; 1992, 97; Dumoulin 1988, 176–8; Buddensiek 2014, 323–4. They think that the reference is to an external god; Woods points out that the interpretation is connected to the passage that comes immediately before this where Aristotle says that there are two ways of reading the expression 'that for the sake of which'. Woods refers to *DA* 415b2, where that for the sake of which can refer to the purpose for which we do something or to the beneficiary for whom we do something. The divine is that for the sake of which in the sense of the purpose as the divine does not need anything. Dirlmeier (1984, 503–4) and Düring (1966) think that it is a reference to *nous*.

a 'Timaios-Platoniker'.[52] However, it is more difficult to argue that at 1249b22 and at b23, where Aristotle speaks of cultivation of the divine and contemplation, the divine refers to *nous* or to the theoretical part of the soul. Buddensiek argues that the cultivation of the divine should be understood as a cultivation of god in the sense of an external god: he points out that the passage recalls Plato's *Laws* 716d, where Plato says that the cultivation of the divine is the best way to achieve happiness.[53] However, the parallelism with Plato's texts does not solve the problem since in Plato's dialogues, we find evidence in favour of the theological interpretation proposed by Buddensiek and others, as well as evidence of the intellectual interpretation of Dirlmeier and others.

As I see it, at *EE* VIII 1249b22, with cultivation of the divine Aristotle refers to a process of self-improvement and self-knowledge. When we engage in a process of knowledge of ourselves, we engage in the cultivation of the divine. This process of self-knowledge leads to contemplation of divine matters and even to god, and is preparatory to this activity. By engaging in a process of knowing ourselves, we engage in a process of self-improving insofar as we exercise the virtues of thinking which are the most divine-like part in us. This process of knowledge and of improvement of ourselves prepares us to contemplate.[54] All the virtues contribute to this process of self-knowledge and self-improvement, and in this sense, the virtues of theoretical thinking and the activity of contemplation are the final cause understood as the aim and the beneficiary of the activities of all the other virtues.[55] With regard

---

[52] Dirlmeier 1984, 504.
[53] Buddensiek 2014, 313–35. Buddensiek argues that the *theôrêtikon* is the beneficiary and that the *spoudaios* is the maker who implements the limit. Cf. Jost (2014b, 287–313) argues that the service of the divine consists in attending to our own moral development.
[54] Gottlieb (2009) arrives at a similar conclusion through a different route: she argues that the *phronimos* must have self-knowledge because this agent needs to know her abilities and worth.
[55] On the idea that a teleological subordination of different capacities binds these capacities together in a unity, see Frey 2015, 144 and Leunissen 2010, 59.

to the interpretation that I propose it does not matter whether the divine mentioned at 1249b15 is an internal principle or god understood as an external god: even if it refers to an external god, we need the virtues of theoretical thinking to contemplate god. This is sufficient to show that the virtues of theoretical thinking and their activities—whether they are directed toward god or not—are the final cause of the activities of all the other virtues.

Additional evidence in favour of TA is provided by the discussion of the limit.[56] The activities of the virtues of theoretical thinking benefit from the *horos* (limit). In VIII.3, Aristotle refers to the limit four times. At *EE* 1249a23, Aristotle says that the doctor must have a limit. This limit determines what is good for health and what is not. Aristotle says that the limit is about actions and choices of natural goods. However, two elements suggest that the virtues of theoretical thinking and their activities are the final cause of this *horos*. First, Aristotle discusses the comparison with the doctor and with health that he proposes at 1249b13–14 to illustrate the relation between *phronêsis* and the virtues of theoretical thinking. That is, the limit is useful for the doctor to bring about health and health is compared few lines later to the theoretical capacity. In light of this comparison, the limit is useful for us to bring about theoretical activity. Second, at *EE* 1249b18–21, Aristotle says that the choice and acquisition of natural goods that best promote the contemplation of the divine is the most beautiful limit. He explains that natural goods should promote theoretical activity and that this is the most beautiful limit. At *EE* 1249b23–5, he explains that being aware as little as possible of the irrational part of the soul is the best limit of the soul.[57] At *EE* 1249b26, *horos* is the limit of *kalokagathia*. These last two references to the limit reinforce the reading of *horos*

---

[56] For a more detailed discussion of the limit, see chapter 3.
[57] Another possible reading proposed by Rowe (2023a) is that we should be aware as little as possible of 'the other' (*allou*) part of the soul, which refers to the part of the soul that does not possess reason.

as something that concerns the entire soul and whose final end is theoretical activity.[58]

Concluding, IA, CA, and TA show that the virtues of theoretical thinking should be included in the Functional Unity of the Virtues. These three arguments show that all the virtues contribute and co-function for the sake of the ultimate end of theoretical activity.

5.3 On the separability of the virtues

Given the cooperation and co-functioning of the virtues of practical thinking, the character virtues, and the virtues of theoretical thinking, one may ask whether it is possible for an agent to have the virtues of theoretical thinking without the virtues of practical thinking and the character virtues, and vice versa. Of course, the *kalos kagathos* needs to have all the virtues, including the virtues of theoretical thinking, the virtues of practical thinking, and the character virtues. In the undisputed books of the *EE*, there is no evidence that shows that one can have the virtues of theoretical thinking and lack the other virtues. Two passages in the common books may initially suggest otherwise. At *EE* V = *NE* VI 1141b2–8, Aristotle explains that *sophia* is *nous* plus *epistêmê*, and is about the most honourable things in nature. He adds that it is for this reason that people say that Anaxagoras, Thales, and similar sages are *sophoi*, but they are not *phronimoi*. He explains that people say this because they observe that these sages know marvellous and difficult things, but they do not know what is advantageous for themselves because they do not investigate human things. I think that the passage does not provide evidence that indeed Anaxagoras and Thales and other sages do not have *phronêsis* and the related virtues. First, in the passage, Aristotle reports what people say rather than explaining his own view. Second, the passage occurs

---

[58] Buddensiek (2014, 313–35) argues for a similar interpretation.

in the context of Aristotle's explanation of the difference between *phronêsis* and *sophia* based on their objects of concern: *phronêsis* is about human matters, *sophia* is about divine and immutable things. In this context, people say that Anaxagoras, Thales, and other sages have *sophia* and not *phronêsis* because they investigate immutable things rather than mutable ones. That is, Anaxagoras, Thales, and other sages disregard what is advantageous for themselves because they value more what is immutable and its investigation. This does not mean that they lack *phronêsis* and the other virtues: they lack *phronêsis* understood as political ability in an ordinary sense. These sages prioritize a higher good, which may turn out to be more advantageous for themselves in the long run.[59]

A few lines after this passage, at 1142a11–16, Aristotle explains that young people can be theoretically wise (*sophoi*), but they cannot be practically wise (*phronimoi*). On a close examination of the passage it is clear that Aristotle qualifies *sophoi*: he says that young people can be geometricians and mathematicians and can be theoretically wise with regard to these things (*sophoi ta toiauta*). Namely, young people are not *sophoi* in the same way in which the *kaloi kagathoi* are *sophoi*. Young people can be *sophoi* in a qualified sense: *sophia* refers to expertise in some fields. Aristotle explains that young people cannot be *phronimoi* because they lack the experience of life.

In the undisputed books of the *NE*, there is little evidence that the virtues of theoretical thinking can be possessed without the other virtues. In the *NE*, the only references to the separability of the virtues appears in *NE* X, and in particular at 1178a22, where Aristotle refers to a higher kind or degree of happiness that is happiness of the contemplative life. As this kind or degree of happiness is discussed it does not seem to require the possession and exercise

---

[59] Natali (1999, footnote 603) refers to *Hippias Major* 281e where there is a similar discussion. He argues that at *NE* X 1179a9–13, Aristotle quotes the moral opinions of Anaxagoras and Solon about who is happy. Natali concludes that these sages should also have the other virtues.

of the virtues of practical thinking and of the character virtues.[60] However, this is a contested issue that involves the long debate on whether happiness should be understood according to the dominant reading or according to the inclusive one.

Even if we accept the idea that the virtues of theoretical thinking can be possessed without the other virtues despite the lack of direct evidence, it is clear that the virtues of theoretical thinking do not function in the same way when they are part of the Functional Unity of the Virtues and when they function without the other virtues that belong to the Functional Unity of the Virtues. *Sophia* functions merely as expertise in specific domains whose objects are immutable and eternal. *Epistêmê* is simply knowledge that can be used for the good or for the bad, but it does not have those additional functions that it has when it interacts with *nous* or with *phronêsis*. The case of *nous* is more complex: in the *EE*, Aristotle does not dedicate a separate analysis to this virtue as he does for the other virtues of thinking in *EE* V. In *De Anima*, Aristotle speaks of a separable *nous*.[61] In the *EE*, *nous* is a virtue that must be possessed with *phronêsis* and that provides the starting points in the practical domain. It is also a virtue that must be possessed as part of *sophia* and provides the starting points in the theoretical domain. Hence, as it is discussed in the *EE*, *nous* seems a virtue that must be possessed always with other virtues.[62]

One may ask whether *phronêsis* and VPD can be possessed without the virtues of theoretical thinking. That is, can there be good agents who do not possess the virtues of theoretical thinking? As I argued, one cannot achieve happiness as this is defined in the *EE* without the virtues of theoretical thinking. *Kalokagathia* is the

---

[60] The relation between the two kinds or degrees of happiness and the discussion of what they consist in are topics much debated by scholars and on which there is no agreement.
[61] *DA* 430a17.
[62] This is compatible with the idea that *nous* comes in two forms: natural virtue and proper virtue. Qua natural virtue, *nous* can be possessed without the other virtues that are part of the whole. I discuss evidence of this in chapter 2.

complete virtue that Aristotle refers to (even though he does not call it *kalokagathia*) in the definition of happiness. It includes all the virtues, comprising also the virtues of theoretical thinking.[63] As I argue in chapter 2, practical *nous* is one of the virtues on which *phronêsis* depends. Hence, the agent who has *phronêsis* must have at least one theoretical virtue: *nous*. One may argue that this agent can have only the practical type of *nous* and does not necessarily have the theoretical type of *nous*. Nothing in the *EE* seems to exclude this option. Hence, there may be cases of agents who have *phronêsis* and VPD and do not have the virtues of theoretical thinking. However, as I showed, the activities of the virtues of theoretical thinking are the final cause of the activities of the other virtues. For this reason, even if we admit the case of agents who have *phronêsis* and VPD, and lack the virtues of theoretical thinking, we must admit that *phronêsis* and the character virtues are not strictly speaking the same virtues that we find in the Functional Unity of the Virtues when they are possessed without the virtues of theoretical thinking. That is, their tasks are limited because they do not function with the virtues of theoretical thinking. In this sense, in order to fulfil their full potential, the virtues should cooperate and be part of the Functional Unity of the Virtues.

5.4 Conclusions

I argued that in the *EE*, the virtues of theoretical thinking co-function with *phronêsis* and VPD: they fulfil tasks that benefit

---

[63] See chapter 6. Wolt (2022, 1–23) argues that in the *EE*, we can distinguish the *phronimos* from the *kalos kagathos*. The *kalos kagathos* possesses all the virtues of character and chooses goods that are praiseworthy. The *phronimos* merely chooses goods that are good by nature but they are not praiseworthy. This agent does not have all the virtues of character. Wolt argues that the *agathos* as this term is used in *EE* VIII.3 refers to someone who is not virtuous. As he sees it, the *agathos* has stable dispositions to do virtuous actions. Wolt argues that in the *EE*, *kalokagathia* has the role that *phronêsis* has in the *NE*.

phronêsis and VPD and they benefit from the activities of *phronêsis* and VPD. I provided three arguments—the Inclusion Argument, the Cooperation Argument, and the Teleological Argument—that show that the virtues of theoretical thinking should be included in the Functional Unity of the Virtues. What emerges from these arguments is that the virtues of theoretical thinking as well as *phronêsis* and VPD do not function in the same way when they are possessed outside the Functional Unity of the Virtues and when they interact with the other virtues in the Functional Unity of the Virtues. Namely, when they are part of the Functional Unity of the Virtues, they have additional tasks and they fulfil their full potential.

6
Kalokagathia: the Functional Unity of the Virtues

The *sophos*, the *phronimos*, the *agathos*, the *spoudaios*, the *epieikês*, and the *kalos kagathos* have all been considered Aristotle's best agent. Nowhere does Aristotle specify exactly if these are all different kinds of best agents or whether they are simply different names for the same kind of best agent. Based on Aristotle's discussion in *EE* V = *NE* VI, and in particular, on his distinction between the political life and the contemplative life in *NE* X, scholars consider the *sophos* to be different from the *phronimos*. The *sophos* has been standardly understood as the contemplator, and it has been argued that the contemplator/*sophos* does not need to be moral.[1] The *phronimos* has been standardly understood as the practically wise person who does not need to have the theoretical virtues.[2] Both these positions are not unanimously agreed upon. The question of who the best agent is tied to the question of what the best life is.

With reference to the *NE*, two primary candidates for the role of best life are the life of contemplation on the one hand, and the life of politics on the other hand. Scholars tend to argue that Aristotle considers the life of contemplation best.[3] On this view, the *NE*'s best

---

[1] Cf. Cooper 1975, ch. 3; Nightingale 2004, 222. Cooper rejected this view in Cooper 1999a, ch. 5. Cf. also Kraut 1989, 6; Walker 2018, ch. 8.
[2] Cf. McDowell 1979, 121–43.
[3] Hardie 1967; Cooper 1975; Kraut 1989.

agent is the *sophos*. Many contributions that shaped virtue ethics in the 1980s, 1990s, and 2000s, however, focused on the political life. In other words, they focused on the ideal of character virtue combined with excellence in deliberation. In this context, it became customary to refer to the *NE*'s best agent as the *phronimos*.[4] Scholars investigated what the *phronimos* knows, what kind of affective and desiderative attitudes the *phronimos* has, and how the *phronimos*' agency is different from the agency of the merely controlled or of the *akratês*.[5] With respect to the person who leads the life of *theôria*, the *sophos*, it is asked to what extent and how the virtues of an active political life are part of Aristotle's ideal. With respect to the life of politics, it is assumed that the person who has the virtues of character in a full or strict sense also has *phronêsis*—practical wisdom.

In *EE*, the best agent is the agent who has all the virtues, and these virtues interact in relevant ways. That is, this agent possesses the unity of the virtues (UoV) understood as Functional Unity. This agent is the *kalos kagathos*: the person who possesses the distinctive and complex virtue of being-beautiful-and-good (*kalokagathia*).[6] The agent who possesses *kalokagathia* is not merely good (*spoudaios* or *agathos*), or decent (*epieikês*), or practically wise (*phronimos*). She is also not uniquely a theorizer (*sophos*).[7] This agent possesses all the virtues that Aristotle discusses in the *EE*.

---

[4] For an influential defense of this view, see McDowell 1979, 121–43. Cooper 1975; Reeve 1992, 97; Wiggins 1988, 237; and Woods 1986, 145–66. Notably, discussions of Aristotle's ethics often refer to the best agent as the *phronimos*, almost independently of the controversial question of whether the best life, according to the *NE*, is the life of *theôria*.

[5] For discussion of the ideal agent in the *NE*, see Drefcinski 1996, 139–53; Curzer 2005, 233–56; Sluiter and Rosen 2008; Hoffman 2010; Hursthouse 2011, 38–57.

[6] For my translation of *kalokagathia*, see introduction, footnote 8.

[7] See introduction, footnote 14, on my translations of Greek masculine nouns and adjectives in a way that aims to include agents of all genders.

Namely, she possesses the character virtues and all the virtues of practical and theoretical thinking and thereby enjoys happiness as defined at the beginning of the *EE*.[8] In the first sentence of the *EE*, Aristotle advances a programmatic claim: that happiness is the best, most beautiful, and most pleasant thing of all. The best agent of the *EE*, the *kalos kagathos*, possesses happiness in this sense. That is, this agent exhibits a complex but unified set of virtues and, likewise, the agent's happiness exhibits a complex but unified set of value properties. *Kalokagathia* can be compared to happiness insofar as both have superlative value: *kalokagathia* is the best of the virtues and happiness is the best activity. To capture the idea of superlative value, I call *kalokagathia* a superexcellence. *Kalokagathia* corresponds, on the level of virtue, to the way in which the Aristotle of the *EE* conceives of *eudaimonia*, happiness. What is more, as I show in the second part of the chapter, *kalokagathia* is the complete virtue that Aristotle refers to (without calling it *kalokagathia*) in the definition of happiness. By claiming that the *kalos kagathos* is the agent who possesses all the virtues, Aristotle argues that excellent thinking and excellent action go together and are both necessary for being the best agent.

In this chapter, I show that Aristotle considers *kalokagathia* a virtue composed by parts and that these parts are all the virtues discussed in the *EE* (section 6.1). I argue that *kalokagathia* is on-off in the sense that it comes about only if a threshold is met (section 6.2). I then move to the notion of complete virtue (section 6.3) and to the place that this notion has in the definition of happiness (section 6.4). By turning to the *Physics* and to the *Metaphysics*, I explain what it means for a virtue to be complete (section 6.5). I conclude by examining some candidates to the role of complete virtue and by showing that only *kalokagathia* meets the stringent criteria (section 6.6). Qua complete virtue, it must comprise all the virtues discussed in the treatise.

---

[8] *EE* I 1219a39–40.

6.1 Kalokagathia and the relation to its parts

EE VIII.3 contains the most extensive Aristotelian discussion of *kalokagathia*.[9] Aristotle uses this notion to refer to the best kind of excellence a person can attain: I call this superlative excellence. What this superlative excellence amounts to, then, is a matter of his substantive ethical proposals. The term *kalokagathia* suggests that this superexcellence combines two excellences: being beautiful (*kalon*) and being good (*agathon*). My translation of *kalon* is intended to be technical. It captures no more and no less than the idea that the *kalon* is, as Aristotle puts this, choiceworthy for itself and praiseworthy for its own sake.[10] My translation of *kalokagathia* as 'being-beautiful-and-good' aims to suggest that in the life of the *kalos kagathos*, beauty and goodness have a prominent place. As I argue, the *kalos kagathos* has all the character virtues and all the virtues of practical and theoretical thinking: for this reason, the *kalos kagathos* has good aims, good relations with other people and with the community, performs good actions, and makes good choices. Insofar as this agent has all the virtues of theoretical thinking, the *kalos kagathos* dedicates time to theoretical activities and contemplates theoretical objects. As I argued in chapter 5, theoretical activity is the final aim of all the other virtues and their activities. Aristotle characterizes theoretical activities and objects as beautiful par excellence. In this sense, beauty, and not only goodness, has a prominent place in the life of the *kalos kagathos*: the life of the *kalos kagathos* aims at *theôria*, which is the most beautiful

---

[9] For the translation of *kalokagathia* and *kalon*, see introduction, footnotes 8 and 17. *Kalokagathia* is discussed in ways that resemble the *EE*'s discussion in *Magna Moralia* 1207b20-08a4. The term *kalokagathia* occurs twice in the *NE* (1124a4, 1179b10), but in this treatise, it does not seem fundamental for Aristotle's project. It occurs once in the *Politics* (1259b34–5). The adjective is found at *Politics* 1270b24, 1271a23, 1293b39, b42, and 1294a18, and in the *Protrepticus* IX 52.28. But in all these occurrences, the adjective is used in the traditional sense of noble birth. Only in the *EE*, *kalokagathia* refers to the superexcellence.
[10] *EE* VIII 1248b19–21.

activity for human beings. In all these senses, this agent and her life are truly beautiful-and-good.[11]

The idea that *kalokagathia* results from the possession of all the virtues is explicitly stated when Aristotle introduces *kalokagathia*. At the beginning of the final chapter of the treatise—*EE* VIII.3 1248b9–10—Aristotle remarks that individual virtues have been discussed throughout the treatise (κατὰ μέρος μὲν οὖν περὶ ἑκάστης ἀρετῆς εἴρηται). Translated literally, Aristotle says that up to now he proceeded 'part by part' (*kata meros*) in addressing each individual virtue.[12] Particular virtues are each by themselves excellences, while at the same time they are (or can be studied as) parts. The mere fact that the virtues are analysed individually earlier in the treatise suggests that, up to a point, they can be studied as individual virtues without this being misleading or confused. But as Aristotle already signals from the beginning of the treatise, and in particular in the Function Argument that leads to the definition of happiness at the beginning of *EE* II, these virtues are also parts of complete virtue, which I interpret it as *kalokagathia*. That is, *kalokagathia* is the Functional Unity of the Virtues. When we have *kalokagathia*, all the virtues interact and co-function in relevant ways. And only when they interact with one another they fulfil their full potential as the virtues that they are.

> (T1) We have spoken earlier about each virtue part by part (*kata meros*); but since we have separately distinguished the capacity of each of them, we have to discuss the virtue composed by them, which we already referred to as being-beautiful-and-good. Now it is evident that whoever truly earns this appellation must have the individual virtues (*tas kata meros aretas*). For it cannot be

---

[11] Scholars who translate *kalon* as 'fine' or 'noble' do not usually focus on theoretical activities and theoretical objects. Cf. Lear 2006; Konstan 2014.

[12] The gloss 'part by part' is justified by the distributive sense of the Greek preposition *kata*.

otherwise in other cases, either. For no one is healthy in his body as a whole (*holon*), yet not in any part (*meros*) of it; rather, all parts, or most parts and the most important ones, should be in the same state as the whole (*holô*).[13]

Aristotle says that *kalokagathia* is composed 'by them' (*ek toutôn*), where *toutôn* refers to the virtues mentioned in the first line of T1. When he says 'we have spoken earlier about each virtue part by part', Aristotle refers to all the virtues that have been discussed in the earlier books of the treatise, and these are all the virtues of thinking and of character.[14] I take it that *ek toutôn* in effect means 'by all of these'. That is, *ek toutôn* refers to the character virtues and to the virtues of practical and theoretical thinking. Insofar as in T1, Aristotle says that *kalokagathia* is composed by these virtues—*ek toutôn*—we can conclude that *kalokagathia* is composed by all the virtues discussed in the treatise.[15] This is supported also by what Aristotle says at *EE* II 1220a3-4. In this passage, he compares good health to the virtue of the soul as *telos*. He explains that good health (*euexia*) results from the virtues taken part by part. That is, it results from the parts of the body being healthy. Aristotle uses a similar Greek expression—*kata morion* ('part by part')—to the one that he uses in T1. Similarly, *kalokagathia* qua virtue of the soul as *telos* results from possessing all the virtues that constitute its parts. The comparison brings further evidence in favour of the idea that *kalokagathia* includes all the virtues as parts.

---

[13] *EE* VIII 1248b9-17.
[14] *EE* II, III, and V.
[15] At 1248b11, Aristotle says that we referred—ἐκαλοῦμεν—to this virtue as *kalokagathia*. Jackson, Ross, Dirlmeier, Donini, Woods, and Reeve read καλοῦμεν: that is, they prefer the present instead of the imperfect. They think that the present is the most plausible reading insofar as a previous reference to *kalokagathia* cannot be found in the *EE*. This reading is in line with the Latin translation that we find in the *Liber de Bona Fortuna*. However, as Rowe notices, this Latin translation is not always reliable and we should prefer the imperfect even though the problem of finding a reference to *kalokagathia* before *EE* VIII.1 remains unsolved. Cf. Rowe 2023b. Inwood and Woolf (2013) read ἐκαλοῦμεν.

Against my reading that *kalokagathia* includes all the virtues, someone could raise the objection that Aristotle explicitly backs away from the claim that *kalokagathia* comprises *all* the virtues. His comparison with health in T1 says that, for someone's body to be healthy as a whole, all, or most, or the most important parts of the body must be healthy.[16] By analogy, this means that for someone to have *kalokagathia* she must have all, or most, or the most important virtues or parts of virtue. One may object that this suggests that there are cases in which the person who is *kalos kagathos* precisely does *not* have all the virtues.

Let me dwell for a moment on the example of health. When we ascribe health to someone, we typically refer to the person as a whole. We may say that someone is healthy after she recovered from a particular illness, say, a fever. But if only the fever had disappeared, and the person still did not feel well, we would not say 'she is healthy'. We only say 'she is healthy' when the person as a whole has recovered. This does not need to mean that the person is perfectly healthy in every possible respect. Instead, we take 'she is healthy' to be true if all, or most, or the most important parts of the body are healthy. Being healthy is a quality of the whole, that is, the body, and in this sense, it is a self-standing quality. However, the quality of the whole cannot exist if it does not exist in all, or most, or the most important of the parts. In the case of being healthy, the well-functioning of the individual parts—all, most, or the most important ones—of the body and their co-functioning produce the state of being healthy.

Now suppose the person who recovered from an illness is mildly allergic to some rare food. Hence she is not perfectly

---

[16] A similar expression is used by Aristotle to qualify which *endoxa* we should consider: both at *EE* VI = *NE* VII 1145b4–6 and in *Topics* 100b21–3, Aristotle says that we should consider the *endoxa* of 'all, the majority, or the wise'. I am grateful to Katja Vogt for pointing out this parallelism to me.

healthy. Still, once she recovered from her illness we will say 'she is healthy'. This is the kind of case that is covered by saying that one is healthy when one is healthy in most or the most important parts. In the case of *kalokagathia*, the same 'relaxed' all-quantifier (as I call Aristotle's specification that we need to be healthy in all, most, or the most important parts of the body) applies in analogous fashion. I submit that there are three ways to interpret the 'relaxed' all-quantifier in light of the analogy with health. First, suppose someone has all the virtues. This includes that she is courageous. Now suppose she has a mild fear of some harmless spider. The perfectly courageous person would not have this fear. And yet, if this mild fear is the only way in which someone falls short with respect to any of the virtues, she can count as having *kalokagathia*. Second, the 'relaxed' all-quantifier refers to the idea that in order to have *kalokagathia*, one must have the most important virtues, which are the virtues properly speaking. That is, agents may lack one or more natural virtues, but as long as they have all the proper virtues—the virtues of character, the virtues of practical thinking, and the virtues of theoretical thinking—they have *kalokagathia*. Third, the 'relaxed' all-quantifier is compatible with the idea that agents may lack one or more specific *technai*—let's say the *technê* of shoemaking—and still have *kalokagathia*. All these readings of the 'relaxed' all-quantifier are plausible and in line with the Functional Unity that I defend.

The 'relaxed' all-quantifier makes Aristotle's notion of *kalokagathia* flexible. It signals that Aristotle is not concerned with an abstract ideal. He is concerned with an ideal that 'real' agents can strive for. And yet, the 'relaxed' all-quantifier does not make this ideal any less demanding with a view to the scope of the relevant excellences. Just as a person who is healthy in the most important parts of her body cannot lack health in any vital organs or other fundamental respects, the person who has the superexcellence cannot lack any of the proper virtues that are part of the Functional Unity.

6.2 *Kalokagathia* as on-off

The comparison between health and *kalokagathia* addresses, moreover, another dimension of this superexcellence. Namely, we may wonder which kind of whole *kalokagathia* is. Specifically, we may ask whether *kalokagathia* is (i) additive, (ii) scalar, or (iii) on-off, as I put this. Let me explain how I understand this threefold distinction. According to (i), the activities of the virtues are not modified by their interaction with other virtues. So far, I showed that the virtues interact and co-function: for this reason, the additive option is not plausible. I include it here for the sake of clarity, and for the purpose of emphasizing that the relevant whole involves a high degree of integration. According to (ii), agents can have all the virtues, and yet have this unified state to greater and lesser degrees. On this model, two agents may possess all the virtues and yet, one of the two may be more *kalos kagathos* than the other. According to (iii), the interpretation that I defend, *kalokagathia* is a whole that is constituted only if a certain threshold is reached, such that the person has all, most, or the most important individual virtues and the virtues co-function in relevant ways.

If *kalokagathia* is an on-off state, one does not become *kalos kagathos* by accumulating more and more positive traits. Instead, the very way in which one's positive traits inter-relate gives rise to a self-standing property that one either has or does not have. As in the healthy body the main organs and the main parts of the body interact in such a way that the result is a healthy individual, in the case of *kalokagathia*, the main parts of the soul and their corresponding virtues need to be in place, interact, and co-function.

The attraction of the scalar model, and the reason why we should consider it, is that our normative assessments of people can be scalar. At times, we call someone simply good or virtuous; but at times, we also say that someone is better than someone else or that she has become more virtuous. And we seem to do the same in the case of health. We may call someone simply healthy; but we may also say we want to develop healthier eating habits or that we used to be healthier when we were younger. However, Aristotle seems to speak of health as on-off rather than scalar: at *EE* IV = *NE* V 1129a15–17, Aristotle says that from health only healthy things result and that we say that someone walks in a healthy way when she walks as a healthy person does. Health is considered the contrary of sickness. The idea is that either one is healthy and she walks as a healthy person does, or she is sick and she walks as a sick person does. Though we may speak of health in scalar terms, this is not the way of ascribing health that Aristotle envisages at *EE* IV = *NE* V 1129a15–17 and in T1. Instead, he invokes ascriptions of health where we say, without qualification, that someone is healthy. *EE* VII 1235b31–7 brings further evidence to this point. Aristotle says that what is beneficial for the healthy body is good for a body without qualification, and that what is pleasant for a healthy body is pleasant for a body without qualification. In this passage, Aristotle does not consider what is good or pleasant for someone who is more or less healthy. Rather, he speaks of the healthy body as simply healthy. What is good and pleasant for the sick body is different from what is good and pleasant for the healthy body. The scalar option, then, does not seem interpretively right. Instead, the thought is that if the conditions of the parts of a whole hit a limit and interact in the relevant way, then the body is healthy and, respectively, the person is *kalos kagathos*. According to my argument, then, *kalokagathia* is an on-off property.

6.3 Complete virtue

I now move to the argument that shows that *kalokagathia* is the complete virtue mentioned in the definition of happiness at *EE* II. In *EE* II, Aristotle says that happiness is activity of a complete life according to complete virtue (*aretê teleia*).[17] In *NE* I, he says that happiness is activity according to the best and most complete (*aristê kai teleiotatê*) virtue.[18] The expression *aretê teleia* can be read in many ways.[19] It can be translated 'complete virtue', 'perfect virtue', or 'final virtue'. I argue below that 'complete virtue' best captures Aristotle's view in the *EE*. Scholars predominantly focus on *aretê teleia* in the *NE*.[20] Two exceptions are Cooper and Kenny, who examine also the complete virtue mentioned in the definition of happiness in the *EE*.[21] Cooper offers a formal characterization of *aretê teleia* as it occurs in the definition of happiness in *EE* II 1219a39–40, namely that it is human excellence as a whole.[22] Kenny offers a substantive identification: *aretê teleia*, he argues, is the virtue of *kalokagathia*.[23] Kenny's view is in fact a specification of Cooper's proposal insofar as he argues that *kalokagathia* is the virtue which is virtue as a whole. By focusing on wholeness, I submit, Cooper showcases *kalokagathia*'s most theoretically challenging feature, which connects the *EE* with Aristotle's *Physics* and *Metaphysics*. My reading goes beyond Kenny's (and Cooper's) work not only because I explore a different route to arrive to the conclusion that *kalokagathia* is the complete virtue mentioned in the *EE*'s definition of happiness. What is more, I base my argument on the premise that Aristotle understands complete and whole—*teleion*

---

[17] *EE* II 1219a39–40, ἡ εὐδαιμονία ζωῆς τελείας ἐνέργεια κατ' ἀρετὴν τελείαν.

[18] *NE* I 1098a17–8. In this passage, Aristotle specifies that complete virtue has to be understood as the best and the most complete. In *NE* I 1100a4, 1101a14, 1102a5–6, Aristotle speaks of complete virtue: in all these occurrences, complete virtue has to be understood as specified in 1098a17–18. That is, it is the best and the most complete virtue.

[19] Cf. Cooper 1975, 100; Kenny 1992, 16; Irwin 2012, 495–528; Destrée (2003, 56) argues that in the *Metaphysics*, *teleios* is connected to *agathos*.

[20] Some of the major contributions to the discussion on happiness and its definition in the two treatises are: Rowe 1971; White 1992; Donini 1994, 98–110; Donini 2014b; Kenny 1992; Kenny 2016.

[21] In addition, in his commentary on the *EE*, Woods (1992, 90) says that in the Eudemian definition of happiness, complete virtue is *kalokagathia*. But he does not offer an argument to support this claim.

[22] Cooper 1975, 100.

[23] Kenny 1992, 19.

and *holon*—in a sense that these expressions have in the *Physics* and in the *Metaphysics*.

In what follows, I develop a set of criteria for virtue's completeness, based on the *EE* and relevant passages from the *Physics* and the *Metaphysics*. By reference to the long-standing discussion about inclusive versus dominant readings, I set up the Inclusion Criterion: virtue is complete only if it includes the character virtues and the virtues of thinking. By reference to wholeness as defined in the *Physics* and in the *Metaphysics*, I defend the Wholeness Criterion: complete virtue must be a whole. Insofar as Aristotle argues that what is complete and whole must have a limit, I propose the Limit Criterion: complete virtue must have a limit.

6.4 The definition of happiness

The much-debated question of which activities—those of theorizing, practical wisdom, the virtues of character, to name the main contenders—make up a happy life matters for present purposes. As I explained in the case of the best agent, also to establish what complete virtue is, we need to determine in what happiness consists. If happiness consists only in theoretical activity, *sophia* is a good candidate for complete virtue. In that case, we would need to specify in which sense *sophia* is complete. If happiness consists both in theoretical and practical activities, complete virtue must be a virtue that includes virtues of character and virtues of practical and theoretical thinking. For present purposes, it is useful to invoke again the so-called dominant and inclusive readings.[24] According to the former, happiness consists in contemplation. According to the latter, the best life includes both contemplation and the exercise of the virtues of character and *phronêsis*.

---

[24] The distinction between a dominant and an inclusive reading is first proposed by Hardie 1968. For a discussion of the debate, see chapter 5.

With regard to the *EE*, the inclusive reading has been considered more plausible.[25] Scholars argue that in the *EE*, the life of the happy agent combines contemplation and the activities of practical wisdom and the character virtues.[26] Notably, in the *EE*, Aristotle does not rank kinds or degrees of happiness and does not discuss a virtue that is most complete. Rather, he simply talks about 'complete virtue' and happiness.

With regard to the *NE*, among defenders of the dominant reading, some scholars argue that the best and most complete virtue is *sophia*, others that it is *nous*.[27] There are also what we may call hybrid views: some scholars argue that the best and most complete virtue is a combination of *sophia* and *phronêsis*.[28] Scholars who support the inclusive reading argue that the best and most complete virtue is a virtue that includes virtues of thinking and of character.[29] In *NE* 1097a25-34, Aristotle says that an end is most complete if it is chosen always as an end and never as a means for something else. Happiness is most complete because it is chosen for its own sake and for nothing else.[30] It is, thereby, the ultimate or chief end, the end for the sake of which other ends are pursued.

---

[25] Even though there are not many studies on the *EE*, comparatively speaking to the *NE*, the discussion of happiness is one of the most investigated topics: cf. Kenny 1992 and Cooper 1975. Among others, Lear (2006), Cooper (1975), and Kenny (1992) think that in the *EE*, happiness includes activity according to the character virtues and contemplation. According to Rowe (1971), there is an incongruity between happiness in *NE* I 7, X 7 and *EE* II 1. As Rowe says, in the *NE*, happiness is 'the actuality of the virtue of the superior part of the soul', and in the *EE*, it is the whole of virtue. Rowe says that in the *NE*, happiness seems to be mostly theoretical while in the *EE*, it is practical and theoretical. Buddensiek (1999, 20) argues that happiness is a whole and many things are necessary to achieve it, but theoretical activity is the most important one.

[26] Cooper (1975) and Kenny (1992) argue that in the *EE*, happiness is activity according to all the parts of the soul.

[27] Among others, Cooper, Kraut, Kenny, and Donini argue that the best virtue is *sophia*. In antiquity, the first to defend this interpretation is Aspasius. Labarrière (2003, 79-107) argues that the best virtue is *nous*. Cf. Cooper 1975; Kraut 1989; Kenny 1992; Donini 1994, 98-110; Destrée 2003.

[28] In antiquity, Eustrate argues that the best virtue is *phronêsis*. Natali (1989) argues that the best virtue is a combination of *phronêsis* and *sophia*.

[29] Cf. Ackrill 1973, 339-59; Destrée 2003.

[30] In *NE* 1097a29 happiness is said to be most complete.

As many scholars argue, this is how completeness or finality is explained if it is happiness—an activity—that is most complete.[31] But what does it mean that a virtue is complete? Let us consider two options: (i) a virtue is complete if it is by itself final, namely insofar as it is the virtue of the activity that most of all is self-sufficient and chosen for its own sake. (ii) A virtue is complete if it does not lack any parts.[32] In this sense, a virtue is complete if it is a whole with all its parts. My hypothesis is that we can distinguish completeness-qua-finality and completeness-qua-unity-of-virtue. On my view, the former characterizes complete virtue in the *NE*, while the latter applies to complete virtue in the *EE*.

6.5 What it means for a virtue to be complete

In *EE* II, Aristotle defines happiness as follows:

> (T2) Happiness, then, is the activity of the good soul. And since happiness is something complete (*teleon*), and a life can be complete (*telea*) or incomplete (*atelês*), and so too virtue (since it can be a whole (*holê*) or a part (*morion*)), and the activity of what is incomplete (*atelôn*) is itself incomplete (*atelês*), it follows that happiness would be the activity of a complete (*teleias*) life in accordance with complete (*teleian*) virtue.[33]

The two expressions—*teleos* (complete) and *holos* (whole)—are connected. Three things are called complete or whole in the passage:

- life can be complete or incomplete;

---

[31] Cf. Kenny 1992, 5, 18; Cooper 1975, 100; Irwin 2012, 495–528.
[32] Cooper (1975) and Irwin (2012, 495–528) argue that in the case of complete virtue, being complete means that the virtue includes all the other virtues.
[33] *EE* II 1219a35–40.

- activity can be complete or incomplete;
- virtue can be complete/whole or incomplete/a part.

What it means for a life to be *telea* is controversial.[34] When it refers to life, I interpret *telea* to refer to a life directed toward its *telos*. That is, a complete life is a life that aims at the highest and best activity for human beings which is contemplation.[35] With regard to activity, Aristotle says that the activity of what is incomplete is itself incomplete. But what does it mean for an activity to be *of* something incomplete (*hê de tôn atelôn energeia*)? In *Metaphysics* 1048b6-9, Aristotle says that activity is activity *of* a *dunamis*: an ability.[36] For example, we may say that there is an activity of the ability of seeing which is seeing. The activity of seeing can be exercised *according to* virtue—with good sight—or without virtue—with poor sight. According to *Metaphysics* 1048b20-35, activities like seeing are always complete. Roughly, this means that the activity of seeing is, at any moment in which is exercised, complete. However, in T2, Aristotle seems to speak of activities in a general sense that admits for activities to be incomplete. For present purposes, I should set aside the discussion of incomplete activities. An activity can be performed according to virtue or not. And this virtue can be complete or incomplete. Hence, there are four combinations: activity of something complete according to complete virtue, activity of something complete according to incomplete virtue, activity of something incomplete according to complete virtue, activity of something incomplete according to incomplete virtue. In the case of happiness, this activity is complete insofar as it is activity of something complete: namely, the ability to do virtuous actions and

---

[34] Irwin 2012, 495–528; Horn 2013, 21–40; Vinje 2023.
[35] An alternative interpretation is that a 'whole' life is either a complete lifespan, including all life stages and ending with death, or it is a sufficiently long lifespan to permit development of excellent activities. For a discussion of this, see Woods 1992, 91; Vinje 2023.
[36] Cf. Kosman 1994, 201.

to contemplate. What is more, this activity is according to complete virtue. While in the case of life and of activity, Aristotle speaks of being *telea* and *atelês*, virtue is said to be *teleia* and *atelês* since it can be *holê* and *morion*. In T2, two lines before the definition of happiness, Aristotle mentions a virtue which is a whole (*holê*). This virtue which is a whole is different from the virtue which is only a part (*morion*). But why is virtue said to be *telea/atelês* since it is *holê/morion*, while life and activity are said to be *telea/atelês* with no further specification? My hypothesis is that with this difference, Aristotle stresses a dimension of the virtue he aims to characterize: this virtue must not only be complete, but also a whole. Conversely, life is *telea/atelês* in the sense of complete or incomplete. In the *EE*, Aristotle does not specify what *teleion* and *holon* mean. In *Metaphysics* 1021b12–22a3, Aristotle defines what is *teleion* as: (i) that which has all its parts; (ii) that which cannot be surpassed in respect to excellence and whose proper excellence does not lack any part; (iii) that which has attained its end. He says that virtue is *teleiôsis*—completion or perfection.[37] In the *Physics*, Aristotle clarifies not only what he means by complete, but also by whole:

> (T3) That of which there is nothing left out, it is complete (*teleion*) or whole (*holon*). For we define a whole precisely as that from which nothing is absent, for example, a 'whole man or a whole chest'. And as with particular wholes, so it is in the main sense (*kuriôs*) [GB: that is, for the whole that is not a part of something else]: the whole is that of which there is nothing left out; whereas that from which something, no matter what, is missing and left outside is not 'all (*apê*)'. And 'whole' and 'complete', if not altogether the same, are close in their nature (*suneggus tên phusin*),

[37] *Metaphysics* 1021b20–21.

and nothing is complete (*teleion*) unless it has an end (*telos*); but an end is a limit (*peras*).[38]

Aristotle says that something is whole or complete when nothing is left out. Something is complete if it has an end and this end is a limit. Limit translates the Greek *peras*.[39] For present purposes, it is sufficient to invoke the definition of limit that Aristotle provides in *Metaphysics* 1022a4–10. Aristotle says that the limit is (a) 'the furthest part of each thing, and the first point outside which no part of a thing can be found, and the first point within which all parts are contained. (b) Any form (*eidos*) of magnitude or of something possessing magnitude. (c) The end of each thing. [. . .] (d) The substance (*ousia*) or essence of each thing.'[40] As (a) suggests, there is continuity among the parts contained within the limit. That is, the parts are connected and identifiable as parts of the same whole insofar as there is a limit that divides what is part of the whole and what is not.

T3 specifies that *teleion* and *holon* are not the same, but they are close in their nature. As Aristotle says in *Physics* 228b13–14: *teleion* and *holon* are close in their nature insofar as they are attributes of what is one.[41] In the *Metaphysics*, Aristotle explains the relative notion of oneness:

(T4) Most things, then, are said to be 'one' because they produce, or possess, or are affected by, or are related to, some other one thing; but some are called 'one' in a primary sense, and one of these is substance. It is one either in continuity or in form or in definition; for we reckon as more than one thing which are not continuous, or whose form is not one, or whose definition is not one. Again, in one sense we call anything whatever 'one' if it is

---

[38] *Physics* 207a8–15, my translation.
[39] LSJ reports 'limit' as possible translation of *peras*, as well as 'end' and 'boundary'.
[40] *Metaphysics* 1022a4–10, trans. by H. Tredennick.
[41] Radice (2011) argues that the two terms are hendiadys.

quantitative and continuous; and in another sense we say that it is not 'one' unless it is a whole (*holon*) of some kind, i.e. unless it is one in form (e.g., if we saw the parts of a shoe put together anyhow, we should not say that they were one—except in virtue of their continuity (*sunecheian*); but only if they were so put together as to be a shoe, and to possess already some one form). Hence the circumference of a circle is of all lines the most truly one, because it is whole and complete (*holê kai teleios*).[42]

The passage is fraught with interpretative difficulties that are not immediately relevant for present purposes. Aristotle addresses the way in which we call substances 'one'. He considers three options: something can be one in terms of continuity, or form, or definition. I am interested in the most ambitious notion of oneness, according to which something is one only if it is a whole, and that is, unless it is one in form. Aristotle uses two examples to illustrate the point. First, consider a shoe: the components of the shoe could be put together in such a way as to be continuous; that would provide the item with the weak oneness of continuity. But the item would not yet be a shoe. For that the components must be put together so that their continuity has the form of a shoe, and thereby the oneness of being a whole. Second, the circumference is said to be whole and complete. It is whole because there is continuity among the different parts that form the circumference: namely, it is a circumference and not a bunch of disconnected points. The circumference is complete insofar as it has a limit—*peras* (as established by what Aristotle says in T3).

In light of all this, virtue is complete when (i) it has all its parts connected in a way that they form a whole; (ii) it has a limit that defines what belongs to the whole; (iii) it is one virtue that has other virtues as genuine parts rather than as a mere bundle that fails to be composed in the way that wholeness requires. Since we

---

[42] *Metaphysics* 1016b7–17, tr. by Tredennick with changes by GB.

are talking about a virtue that has other virtues as parts, it seems plausible to say that the virtues that are parts are connected if they interact and co-function according to the ideas of Functional Unity and Additive Functionality.

6.6 What is the complete virtue of the *EE*'s definition of happiness?

Prima facie, *megalopsychia* (magnanimity), *dikaiosunê* (justice), *phronêsis*, *sophia*, and *kalokagathia* are candidates for the role of complete virtue as it appears in the *EE*'s definition of happiness.[43] Each of these virtues meets some important criteria: *megalopsychia* is called the strongest and greatest state, and it must be possessed together with some virtues; *dikaiosunê* is, albeit with qualification, called complete virtue; *phronêsis* forms a unity with the character virtues and the virtues of practical thinking; *sophia* includes already two virtues—*nous* and *epistêmê*; and *kalokagathia* is called complete and whole. When Aristotle ascribes any of these virtues to a person, it is clear that he intends it as high praise. Each virtue is a comprehensive accomplishment, which pertains to important domains of life. Nevertheless, only *kalokagathia* meets the stringent criteria (Inclusion, Wholeness, and Limit) for complete virtue.

Magnanimity and justice are the least promising candidates. They fail to meet what, earlier, I called the Inclusion Criterion. Namely, scholars agree that in the *EE*, happiness includes both activities according to the character virtues and activities according to the virtues of practical and theoretical thinking. In line with this reading, complete virtue should include both the virtues of character and the virtues of thinking. Magnanimity and justice,

---

[43] Décarie considers as candidates for the role of complete virtue justice, *sophia*, and *kalokagathia*. Décarie 1975, 60–76.

however, are virtues of character that do not include the virtues of thinking.

In the *EE*, the discussion of magnanimity differs in some respect from the more widely studied discussion of this virtue in the *NE*.[44] In *EE* II 1221a10, magnanimity is included in the list of vices and virtues: it is the mean between conceitedness and weakheartedness.[45] Even if the third item of each line of the list, that is, all the virtues, including magnanimity, was not Aristotelian, magnanimity is discussed in book III, which is about the virtues of character. Hence, it is undoubtedly a virtue of character. This is sufficient reason against the identification of complete virtue and magnanimity; but it is not the only reason.

Aristotle says that magnanimity is the greatest and strongest (*kratistê*) state.[46] At first sight, this claim seems to speak in favour of the identification of magnanimity with the complete virtue mentioned in the definition of happiness. Aristotle says:

(T5) Moreover magnanimity even seems to follow (*akolouthein*) all the virtues. And correctly judging what is great and small among good things is praiseworthy; and the great goods are thought to be those pursued by the possessor of the strongest state regarding such matters, the strongest state being magnanimity. What virtue in each sphere does is judge the greater and the lesser correctly; as the wise person and as virtue would bid. Hence all of the virtues will accompany (*hepesthai*) magnanimity, or it will accompany all of them.[47]

---

[44] *NE* 1124a1–2. In the *NE*, Aristotle points out that *megalopsychia* is the adornment (*kosmos*) of the virtues. Scholars debate on how to understand this claim: they suggest that either *megalopsychia* is not a virtue at all, or it includes all the virtues and somehow perfects them. Curzer (2012) argues that Aristotle's notion of *megalopsychia* is an attempt to reconcile the Homeric virtue of grandeur with his new virtue of moderation.

[45] Rowe (2023a) puts the third column of the list in round brackets to signal that there is something suspect about the text. The disposition of the items in columns and the items of the third column are probably not Aristotelian.

[46] *EE* III 1232a34.

[47] *EE* III 1232a31–8: with Rowe and Walzer and Mingay, I delete εἶναι ἡδέα at 1232a34–5.

Magnanimity follows (*akolouthein*) all the virtues and all the virtues accompany (*hepesthai*) it. Aristotle does not specify whether he is talking about all the character virtues or all the virtues, including the virtues of practical and of theoretical thinking. However, the passage occurs in *EE* III, which is a book dedicated to the virtues of character. Hence, we may suppose that Aristotle is talking about the virtues of character: these are the virtues that accompany magnanimity. The verb *akolouthein*—to follow—signals that magnanimity occurs with the other virtues, but it does not say that it includes the virtues. In addition, there is no indication that magnanimity includes the virtues of thinking.[48] Magnanimity must be possessed with practical wisdom (and with the virtues on which practical wisdom depends)—even though it does not include it— insofar as there cannot be virtues of character in the proper sense without practical wisdom.[49] In T5, Aristotle says explicitly that the magnanimous and the *phronimos* (the wise person) are able to judge the greater and the smaller correctly. The magnanimous has practical wisdom, but nothing is said regarding the virtues of theoretical thinking.[50]

The magnanimous is characterized by the capacity to judge correctly what has value in life. In T5, Aristotle says that the magnanimous is the measure of great goods insofar as this agent pursues great goods. The magnanimous does not care about life or wealth.[51] This agent cares only about honour. Gauthier argues that there are important differences between the discussion of magnanimity in the *NE* and in the *EE*: in the *NE*, magnanimity is characterized by

---

[48] Polansky and Stover 2003. Crisp 2006, 158–78.
[49] Cf. chapter 3. *EE* III 1234a24–37; *EE* V = *NE* VI 1144b17.
[50] Aristotle distinguishes a particular form of *megalopsychia* and a more general form of *megalopsychia*. In his discussion of this virtue, he focuses on the particular form. The more general form is not discussed and is a virtue of character, so it could be excluded as candidate for the role of complete virtue. Cf. *EE* III 1232b24–6. Cooper argues that this distinction between a general and a particular form is introduced to solve the tension between *megalopsychia* as the virtue of doing great deeds and the virtue of acting moderately. Cf. Cooper 1975, 196.
[51] *EE* III 1232b11.

self-sufficiency, while in the *EE*, it is characterized by honour.[52] In agreement with Gauthier, I think that honour has a special role in the discussion of magnanimity in the *EE*. This relation with honour is an important element that disqualifies magnanimity from the role of complete virtue mentioned in the definition of happiness.

(T6) Magnanimity is the best disposition concerning the choice and the use of honour and the other honourable goods, and it is with regard to this and not to what is useful that we define the magnanimous. At the same time the most praiseworthy disposition is the mean. Clearly, then, magnanimity too would be a mean.[53]

Magnanimity is defined as the best disposition in relation to the choice and use of honour. The same expressions 'choice and use' appears in *EE* VIII where Aristotle talks about natural goods.[54] As Aristotle says in *EE* VIII 1248b29, honour is a natural good. While another plausible candidate for the role of complete virtue—*kalokagathia*—allows us to choose and use all the natural goods in a way that promotes contemplation, magnanimity is the virtue of choosing and using honour and honourable goods. However, there is no mention of contemplation as the final purpose of this choice and use of honour and honourable goods. This is a further argument that speaks against the identification of magnanimity with the virtue mentioned in the definition of happiness: magnanimity does not have any explicit relation to contemplation.

---

[52] Gauthier 1951; Rees 1971, 231–45. Cf. Schmidt 1967, 149–68. Cf. *NE* 1124a4. In the *NE*, Aristotle says that *megalopsychia* cannot be possessed without *kalokagathia*. If *kalokagathia* is conceived in the same way as in the *EE*, this means that *megalopsychia* cannot be possessed without all the virtues of character and all the virtues of practical and theoretical thinking. However, this does not seem to be in line with how Aristotle conceives of this virtue in the *NE* (in 1079b10, Aristotle mentions *kalokagathia*, but he does not elucidate what he understands with this virtue except perhaps that if one possesses it, this agent is a lover of the beautiful).

[53] *EE* III 1233a4–8.

[54] *EE* VIII 1249b18.

Justice (*dikaiosunê*) does not satisfy the Inclusion Criterion: in Aristotle's reinterpreted Thrasymachean formulation, justice is the 'good of the other'.[55] It includes all the virtues, but merely in a qualified sense, namely insofar as virtuous action relates to others. In *EE* IV = *NE* V, Aristotle calls justice complete virtue.[56] He says explicitly that justice is a whole (*holon*).[57] That is, though justice does not meet the Inclusion Criterion, it has a kind of completeness.

> (T7) This form of justice is complete virtue, not however without qualification but in relation to other people. That is why justice is often thought to be the strongest virtue, and 'neither Evening star nor Morning star is so wondrous'. And we affirm the old saying: 'Justice contains within it all of virtue together.' It is complete virtue to the highest degree because it is the use of complete virtue. And it is complete because one who possesses it has the capability to use virtue not just on one's own behalf but in relation to others.[58]

Justice is said to be, as magnanimity, the strongest of the virtues. Aristotle quotes Theognis who says that justice is all virtues together. Aristotle does not agree with Theognis. Instead he develops his own proposal, according to which justice is specifically concerned with our relation to others. Justice contains all the virtues, and is the use—*chrêsis*—of complete virtue, insofar as the agent relates not only to herself but also to others. This makes justice complete in a qualified sense and not in an unqualified sense (*haplôs*).

Let us move to more plausible candidates: *phronêsis*, *sophia*, and *kalokagathia*. Aristotle says that *phronêsis* (practical wisdom)

---

[55] In *EE* II 1221a4, justice is listed among the character virtues. It is the mean between profit and loss. But as I pointed out, the list of the virtues that appears in this section of the text is probably not Aristotelian.
[56] *EE* IV = *NE* V 1129b26.
[57] *EE* IV = *NE* V 1130b18.
[58] *EE* IV = *NE* V 1129b26–33.

always functions in conjunction with the character virtues.[59] I showed in chapters 2 and 3 that *phronêsis* depends on practical intelligence, good deliberation, comprehension, consideration, and the character virtues. However, Aristotle does not say that practical wisdom includes all the virtues. It certainly does not include the virtues of theoretical thinking nor does it depend on them. Aristotle says that *phronêsis* prescribes (*epitattei*) for the sake of theoretical wisdom.[60] That is, practical wisdom 'serves' or 'prepares the ground' for theoretical wisdom: *sophia*. Practical wisdom cannot be the complete virtue mentioned in the definition of happiness in the *EE* insofar as it does not include *sophia*—and this is clear insofar as it prescribes for its sake.[61]

One of the most promising candidates for the role of complete virtue is *sophia* (theoretical wisdom). *Sophia* includes already two virtues: *epistêmê* and *nous*. Yet one passage clearly excludes *sophia*. In *EE* V = *NE* VI 1144a1–6, Aristotle says that *sophia* is *part* of complete virtue.

(T8) These states [GB: that is, theoretical wisdom and practical wisdom] must be choiceworthy in their own right, since each is certainly the virtue of its own part of the soul, even if neither of them accomplishes anything. Next, they do indeed accomplish things, not in the way that medical knowledge brings about health but in the way that health does. That is how theoretical wisdom (*sophia*) causes happiness, since theoretical wisdom is a part of the whole virtue and by being possessed and by being active it makes a person happy.[62]

---

[59] *EE* V = *NE* VI 1144a30; 1144b15–17.
[60] *EE* V = *NE* VI 1145a7; *EE* VIII 1249b15–16.
[61] Cf. Cooper 1975, 121. In addition, in *MM* 1184a34, Aristotle says that practical wisdom is not complete because when one acquires this virtue, one still wants and needs other things. In *MM* 1198b12–18, practical wisdom is called the steward of *sophia*.
[62] *EE* V = *NE* VI 1144a1–6.

Aristotle introduces a distinction between two ways in which something can be productive of something or, in other words, accomplish something. His comparandum is once again health. Medicine brings about health in one way; in another way, health brings about health. If someone is sick, medicine can produce health. If someone is healthy, however, then it is in the nature of being healthy that health sustains itself. In that sense, health brings about health. This is the very sense, according to T8, in which theoretical and practical wisdom are productive. They are ways of being active which sustain themselves. And hence it is not just true to say that they bring about themselves; insofar as one can engage in excellent activities such as contemplation and activities that display practical wisdom, they bring about happiness. At the conclusion of this line of thought, Aristotle makes the claim that interests us here: *sophia* is part of complete virtue.[63] This shows that *sophia* is not the complete virtue mentioned in the *EE*'s definition of happiness. Insofar as *EE* V = *NE* VI 1144a1–6 occurs in one of the so-called common books, it may also raise a problem for the interpretation of complete virtue in the *NE*. That is, if *sophia* is said to be part of complete virtue, how can it be the most complete virtue of the *NE*? The answer to this question is not clear. One way to solve the problem is to consider the common books—or at least this passage—as part of the philosophical argument in the *EE*. Another way to read the passage is that *sophia* is *teleion* in the sense of final rather than complete.[64]

Kalokagathia is the most promising candidate for being the complete virtue mentioned in the definition of happiness. As the analysis of T1 and the comparison with health show, *kalokagathia* is composed of *all* the virtues discussed so far in the treatises.[65]

---

[63] Aristotle compares theoretical wisdom to health. Cf. Burnet 1900, 283; Joachim 1951, 216–17; Reeve 1992, 95.

[64] Cooper argues that *sophia* is most final insofar as the activity of contemplation does not need other goods. Cf. Cooper 1975, 118.

[65] Bonasio 2020, 27–57. Kenny, Buddensiek, Monan, and Gastaldi argue that *kalokagathia* includes the virtues of thinking. Verdenius, and Moraux and Harlfinger argue that it does not include the virtues of thinking. On *kalokagathia* as complete

Insofar as *kalokagathia* is composed of all the virtues of character and of all the virtues of thinking, it meets the Inclusion Criterion. In *EE* VIII.3, Aristotle says that *kalokagathia* is complete virtue:

> (T9) Goods are beautiful when the aim in acting and choosing them is beautiful. That is why the natural goods are beautiful for the beautiful-and-good person. For the just is beautiful and this in the sense of what accords with worth; this person is worthy of these things. What suits him is also beautiful, and these things (wealth, high-born status, and power) are suitable for him. Consequently for the beautiful-and-good person the same things are both advantageous and beautiful. But for most people there is a discrepancy here. Things which are good without qualification are not good for them too, but they are good for the good person; but for the beautiful-and-good person they are also beautiful, since he performs many beautiful actions on their own account. But he who thinks that he ought to possess the virtues for the sake of external goods performs beautiful actions only incidentally. Hence being beautiful-and-good is complete virtue.[66]

The last sentence of the passage sums up several reasons for the claim that *kalokagathia* is complete virtue. All these reasons are connected to the beautiful. First of all, Aristotle says that the so-called natural goods are not only good for the agent who possesses *kalokagathia*, but they are also beautiful. Second, the beautiful is the ultimate motivation for the actions and choices of the *kalos kagathos*. Third, the agent who possesses *kalokagathia* is worthy (*axios*) of things beautiful such as the just, the suitable, wealth,

---

virtue, cf. Kenny 1992, 94. Arius Didymus describes *kalokagathia* as *aretē teleia*: see the discussion in Kenny 2016, ch.1.

[66] *EE* VIII 1249a6–17. I accept Spengel's reading at 1249a13. Cf. Bonasio 2021, 123–42. At 1249a6, I translate *kala* 'beautiful' to stress the parallelism with *kalos kagathos*, which is evident in the Greek. On my translation of *kalokagathia*, see introduction, footnote 8.

high-born status, and power. Fourth, things that are advantageous (*sumpheronta*) are also beautiful for this agent. For the many, there is a discrepancy between what is advantageous and what is beautiful. Finally, beautiful actions are done for their sake and not for the sake of acquiring external goods. The virtue of *kalokagathia* allows agents who possess it to have a special relation with the beautiful. This is due to the very nature of *kalokagathia*, as the name of this virtue suggests. What matters for present purposes is that Aristotle discusses the relation to the beautiful as evidence that *kalokagathia* is complete virtue. As part of the definition of *teleion* that Aristotle offers in *Metaphysics* 1021b12–22a3, Aristotle says that what is *teleion* cannot be surpassed in respect to excellence. As T9 shows, *kalokagathia* cannot be surpassed in respect to excellence. That is, for the agent who has *kalokagathia* things are not only good, but they are also beautiful. And the beautiful is the final aim of actions and choices. Insofar as all the virtues that compose *kalokagathia* co-function in order to attain one common end— the beautiful—there is continuity among the parts that constitute the whole of *kalokagathia*. This meets the definition of being one and whole given in *Metaphysics* 1016b7–18. In light of this and of what said in T9 in relation to being composed by all the virtues, *kalokagathia* meets the Wholeness Criterion.

Another element in favour of the idea that *kalokagathia* is the complete virtue of the definition of happiness is the discussion of the limit (*horos*), which I already analysed in chapter 3. Aristotle says that there is a *horos* of *kalokagathia*.[67] The limit of *kalokagathia* entails that (i) we perceive the irrational part of the soul as little as possible,[68] and that (ii) we are able to choose and acquire the

---

[67] *EE* VIII 1249b26. Cf. Peterson 1988, 233–50.
[68] The 'irrational' part translates the term ἀλόγου. An alternative reading of the manuscripts (defended by Rowe 2023a) is ἄλλου—namely 'the other part' of the soul.

natural goods in a way that promotes contemplation. In *EE* VIII 1249b14, Aristotle mentions explicitly *to theôrêtikon*—the theoretical capacity. This seems to be the *archê*—principle—to which we need to subordinate. In *EE* VIII 1249b19, Aristotle says that the choice and the acquisition of natural goods should promote the *theou theoria*: the contemplation of the divine. The choice and acquisition of natural goods is the most beautiful limit because it promotes the most beautiful activity, namely contemplation.[69] The limit is characterized as the limit of *kalokagathia*. All this shows that *kalokagathia* meets the Inclusion Criterion: that is, the final aim of this virtue is theoretical contemplation and the virtues of theoretical thinking must be included in *kalokagathia* in addition to the virtues of character and practical wisdom (which are necessary for the aim of our actions to be beautiful).

Regarding the completeness of *kalokagathia*, in T3, in the *Physics*, Aristotle says that something is complete when it has an end and the end is a limit: *peras*. *Peras* and *horos* are two different terms, but they are closely connected and for present purposes, they can be treated as synonyms.[70] As Aristotle states, *kalokagathia* has a *horos*. This is enough to show that *kalokagathia* meets the Limit Criterion. Insofar as it satisfies the Inclusion, Wholeness, and Limit Criteria, *kalokagathia* is the most plausible candidate for being the complete virtue mentioned in the definition of happiness.

---

[69] Buddensiek (2014) argues for a similar interpretation.

[70] LSJ reports that *horos* can be translated as 'standard', 'limit', and 'measure'. Ancient commentators stress the connection between *peras* and *horos*. Simplicius, in his *Commentary on On the Soul* at 407a18, mentions *horos* and *peras* in nearby passages: he calls *peras* the limit of the line and *horos* the limit of the whole structure which is also its form. In the same passage, he talks about *holon*—the whole—of which *peras* is the limit. Cf. Simplicius, *Commentary on On the Soul*, tr. by Urmson, footnote 207 and 187, 73–4. Of course, Aristotle may understand *peras* and *horos* in *De Anima* in a way that is not consistent with how he understands them in the *EE*. Steel argues that *horos* is that by which the essence of something is constituted and determined. He says that it is used interchangeably with *eidos*. Steel lists both *horos* and *peras* as possible translations of boundary (Simplicius, *On Aristotle on the Soul* 3.6–13, tr. by Steel).

6.7 Conclusions

In this chapter, I argued that *kalokagathia* includes all the virtues discussed in the *EE*. For this reason, it is the Functional Unity of the Virtues. First, I analysed the beginning of *EE* VIII.1, where we find the first explicit reference to *kalokagathia*. I showed that this passage elucidates that *kalokagathia* is a virtue composed of all the other virtues. Second, I argued that the comparison between *kalokagathia* and health shows that *kalokagathia* admits a 'relaxed' all-quantifier that renders the notion of *kalokagathia* flexible. Third, I investigated the complete virtue mentioned in the Eudemian definition of happiness. I focused on three criteria: complete virtue is virtue that includes *all* the virtues qua parts, and all its parts are connected so that they form a whole. What is more, complete virtue has a limit. I analysed the accounts of complete/final (*teleion*), whole (*holon*), one, and limit that Aristotle offers in the *Physics* and in the *Metaphysics*. In light of these accounts, I examined some possible candidates for the role of complete virtue in the *Eudemian Ethics*. I considered magnanimity and justice: qua virtues of character they must be ruled out, though they have some relevant features. Next, I turned to two virtues of thinking: *phronêsis* and *sophia*. Even though these two virtues must be possessed with other virtues, they fail to meet the Inclusion, Wholeness, and Limit Criteria. Finally, I brought evidence in favour of the idea that *kalokagathia* is the complete virtue that Aristotle refers to in the definition of happiness insofar as it meets all the criteria. *Kalokagathia* includes all the virtues of Aristotle's *EE*. With this analysis of *kalokagathia*, my argument in favour of the Functional Unity of the Virtues is complete.

Conclusion

In this book, I distinguished three unities of the virtues: the unity of the practical virtues, the unity of all the virtues of theoretical thinking, and the Functional Unity of all the Virtues as parts of *kalokagathia*. The unity of the practical virtues and the unity of the virtues of theoretical thinking are included in the Functional Unity. According to my proposal the virtues can be individuated and are not all versions of the same virtue. However, they cannot be fully functioning virtues unless they are part of the Functional Unity of the Virtues. My perspective distinguishes the virtues in virtues that are wholes and virtues that are parts, as well as in dependent virtues and virtues on which other virtues depend. The virtues are organized in a hierarchy where *kalokagathia*, *sophia*, and *phronêsis* direct and, in a way, command the other virtues. The virtues that are parts of *kalokagathia* and *sophia* are fundamental for these virtues to come about and to function. In a similar way, the virtues on which *phronêsis* depends are fundamental for *phronêsis* to come about and to function. This approach to the virtues adds a new perspective not only on how we understand the virtues, but also on how the virtues function. That is, the virtues are states that can acquire additional functions depending on the virtues with which they interact. This does not mean that the virtues should be understood in a scalar way in the sense that one can be more or less virtuous: there is no evidence in favour of this interpretation of the virtues in Aristotle's texts. On the view that I defend, when the virtues are not part of the unity, they are somehow functionally deficient versions of themselves.

In chapter 1, I prepared the ground for the Functional Unity of the Virtues by arguing that there is a unity of the parts of the soul. Insofar as the parts of the soul are interrelated, the virtues and the activities associated to the parts are interrelated as well. Moreover, insofar as the parts of the soul are hierarchically ordered, there is a hierarchy of the virtues that belong to the parts. The virtues of thinking command and direct the virtues of character. On their turn, the virtues of thinking cannot function at the best if the virtues of character are not present. In this sense, the Functional Unity of the Virtues is a whole hierarchically structured. It is a unity in which the virtues co-function. This unity is *kalokagathia*. As I see it, the proposal that I developed in this book sheds light on:

1. the unity of the virtues (UoV) in Aristotle's ethics;
2. the notion of the excellent agent who has all the virtues;
3. the distinctive philosophical proposal of the *EE*.

C.1 The Unity of the Virtues: ancient and contemporary debates

Contemporary philosophers regard the UoV as a thesis difficult to defend that goes against what we observe and experience. They consider it the least plausible and appealing among the theses defended by ancient philosophers. The idea that all the character virtues must be possessed together has been the target of strong criticism.[1] There are recent attempts to defend this thesis.[2] However,

---

[1] See the discussion in Badhwar 1996, 306–29. Badhwar as well as Hursthouse (1999), Wolf (2007, 145–67), Russell (2009), and Watson (1984, 57–74) highlight some problems of the UoV, but try to propose some limited versions of it. Williams (1985, 36) considers the idea that we can possess some virtues without possessing all the other virtues a platitude. Driver (2001) rejects the idea that the character virtues require practical wisdom.

[2] For an overview, see Wilson 2021, 9835–54. Wilson distinguishes the Standard Unity according to which in order to possess one virtue we must possess them all, from the Strong Unity according to which all virtues are one. He divides the standard unity

all these attempts reduce the UoV to a weak unity or to a limited unity. Some scholars divide the virtues in areas of influence. They argue that one does not need to have all the virtues that belong to the same area, but it is enough to possess at least one virtue per area.[3] Other scholars suggest that the scope of the virtues should be broaden to such an extent that just actions are also courageous and so forth.[4] Halper distinguishes psychic and proper virtues: according to his view, agents need to possess psychic virtues (understood as dispositions rather than virtues exercised in actuality), but they do not need to possess proper virtues.[5] Toner argues that the idea that we must possess all the virtues is limited to the cardinal virtues.[6] In addition, he points out that for this unity to be plausible we must understand the virtues as *satis* concepts.[7] That is, for Toner, it is sufficient to be virtuous enough as opposed to be completely virtuous in order to have the virtues. As I see it, even though the proposal is attractive, the idea of the virtues as *satis* concepts is not Aristotelian.

Most proposals in contemporary debates focus on the unity of all the character virtues, or on the unity of the character virtues

in Standard Unity Limited, according to which in order to have a virtue in one domain we need practical wisdom in that domain (cf. Badhwar 1996, 306–29); Standard Unity Decency, according to which in order to possess one virtue we need moral decency; Standard Unity Cardinal exemplified by Toner 2014, 207–27; Standard Unity Cluster, according to which the possession of one virtue in a cluster implies the possession of all the virtues in that cluster. Wilson argues that a defender of the Standard Unity of the intellectual virtues faces the same challenges of the defender of the Standard Unity of the moral virtues.

[3] Kraut 1988, 79–86. A similar solution has been proposed by Drefcinski 2006, 201–10.
[4] This option has been explored with regard to the Socratic/Platonic Unity of Virtue but is relevant also for discussions of the Aristotelian UoV. See Irwin 1977 and Penner 1992, 1–27.
[5] Halper 1999, 115–43.
[6] Toner 2014, 207–27.
[7] He posits two requirements: (1) that there is a threshold above which we consider people virtuous and (2) that it is sufficient to be virtuous enough in order to be virtuous. These requirements are shared by almost all contemporary interpretations of the UoV. However, these requirements are not shared by ancient proposals of the UoV: for the ancients, the virtues do not come in degrees.

and *phronêsis*.[8] That is, they focus only on the practical side of the UoV. With some variations, they discuss a paradigmatic counterexample: the person who is excellent in one respect, but not tout court. Think about the courageous agent who does not have the virtue of temperance.[9] As this example shows, the criticism of these contemporary philosophers is directed to the unity of all the character virtues, and not to the unity of character virtues and *phronêsis*. As I showed, scholars who focus on ancient philosophy often think about the UoV as unity of character virtues and *phronêsis*. Differently from this broader strand that conceives of the UoV as unity of *phronêsis* and the character virtues, in my reconstruction of the Functional Unity of the Virtues, I considered not only the virtues of practical thinking and the character virtues, but also the virtues of theoretical thinking.[10] I hope that this proposal will draw attention, especially in debates on Aristotle's ethics and in contemporary debates inspired by Aristotle, to the fundamental role of theoretical thinking in living a good life, and to the interaction between theoretical and practical domains.

Two contemporary proposals in virtue ethics/virtue epistemology pay particular attention to the virtues of thinking in the UoV. First, Wolf argues that the UoV is plausible only if we understand it as unity of the character virtues and knowledge.[11] That is, in order to possess any of the virtues we need knowledge necessary for all the virtues. She characterizes this knowledge as knowledge of value which is intrinsically comparative: in order to know the value of something we have to possess knowledge of value of other things. In this sense, she argues that we must understand the UoV

---

[8] Dahl 1984; Irwin 1988a, 61–78; Badhwar 1996, 306–29; Halper 1999; Natali 2001; Annas 2011; Russell 2014.
[9] This opposition is already detected by Plato in the *Statesman* 306a5–11. Cf. Giavatto 2014, 91–119.
[10] To my knowledge, Delcomminette and Collette-Dučić 2014 is the only attempt to offer an overview of how the UoV is understood in ancient philosophy from Xenophon to Augustine.
[11] Wolf 2007, 145–67.

as a unity of knowledge. Second, Wilson defends what he calls an Intellectual Strong Unity Substance according to which the intellectual virtues are all parts or applications of one virtue: the love of wisdom.[12] He individuates two conceptions of what the intellectual virtues are that are prominent in contemporary debates: according to the reliabilist conception, these virtues are 'features of an agent that produce epistemically valuable states'.[13] Some examples are true belief and knowledge. According to the responsibilist conception, they are 'character traits that involve epistemically valuable motivations'.[14] Some examples are open-mindedness and intellectual humility. Wilson understands the intellectual virtues according to the responsibilist conception. His proposal is important insofar as it brings attention to the unity of the intellectual virtues. Wilson explores a route similar to the one that I developed in my book. That is, Wilson considers the virtues parts of a whole. But his proposal is still far away from the full unity of all the virtues that I defended in the book. What is more, he conceives of the parts of the love of wisdom as versions of the same virtue instead of distinct virtues.

As I conceive the Functional Unity of the Virtues, all virtues are states of the soul—or we may say, they are states of the mind—and when we have them all we have a unified soul or a unified mind. When we possess all the virtues, the virtues fulfil their full potential with the result that we are better in the practical domain as well as in the theoretical one. I hope to have shown that for what concerns Aristotle's proposal, the UoV acquires plausibility if it is conceived as Functional Unity of the Virtues. That is, it acquires plausibility if we think that in order to act aiming at the good we need to be excellent not only in the practical domain, but also in the theoretical

---

[12] Wilson 2021, 9835–54. In contemporary debates, love of wisdom, also called love of knowledge, is considered an intellectual virtue (Roberts and Wood 2007, ch. 6; Baehr 2011, 94).
[13] Wilson 2021, 9835–54.
[14] Wilson 2021, 9835–54; Battaly 2014, 117–18.

one. Being excellent theoretical thinkers offers us a broader and better perspective on how to live a good human life.

C.2 Excellent agents

According to the proposal that I defended in the book, Aristotle's excellent agent is not the *phronimos*, but the *kalos kagathos*. That is, the agent who is the best at virtuous actions and at theoretical thinking is the agent who possesses the Functional Unity of the Virtues. The virtues that this agent possesses function at their best insofar as they interact with all the other virtues in relevant ways. Irwin recently argues that according to the perspective of *EE* VIII.3, the *kalos kagathos* and the good person (*agathos*) are the same.[15] For Irwin, Aristotle offers different descriptions of these two agents: the good person is defined as the person for whom natural goods are good. This person needs to have all the virtues. The *kalos kagathos* is defined as the person who has goods that are beautiful and praiseworthy in themselves, and engages in beautiful actions for their own sake.[16] As Irwin argues, these two descriptions are compatible with the idea that these two kinds of agent are the same.

---

[15] Irwin 2022, 188–207.

[16] Irwin's proposal (2022, 188–207) is in part based on his rejection of Spengel's conjecture at *EE* VIII 1249a13: τῷ δ<ὲ καλῷ κ>ἀγαθῷ. If we reject the conjecture, the claim in this passage is that natural goods are beautiful for the good agent. That is, natural goods are beautiful both for the good agent and for the *kalos kagathos*. This idea together with the idea that the virtues, which the good agent possesses, require that we engage in beautiful actions for their own sake ends up collapsing the distinction between the good agent and the *kalos kagathos*. Differently from Irwin, I accept Spengel's conjecture according to which the natural goods are beautiful for the *kalos kagathos*, and they are only good and not beautiful for the merely good agent. If we do not accept the conjecture in the passage, Aristotle would move abruptly from contrasting the *kalos kagathos* with the good agent to the idea that natural goods are beautiful for the *kalos kagathos* as well as for the good person. The flow of the argument seems to me to speak in favour of accepting the conjecture, which is accepted by Rowe (2023a), Walzer and Mingay (1991), and Susemihl (1884). Irwin observes that this apparent incoherence of the passage is explained with reference to the idea defended at 1248b38–49a3 that the Spartans are wild and not good because these agents pursue virtue for the sake of the natural goods. Irwin concludes that the good and the *kalos kagathos* are the same person. I agree

As I see it, the Functional Unity of the Virtues that I defended in the book shows that the *kalos kagathos* is the excellent agent of Aristotle's *EE* because this agent has all the virtues, including the virtues of theoretical thinking. That is, this agent is not merely the *phronimos* in the sense that he is not merely the agent who has *phronêsis* and the virtues on which *phronêsis* depends. The *kalos kagathos* has not only the character virtues, *phronêsis*, and the virtues of practical thinking, but also the virtues of theoretical thinking. Irwin shows that in *EE* VIII.3, Aristotle contrasts the *kalos kagathos* and the *agathos* on the basis of their relation to the beautiful. However, as I see it, throughout the *EE*, the *agathos* does not consistently refer to the agent described in *EE* VIII.3. As I explained in chapter 6, Aristotle often uses *sophos*, *phronimos*, *agathos*, *epieikês*, and *spoudaios* in a generic sense to refer to the best agent. But at times, the *phronimos* is used to refer to the agent who has *phronêsis* and the virtues on which *phronêsis* depends, and the *sophos* is used for the agent who has *sophia* and its parts. This seems to suggest that the *agathos* as this agent is referred to in *EE* VIII.3, coincides with the *phronimos*, namely with the agent who has *phronêsis* and the virtues on which *phronêsis* depends. In this sense, the *phronimos/agathos* is contrasted with the *kalos kagathos*, who has *phronêsis* and the virtues on which *phronêsis* depends, and *sophia* and its parts. If understood in this way, being *kalos kagathos* is a very ambitious ideal.

One may object that there is almost no one able to be *kalos kagathos*. Namely, the Functional Unity of the Virtues is an ideal impossible to achieve. It is true that most of us are not *kaloi kagathoi*. And yet, even if being *kalos kagathos* is only an ideal, it

with Irwin that the Spartans cannot be genuinely good in the sense of virtuous. But I disagree on his proposals that natural goods are beautiful for the good person and that the good person and the *kalos kagathos* are the same person. For a recent defence of reading *agathoi* instead of *agrioi*, see Bobonich 2023, 172–93. Bobonich argues that the *agathos* and the *kalos kagathos* are different.

is still worthy to think about it and about the Functional Unity of the Virtues as aims that guide our lives. As I argued in chapter 6, Aristotle compares *kalokagathia* to health. There may be very few people who are perfectly healthy, and yet, health is still an important value that guides our choices and behaviours. As in the case of health, we are healthy when all, most, or the most important parts of our body and mind are healthy; in a similar way, we are *kaloi kagathoi* when we have all, most, or the most important virtues (which are the character virtues, and the virtues of practical and theoretical thinking). This 'relaxed' all-quantifier makes the notion of *kalokagathia* somehow flexible. According to my reconstruction, for the non-fully virtuous agent (most of us), if we possess some virtues, these virtues do not fulfil their full potential and do not function at their best. In other words, we do not possess the Functional Unity of the Virtues. But there is still a certain level of interaction among the virtues. And the Functional Unity of the Virtues that I defended highlights that this interaction is fundamental in order to become fully virtuous. Even if it is ambitious, the Functional Unity of the Virtues is important for the non-fully virtuous agent to understand how to develop the virtues: we cannot develop one virtue at a time, but we must develop all the virtues together. What is more, the interactions and connections among the virtues are necessary to become fully virtuous. As I showed, there is a strong connection between theoretical and practical domains: becoming excellent in one domain supports also excellence in the other domain. This view goes against our contemporary way of conceiving of someone excellent only in one or some domains or in one respect. This specialized view of excellency is foreign to Aristotle and to how the ancients conceived of being excellent. For the ancients, being excellent means being excellent in all domains. It refers to excellency tout court—or at least with minimal exceptions—insofar as it is a state of the soul that characterizes everything that agents do, how they think, and how they relate to other people.

C.3 The distinctive philosophical proposal of the *EE*

Scholarly interest in the *EE* has often been directed at individual sections of the treatise and has been mostly comparative: namely, scholars examine the *EE* to determine whether the common books belong to this treatise or to the *NE*, or they look at ways in which the *EE* differs from the *NE*.[17] In this sense, the *NE* is the main reference and is considered 'The Aristotelian Ethics'.[18] In this book, I approached the *EE* as a treatise in its own right that proposes a coherent and unified argument. That is, I focused on the philosophical proposal of the *EE* as a whole and in itself, and I reconstructed the argument in favour of the Functional Unity of the Virtues that Aristotle develops in this treatise. I hope that what I pursued in this book together with recent contributions on the *EE* and with a new Greek edition of the text will promote a new interest in the *EE* as a treatise that is not only worthy to consider in itself for its philosophical proposal, but as fundamental to understand Aristotle's ethics as a whole, and its relation to the philosophical proposals of other ancient philosophers. The proposal that I developed in the book challenges the view that the *NE* gives us a full picture of what Aristotle's ethics is about and that the *EE* is useful only to compare it with the *NE* to detect incoherences or similarities. As I argued in the book, Aristotle's ethics constitutes a multifarious picture of which the *EE* is a fundamental part. What is more, the philosophical proposal of the *EE* that I reconstructed offers a distinctive view of the mind as unified and of the virtues as standing in a network of interactions that can generate new ideas in contemporary debates beyond ancient philosophy.

---

[17] Cf. Rowe 1971; Kenny 1978/2016; Kenny 1992; Donini 2014a; Di Basilio 2022.
[18] Kenny (2016) challenges this perspective.

Bibliography

Achtenberg, Deborah. 'The Role of the Ergon Argument in Aristotle's *Nicomachean Ethics*', in J. P. Anton, A. Preus (eds.), *Essays in Ancient Greek Philosophy, IV*, Albany: State University New York Press, 1991, 59–72.

Achtenberg, Deborah. *Cognition of Value in Aristotle's Ethics: Promise of Enrichment, Threat of Destruction*, Albany: State University of New York Press, 2002.

Ackrill, John L. (trans. and notes). *Aristotle's Ethics*, New York: Humanities Press, 1973.

Ackrill, John L. 'Aristotle's Theory of Definition: Some Questions on *Posterior Analytics* II 8–10', in E. Berti (ed.), *Aristotle on Science: The Posterior Analytics*, Padova: Editrice Antenore, Proceedings of the Eight Symposium Aristotelicum held in Padua from 7 to 15 September 1981, 359–84.

Ackrill, John L. 'Aristotle on Eudaimonia', in A. O. Rorty (ed.), *Essays on Aristotle's Ethics*, Berkeley: University of California Press, 1980, 15–34.

Adamson, Peter. 'Posterior Analytics 2.19: a Dialogue with Plato?' *Bulletin of the Institute of Classical Studies*, Supplement, 107, 2010, 1–19.

Adkins, Arthur W. H. '*Theôria* versus *Praxis* in the *Nicomachean Ethics* and the *Republic*', *Classical Philology* 73, 4, 1978, 297–313.

Allan, Donald. 'Review of Dirlmeier 1962', *Gnomon* 38, 1966, 138–49.

Annas, Julia. *The Morality of Happiness*, New York: Oxford University Press, 1993.

Annas, Julia. *Intelligent Virtue*, Oxford: Oxford University Press, 2011.

Anscombe, Elizabeth. 'Thought and Action in Aristotle: What Is Practical Truth?' in R. Bambrough (ed.), *New Essays on Plato and Aristotle*, London: Routledge, 1965, 143–58.

Anscombe, Elizabeth. 'Practical Truth', in J. Dolan (ed.), *Working Papers in Law, Medicine and Philosophy*, Minneapolis, 1993. Reprinted in *Logos* 2, 1999, 68–76, and in M. Geach and L. Gormally (eds.), *Human Life, Action and Ethics: Essays by G. E. M. Anscombe*, Exeter: Imprint Academic, 2005, 149–60.

Aquinas, Thomas. *Commentary on Aristotle's Nicomachean Ethics*, trans. by C. I. Litzinger, Notre Dame: Dumb Ox Books, 1993.

Von Arnim, Hans. *Die drei Aristotelischen Ethiken*, Vienna: Hölder-Pichler-Tempsky, 1924.

BIBLIOGRAPHY

Von Arnim, Hans. *Das Ethische in Aristoteles' Topik*, Vienna: Hölder-Pichler-Tempsky, 1927.
Aubenque, Pierre. *La prudence chez Aristote*, Paris: Presses Universitaires de France, 2014.
Austin, John L. 'Agathon and Eudaimonia in the Ethics of Aristotle', in J. M. E. Moravcsik (ed.), *Aristotle, Critical Essays*, New York: Anchor Books, 1967, 261–97.
Badhwar, Neera. 'The Limited Unity of Virtues', *Nous* 30, 3, 1996, 306–29.
Baehr, Jason. *The Inquiring Mind*, Oxford: Oxford University Press, 2011.
Baghadassarian, Fabienne. 'Les deux sens de la cause finale chez Aristote et le cas des êtres immobiles', last accessed in April 2024, http://aitia.hypotheses.org/publications/textes.
Baker, Samuel H. 'Aristotle on the Nature and Politics of Medicine', *Apeiron* 54, 4, 2021, 411–49.
Barnes, Jonathan. 'Aristotle's concept of mind', *Proceedings of the Aristotelian Society* 72, 1971, 101–14.
Barnes, Jonathan. *Aristotle's Posterior Analytics*, Oxford: Oxford University Press, 1994.
Barnes, Jonathan. 'Introduzione', in M. Mignucci (ed.), *Aristotele. Analitici Secondi*, Roma-Bari: Laterza, 2007, 7–30.
Barney, Rachel. 'Aristotle's Argument for a Human Function', *Oxford Studies in Ancient Philosophy* 34, 2008, 293–322.
Battaly, Heather. *Virtue*, Chichester: Polity, 2014.
Beere, Jonathan. *Doing and Being: an Interpretation of Aristotle's Metaphysics Theta*, New York: Oxford University Press, 2009.
Bobonich, Chris. 'Aristotle's Ethical Treatises', in R. Kraut (ed.), *The Blackwell Guide to Aristotle's Nicomachean Ethics*, Oxford: Blackwell, 2006, 12–36.
Bobonich, Chris. 'Why Should Philosophers Rule? Plato's *Republic* and Aristotle's *Protrepticus*', *Social Philosophy and Policy* 24, 2, 2007, 153–75.
Bobonich, Chris. 'The Good and the Wild at Aristotle Eudemian Ethics 8.3?' *Classical Philology* 118, 2, 2023, 172–93.
Bonasio, Giulia. 'Kalokagathia and the Unity of the Virtues in the *EE*', *Apeiron* 53, 1, 2020, 27–57.
Bonasio, Giulia. 'Natural Goods in the *Eudemian Ethics*', *Ancient Philosophy* 41, 1, 2021, 123–42.
Bonasio, Giulia. 'Complete Virtue', in G. Di Basilio (ed.), *Investigating the Relationship between Aristotle's Eudemian and Nicomachean Ethics*, New York: Routledge, 2022, 172–88.
Bostock, David. *Aristotle's Ethics*, Oxford: Oxford University Press, 2000.
Broadie, Sarah. *Ethics with Aristotle*, New York: Oxford University Press, 1994.
Broadie, Sarah. 'Practical Truth in Aristotle', *Oxford Studies in Ancient philosophy* 57, 2020, 249–71.

Broadie, Sarah, Rowe, Christopher (trans. and commentary). *Aristotle: Nicomachean Ethics*, Oxford: Oxford University Press, 2002.
Bronstein, David. *Aristotle on Knowledge and Learning*, Oxford: Oxford University Press, 2016.
Brown, Lesley. 'Why Is Aristotle's Virtue of Character a Mean?' in R. Polansky (ed.), *Cambridge Companion to Aristotle's Nicomachean Ethics*, Cambridge: Cambridge University Press, 2014, 64–80.
Buddensiek, Friedemann. *Die Theorie des Glücks in Aristoteles' Eudemischer Ethik*, Göttingen: Vandenhoeck & Ruprecht, 1999.
Buddensiek, Friedemann. 'Contemplation and Service of the God', in P. Destrée, M. Zingano (eds.), *Theoria, Studies on the Status and Meaning of Contemplation in Aristotle's Ethics*, Louvain: Peeters, 2014, 313–35.
Buddensiek, Friedemann. 'The Ergon Argument of the Eudemian and the Nicomachean Ethics', in G. Di Basilio (ed.), *Investigating the Relationship between Aristotle's Eudemian and Nicomachean Ethics*, New York: Routledge, 2022, 34–48.
Burnet, John. *The Ethics of Aristotle*, London: Metheuen, 1900.
Burnyeat, Myles. 'Aristotle on Understanding Knowledge', in E. Berti (ed.), *Aristotle on Science: The Posterior Analytics*, Padova: Editrice Antenore, Proceedings of the Eight Symposium Aristotelicum held in Padua from 7 to 15 September 1981, 97–139.
Burnyeat, Myles. 'Epistêmê', in B. Morison, K. Ierodikonou (eds.), *Epistêmê, etc.*, New York: Oxford University Press, 2011, 3–29.
Bywater, Ingram (ed.). *Aristotelis Ethica Nicomachea*, Oxonii: Clarendon Press, 1894.
Callard, Agnes. 'Enkratēs Phronimos', *Archiv für Geschichte der Philosophie* 99, 1, 2017, 31–63.
Charles, David. 'Aristotle on Well-Being and Intellectual Contemplation', *The Aristotelian Society* 73, 1, 1999, 205–23.
Cohoe, Caleb. 'Knowing in Aristotle: Part 1: *Epistêmê, Nous*, and Non-Rational Cognitive States', *Philosophy Compass* 17, 1, 2022, 1–13.
Collette-Dučić, Bernard, Delcomminette, Sylvain (eds.), *Unité et origine des vertus dans la philosophie ancienne*, Bruxelles: Ousia, 2014.
Cooper, John. *Reason and the Human Good*, Indianapolis: Hackett, 1975.
Cooper, John. 'Hypothetical Necessity and Natural Teleology', in A. Gotthelf, J. G. Lennox (eds.), *Philosophical Issues in Aristotle's Biology*, New York: Cambridge University Press, 1987, 243–74.
Cooper, John. 'The Unity of Virtue', *Social Philosophy and Policy* 15, 1, 1998, 233–74.
Cooper, John. 'Contemplation and Happiness: a Reconsideration', in J. Cooper (ed.), *Reason and Emotion*, Princeton, NJ: Princeton University Press, 1999a, 212–36.

Cooper, John. 'Reason, Moral Virtue and Moral Value', in M. Frede, G. Striker (eds.), *Rationality in Greek Thought*, Oxford: Oxford University Press, 1999b, 81–114.

Corcilius, Klaus, Gregoric, Pavel. 'Separability vs Difference: Parts and Capacities of the Soul in Aristotle', *Oxford Studies in Ancient Philosophy* 39, 2010, 81–119.

Corrigan, Kevin. *Love, Friendship, Beauty and the Good*, Eugene: Veritas, 2018.

Crisp, Roger. 'Aristotle's Inclusivism', *Oxford Studies in Ancient Philosophy*, 12, 1993, 111–36.

Crisp, Roger (trans.). *Nicomachean Ethics*, Cambridge: Cambridge University Press, 2000.

Crisp, Roger. 'Aristotle on Greatness of Soul', in R. Kraut (ed.), *Blackwell Guide to Aristotle's Nicomachean Ethics*, Oxford: Blackwell, 2006, 158–78.

Crisp, Roger. 'Nobility in the Nicomachean Ethics', *Phronesis* 59, 2014, 231–45.

Curzer, Howard J. 'How Good People Do Bad Things. Aristotle on the Misdeeds of the Virtuous', *Oxford Studies in Ancient Philosophy* 28, 2005, 233–56.

Curzer, Howard J. *Aristotle and the Virtues*, Oxford: Oxford University Press, 2012.

Dahl, Norman O. *Practical Reason, Aristotle and Weakness of Will*, Minneapolis: University of Minnesota Press, 1984.

Dahl, Norman O. 'Contemplation and *Eudaimonia* in the *Nicomachean Ethics*', in J. Miller (ed.), *Aristotle's Nicomachean Ethics*, Cambridge: Cambridge University Press, 2011, 66–91.

De Luise, Fulvia, Farinetti, Giuseppe. *Storia della felicità. Gli antichi e i moderni*, Torino: Einaudi, 2001.

Décarie, Vianney. 'Vertu totale, vertu parfaite et *kalokagathia* dans l'Éthique à Eudème', in G. B. Madison (ed.), *Sens et Existence*, Paris: Éditions du Seuil, 1975, 60–76.

DePaul, Michael, Zagzebski, Linda (eds.). *Intellectual Virtue*, New York: Oxford University Press, 2003.

Deslauriers, Marguerite. 'How to Distinguish Aristotle's Virtues', *Phronesis* 47, 2, 2002, 101–1.

Destrée, Pierre. *Aristote, Bonheur et Vertus*, Paris: Presses Universitaires de France, 2003.

Destrée, Pierre, Zingano, Marco (eds.), *Theoria, Studies on the Status and Meaning of Contemplation in Aristotle's Ethics*, Leuven: Peeters, 2014.

Devereux, Daniel T. 'The Unity of the Virtues in Plato's *Protagoras* and *Laches*', *The Philosophical Review* 101, 4, 1992, 765–89.

Devereux, Daniel T. 'Theôria and Praxis in Aristotle's Ethics', in P. Destrée, M. Zingano (eds.), *Theoria, Studies on the Status and Meaning of Contemplation in Aristotle's Ethics*, Louvain: Peeters, 2014, 159–20.

Di Basilio, Giulio (ed.). *Investigating the Relationship between Aristotle's Eudemian and Nicomachean Ethics*, Oxford: Routledge, 2022.

Dirlmeier, Franz (trans. and notes). *Aristoteles: Eudemische Ethik*, Berlin: Akademie Verlag, 1984.

Donini, Pierluigi. 'Due libri su eudaimonia in Aristotele', *Phronesis* 39, 1994, 98–110.

Donini, Pierluigi (trans. and notes). *Aristotele: Etica Eudemia*, Roma-Bari: Laterza, 1999.

Donini, Pierluigi. *Abitudine e saggezza*, Alessandria: Edizioni dell'Orso, 2014a.

Donini, Pierluigi. 'Happiness and *Theôria* in Books I and X of the *Nicomachean Ethics*', in P. Destrée, M. Zingano (eds.), *Theoria, Studies on the Status and Meaning of Contemplation in Aristotle's Ethics*, Louvain: Peeters, 2014b, 7–21.

Dover, Kenneth. 'Fathers, Sons, and Forgiveness', *Illinois Classical Studies* 16, 1991, 173–82.

Drefcinski, Shane. 'The Fallible *phronimos*', *Ancient Philosophy* 16, 1996, 139–53.

Drefcinski, Shane. 'A Different Solution to an Alleged Contradiction in Aristotle's Nicomachean Ethics', *Oxford Studies in Ancient Philosophy* 30, 2006, 201–10.

Driver, Julia. *Uneasy Virtue*, Cambridge: Cambridge University Press, 2001.

Dumoulin, Bertrand. 'Sur l'éthique théonome du premier Aristote', *Les études philosophiques* 2, 1988, 167–81.

Düring, Ingmar. *Aristoteles, Darstellung und Interpretation seines Denkens*, Heidelberg: Winter, 1966.

Dybikowski, James. 'Is Aristotelian Eudaimonia Happiness?' *Dialogue* 20, 1981, 185–200.

Eriksen, Trond B. *Bios Theoretikos: Notes on Aristotle's Nicomachean Ethics X.6-8*, Oslo: Universitetsforlaget, 1976.

Eustrace, *Eustratii et Michaelis et anonyma in Ethica Nicomachea commentaria*, G. Heylbut (ed.), Reimer: Berolini, 1892.

Ferejohn, Michael. 'The Unity of Virtue and the Objects of Socratic Inquiry', *Journal of the History of Philosophy* 20, 1, 1982, 1–21.

Ferejohn, Michael. 'Socratic Virtue as the Parts of Itself', *Philosophy and Phenomenological Research* 44, 3, 1983-4, 377–88.

Festa, Nicola (ed.). *Iamblichi. De communi mathematica scientia*, Leipzig, 1981.

Fine, Gail. 'Aristotle on Knowledge', in G. Fine (ed.), *Essays in Ancient Epistemology*, New York: Oxford University Press, 2021, 221–42.

Foot, Philippa. 'Virtues and Vices', in P. Foot (ed.), *Virtues and Vices and Other Essays in Moral Philosophy*, Berkeley: University of California Press, 1978, 1–19.

BIBLIOGRAPHY

Frede, Dorothea. 'A Swarm of Virtues: On the Unity and Completeness of Aristotle's Scheme of Character-Virtues', in M. Lee (ed.), *Strategies of Argument: Essays in Ancient Ethics, Epistemology, and Logic*, New York: Oxford University Press, 2014, 83–103.

Frede, Dorothea. 'On the So-Called Common Books of the *Eudemian* and the *Nicomachean Ethics*', *Phronesis* 64, 2019, 84–116.

Frede, Dorothea. *Aristoteles. Band 6. Nikomachische Ethik*, Berlin: De Gruyter, 2020.

Frey, Christopher. 'Two Conceptions of Soul in Aristotle', in D. Ebrey (ed.), *Theory and Practice in Aristotle's Natural Science*, Cambridge: Cambridge University Press, 2015, 137–60.

Frey, Christopher. 'Aristotle's on the Soul Unity', in C. M. Cohoe (ed.), *Aristotle on the Soul*, Cambridge: Cambridge University Press, 2022, 88–103.

Furley, David. 'What Kind of Cause Is Aristotle's Final Cause?' in M. Frede, G. Striker (eds.), *Rationality in Greek Thought*, Oxford: Clarendon Press, 1996, 59–81.

Gabbe, Myrna. 'Aristotle on the Starting Points of Motion in the Soul', *Phronesis* 57, 4, 2012, 358–79.

Gadamer, Hans G. 'The Problem of Historical Consciousness', in P. Rabinow and W. M. Sullivan (eds.), *Interpretive Social Science*, Berkeley: University of California Press, 1979, 82–141.

Gardiner, Stephen. 'Aristotle's Basic and Non-Basic Virtues', *Oxford Studies in Ancient Philosophy* 20, 2001, 261–96.

Gardiner, Stephen. *Virtue Ethics Old and New*, Ithaca, NY: Cornell University Press 2005.

Gartner, Corinne. 'Aristotle on Understanding and Practical Wisdom', in N. D. Smith (ed.), *Knowledge in Ancient Philosophy*, London: Bloomsbury, 2019, 125–14.

Gastaldi, Silvia. *Bios Hairetotatos. Generi di vita e felicità in Aristotele*, Napoli: Bibliopolis, 2003.

Gauthier, René A. *Magnanimité*, Paris: Vrin, 1951.

Gauthier, René A. *La morale d'Aristote*, Paris: Presses Universitaires de France, 1958.

Gauthier, René A., Jolif, Jean Y. (trans. and commentary). *Aristote: l'Éthique à Nicomaque*, Louvain-Paris: Presses Universitaires de France, 1959.

Gavray, Marc-Antoine. 'Unité et origine des vertus dans le *Protagoras*', in B. Collette-Dučić, S. Delcomminette (eds.), *Unité et origine des vertus dans la philosophie ancienne*, Bruxelles: Ousia, 2014, 39–65.

Giavatto, Angelo. 'Unité et articulations de la vertu dans le *Politique* et dans les *Lois* de Platon', in B. Collette-Dučić, S. Delcomminette (eds.), *Unité et origine des vertus dans la philosophie ancienne*, Bruxelles: Ousia, 2014, 91–119.

Gladigow, Burkhard. *Sophia und Kosmos: Untersuchungen zur Frühgeschichte von σοφός und σοφίη*, Hildesheim: Olms, 1965.

Gosling, Justin B. C., Taylor, C. C. W. *The Greeks on Pleasure*, Oxford: Oxford University Press, 1982.

Gotthelf, Allan. 'Understanding Aristotle's Teleology', in R. F. Hassing (ed.), *Final Causality in Nature and Human Affairs*, Washington: Catholic University of America Press, 1997, 71–83.

Gotthelf, Allan. *Teleology, First Principles and Scientific Method*, New York: Oxford University Press, 2012.

Gottlieb, Paula. *The Virtues of Aristotle's Ethics*, New York: Cambridge University Press, 2009.

Grant, Alexander. *The Ethics of Aristotle*, London: Longmans, 1874.

Green, Jerry. 'Self-Love in the Aristotelian Ethics', *Newsletter for the Society of Ancient Greek Philosophy* 11, 2010, 12–18.

Greenwood, Leonard H. G. *Aristotle, Nicomachean Ethics. Book Six*. Cambridge: Cambridge University Press, 1909.

Halper, Edward. 'The Unity of Virtues in Aristotle', *Oxford Studies in Ancient Philosophy* XVII, 1999, 115–44.

Henry, David, Nielsen, Karen M. (eds.), *Bridging the Gap between Aristotle's Science and Ethics*, Cambridge: Cambridge University Press, 2015.

Hardie, William F. R. 'The Final Good in Aristotle's Ethics', in J. M. E. Moravcsik (ed.), *Aristotle: A Collection of Critical Essays*, Garden City: Anchor Books, 1967, 277–95.

Hardie, William F. R. *Aristotle Ethical Theory*, Oxford: Clarendon Press, 1968.

Harlfinger, Dieter, Moraux, Paul (ed.). *Die Überlieferungsgeschichte der Eudemischen Ethik*, Symposium Aristotelicum, Berlin: Akademie Verlag, 1971.

Hoffman, Magdalena. *Der Standard des Guten bei Aristoteles. Regularität im Umbestimmten*, Freiburg-Munich: Alber 2010.

Horn, Christof. 'Eine Schwalbe macht noch keinen Frühling', in W. Mesch (ed.), *Glück, Tugend, Zeit*, Stuttgart: Verlag J.B. Metzler, 2013, 21–40.

Hursthouse, Rosalind. *On Virtue Ethics*, Oxford: Oxford University Press, 1999.

Hursthouse, Rosalind. 'What Does the Aristotelian *Phronimos* Know?' in L. Jost, J. Wuerth (eds.), *Perfecting Virtues*, Cambridge: Cambridge University Press 2011, 38–57.

Hutchinson, Douglas S. *The Virtues of Aristotle*, New York: Routledge, 1986.

Hutchinson, Douglas S. 'Ethics', in J. Barnes (ed.), *The Cambridge Companion to Aristotle*, Cambridge: Cambridge University Press, 1995, 195–232.

Iamblichus, *Protrepticus* ad fidem codicis Florentini, Hemenegildo Pistelli (ed.), Leipzig: Bibl. Teubn., 1888, reprinted Stuttgart, 1967.

Inwood, Bred, Woolf, Raphael (trans. and notes). *Aristotle: Eudemian Ethics*, Cambridge: Cambridge University Press 2013.

Irwin, Terence H. 'Aristotle on Reason, Desire and Virtue', *Journal of Philosophy* 72, 17, 1975, 567-78.
Irwin, Terence H. *Plato's Moral Theory*, Oxford: Clarendon Press, 1977.
Irwin, Terence H. 'First Principles in Aristotle's Ethics', *Midwest Studies in Philosophy* 3, 1, 1978, 252-72.
Irwin, Terence H. (trans.). *Aristotle: Nicomachean Ethics*, Indianapolis: Hackett Publishing, 1985.
Irwin, Terence H. 'Disunity in the Aristotelian Virtues', in J. Annas and R. Grimm (eds.), *Oxford Studies in Ancient Philosophy*, 1988a, 61-78.
Irwin, Terence H. *Aristotle's First Principles*, Oxford: Oxford University Press, 1988b.
Irwin, Terence H. 'The Sense and Reference of *Kalon* in Aristotle', *Classical Philology* 105, 4, Special Issue on Beauty, Harmony and the Good, 2010, 381-96.
Irwin, Terence H. 'Beauty and Morality in Aristotle', in J. Miller (ed.), *Aristotle's Nicomachean Ethics: A Critical Guide*, Cambridge: Cambridge University Press, 2011, 239-53.
Irwin, Terence H. 'Conceptions of Happiness in the *Nicomachean Ethics*', in C. Shields (ed.), *The Oxford Handbook of Aristotle*, New York: Oxford University Press, 2012, 495-528.
Irwin, Terence H. 'The Wild and the Good: Conditions for Virtue in the *Eudemian Ethics*', in G. Di Basilio (ed.), *Investigating the Relationship between Aristotle's Eudemian and Nicomachean Ethics*, Oxford: Routledge, 2022, 188-207.
Jaeger, Werner. *Aristotle: Fundamentals of the History of His Development*, Oxford: Clarendon Press, 1948.
Jenks, Rod. *Plato on the Unity of the Virtues*, Lanham: Lexington Books, 2022.
Jimenez, Marta. *Aristotle on Shame and Learning to Be Good*, Oxford: Oxford University Press, 2021.
Jirsa, Jakub. 'Divine Activity and Human Life', *Rhizomata* 5, 2, 2017, 210-38.
Joachim, Harold H. *Aristotle, The Nicomachean Ethics: A Commentary*, Oxford: Oxford University Press, 1951.
Johnson, Monte. *Aristotle on Teleology*, Oxford: Clarendon Press, 2005.
Jost, Lawrence. 'Aristotle's Ethics: Have We Been Teaching the Wrong One?' *Teaching Philosophy* 6, 4, 1983, 331-40.
Jost, Lawrence. 'The *EE* and Its Controversial Relationship to the *NE*', in R. Polansky (ed.), *Cambridge Companion to Aristotle's Nicomachean Ethics*, Cambridge: Cambridge University Press, 2014a, 410-25.
Jost, Lawrence. 'Theos, Theôria and Therapeia in Aristotle's Ethical Endings', in P. Destrée, M. Zingano (eds.), *Theoria: Studies on the Status and Meaning of Contemplation in Aristotle's Ethics*, Louvain: Peeters, 2014b, 287-313.
Kapp, Ernst. *Das Verhältnis der Eudemischen zur Nikomachischen Ethik*, Berlin: Schade, 1912.

Karbowski, Joseph. 'Aristotle on the Deliberative Abilities of Women', *Apeiron* 47, 4, 2014, 435-60.
Karbowski, Joseph. *Aristotle's Method in Ethics*, Cambridge: Cambridge University Press, 2019.
Kenny, Anthony. *The Aristotelian Ethics*, Oxford: Oxford University Press, 2016, first edition: 1978.
Kenny, Anthony. *Aristotle on the Perfect Life*, Oxford: Clarendon Press, 1992.
Kenny, Anthony. 'Practical Truth in Aristotle', in B. Morison, K. Ierodiakonou (eds.), *Epistêmê, etc. Essays in Honour of Jonathan Barnes*, Oxford: Oxford University Press, 2011, 277-84.
Kent, Bonnie. 'Moral Growth and the Unity of the Virtues', in D. Carr, J. Steutel (eds.), *Virtue Ethics and Moral Education*, London: Routledge 1999, 109-24.
Konstan, David. *Beauty: The Fortunes of an Ancient Greek Idea*, New York: Oxford University Press, 2014.
Korsgaard, Christine. 'Aristotle and Kant on the Source of Value', *Ethics* 96, 1986, 486-505.
Korsgaard, Christine. 'Aristotle's Function Argument', in C. M. Korsgaard, *The Constitution of Agency*, Oxford: Oxford University Press, 2008, 129-50.
Kosman, Aryeh. 'The Activity of Being in Aristotle's *Metaphysics*', in T. Scaltsas, D. Charles, M. L. Gill (eds.), *Unity, Identity and Explanation in Aristotle's Metaphysics*, Oxford: Clarendon Press, 1994, 195-213.
Kosman, Aryeh. 'The Divine in Aristotle's Ethics', *Animus* 13, 2009, 101-107.
Kosman, Aryeh. *Virtues of Thought*, Cambridge: Harvard University Press, 2014.
Kraut, Richard. 'The Peculiar Function of Human Beings', *Canadian Journal of Philosophy* 9, 1979, 467-78.
Kraut, Richard. 'Comments on "Disunity in the Aristotelian Virtues"', *Oxford Studies in Ancient Philosophy*, suppl. 1988, 79-86.
Kraut, Richard. *Aristotle on the Human Good*, Princeton, NJ: Princeton University Press, 1989.
Kraut, Richard. 'An Aesthetic Reading of Aristotle's Ethics', in V. Harte, M. Lane (eds.), *Politeia in Greek and Roman Philosophy*, Cambridge: Cambridge University Press, 2013, 231-50.
Labarrière, Jean L. 'Comment vivre la vie de l'esprit ou être le plus soi-même?' in P. Destrée (ed.), *Aristote. Bonheur et Vertus*, Paris: Presses Universitaires de France, 2003, 79-107.
Lännström, Anna. *Loving the Fine: Virtue and Happiness in Aristotle's Ethics*, Notre Dame: University of Notre Dame Press, 2006.
Lawrence, Gavin. 'Human Good and Human Function', in R. Kraut (ed.), *The Blackwell Guide to Aristotle's Nicomachean Ethics*, Oxford: Blackwell, 2006, 37-57.

Lawrence, Gavin. 'Acquiring Character: Becoming Grown-Up', in M. Pakaluk, G. Pearson (eds.), *Moral Psychology and Human Action*, New York: Oxford University Press, 2011, 233–84.

Lear, Gabriel R. *Happy Lives and the Highest Good*, Princeton, NJ: Princeton University Press, 2006.

Lear, Gabriel R. 'Approximation and Acting for an Ultimate End', in P. Destrée, M. Zingano (eds.), *Theoria, Studies on the Status and Meaning of Contemplation in Aristotle's Ethics*, Louvain: Peeters, 2014, 61–89.

Lear, Gabriel R. 'Aristotle on Moral Virtue and the Fine', in R. Kraut (ed.), *Blackwell Guide to Aristotle's Nicomachean Ethics*, Oxford: Blackwell, 2015, 116–37.

Lee, Roy. 'The Function Argument in the Eudemian Ethics', *Ancient Philosophy* 42, 1, 2022, 191–214.

Leighton, Stephen R. '*Eudemian Ethics* 1220b11–13', *Classical Quarterly* 34, 1984, 135–8.

Lemos, John. 'The Unity of the Virtues and Its Recent Defenses', *Southern Journal of Philosophy* 31, 1993, 85–106.

Lennox, James G. 'Aristotle on the Biological Roots of Virtue', in D. Henry, K. M. Nielsen (eds.), *Bridging the Gap between Aristotle's Science and Ethics*, Cambridge: Cambridge University Press, 2015, 193–214.

Leunissen, Mariska. *Explanation and Teleology in Aristotle's Science of Nature*, Cambridge: Cambridge University Press, 2010.

Leunissen, Mariska. 'Aristotle on Natural Character and Its Implications for Moral Development', *Journal of the History of Philosophy* 50, 4, 2012, 507–30.

Leunissen, Mariska. *From Natural Character to Moral Virtue in Aristotle*, New York: Oxford University Press, 2017.

Long, Alex A. 'Aristotle on Eudaimonia, Nous and Divinity', in J. Miller (ed.), *Aristotle's Nicomachean Ethics*, Cambridge: Cambridge University Press, 2011, 176–94.

Lorenz, Hendrik. 'Virtue of Character in Aristotle's *Nicomachean Ethics*', *Oxford Studies in Ancient Philosophy* 37, 2009, 177–212.

Lorenz, Henrik. 'Aristotle's Analysis of Akratic Action', in R. Polansky (ed.), *Aristotle's Nicomachean Ethics*, Cambridge: Cambridge University Press, 2014, 242–62.

Louden, Robert B. 'What Is Moral Authority? *Euboulia, Sunesis* and *Gnôme* vs *Phronêsis*', *Ancient Philosophy* 17, 1997, 103–18.

Lyons, John. *Structural Semantics: An Analysis of Part of the Vocabulary of Plato*, Oxford: Blackwell, 1963.

Mazzarelli, Claudio (trans.). *Aristotele. Etica Nicomachea*, Milano: Rusconi, 1979.

McDowell, John Henry. 'Virtue and Reason', in N. Sherman (ed.), *Aristotle's Ethics. Critical Essays*, Lanham, MD: Rowman and Littlefield, 1979, 121–43.

McDowell, John Henry. 'The Role of Eudaimonia in Aristotle's Ethics', in A. O. Rorty (ed.), *Essays on Aristotle's Ethics*, Berkeley: University of California Press, 1980, 359–76.

McDowell, John Henry. *Mind, Value, and Reality*, Cambridge: Harvard University Press, 1998.

Monan, J. Donald. *Aristotle on Moral Knowledge*, Oxford: Clarendon Press, 1968.

Morel, Pierre Marie. 'Vertu éthique et rationalité pratique chez Aristote. Note sur la notion d'*hexis prohairetikê*', *Philonsorbonne* 11, 2017, 141–53.

Morel, Pierre Marie. *La nature et le bien*, Louvain: Peeters, 2021.

Morison, Benjamin. 'An Aristotelian Distinction between Two Types of Knowledge', *Proceedings of the Boston Colloquium in Ancient Philosophy* XXVII, 2011, 29–57.

Moss, Jessica. 'Virtue Makes the Goal Right: Virtue and Phronêsis in Aristotle's Ethics', *Phronesis* 56, 2011, 204–61.

Moss, Jessica. *Aristotle on the Apparent Good*, Oxford: Oxford University Press, 2014.

Müller, Anselm Winfried. *Praktisches Folgern und Selbstgestaltung bei Aristoteles*, Freiburg: Alber, 1982.

Müller, Anselm Winfried. 'Aristotle's Conception of Ethical and Natural Virtue: How the Unity Thesis Sheds Light on the Doctrine of the Mean', in J. Szaif, M. Lutz-Bachmann (eds.), *What Is Good for a Human Being: Human Nature and Values*, Berlin: De Gruyter, 2004, 18–53.

Müller, Jozef. 'Aristotle on Vice', *British Journal of the History of Philosophy* 23, 2015, 459–77.

Murgier, Charlotte. *Éthiques en dialogue, Aristote lecteur de Platon*, Paris: Vrin, 2014.

Nagel, Jennifer. 'Factive and Nonfactive Mental State Attribution', *Mind & Language* 32, 2017, 525–44.

Nagel, Thomas. 'Aristotle on Eudaimonia', *Phronesis* 17, 3, 1972, 252–59.

Natali, Carlo. *La saggezza di Aristotele*, Napoli: Bibliopolis, 1989 (trans. *The Wisdom of Aristotle*, Albany: SUNY Press 2001).

Natali, Carlo (trans. and notes). *Etica Nicomachea*, Roma-Bari: Laterza, 1999.

Natali, Carlo, 'The Book on Wisdom', in R. Polansky (ed.), *The Cambridge Companion to Aristotle's Nicomachean Ethics*, Cambridge, New York: Cambridge University Press, 2014, 180–202.

Natali, Carlo. *Il metodo ed il trattato*, Roma: Edizioni di Storia e Letteratura, 2017.

Needler, Mary C. *The Relation of the Eudemian to the Nicomachean Ethics of Aristotle*, Chicago: Chicago University Press, 1926.

Nielsen, Karen M. 'Aristotle on Principles in Ethics: Political Science as the Science of the Human Good', in D. Henry, K. Nielsen (eds.), *Bridging*

the Gap between Aristotle's Science and Ethics, Cambridge: Cambridge University Press, 2015, 29–49.
Nielsen, Karen M. 'Vice in the Nicomachean Ethics', Phronesis 62, 2017, 1–25.
Nielsen, Karen M. 'Phronêsis and Excellence of Deliberation in EN VI', Revue de philosophie ancienne 2, 2020, 291–318.
Nielsen, Karen M. 'Decision in the Eudemian Ethics', in G. Di Basilio (ed.), Investigating the Relationship between Aristotle's Eudemian and Nicomachean Ethics, Oxford: Routledge, 2022, 80–101.
Nightingale, Andrea. Spectacles of Truth: Theôria in its Cultural Context, Cambridge: Cambridge University Press, 2004.
Nussbaum, Martha C. 'Nature, Function and Capability: Aristotle on Political Distribution', Oxford Studies in Ancient Philosophy, supp. volume, 1988a, 145–84.
Nussbaum, Martha C. 'Non-relative Virtues: An Aristotelian Approach', Midwest Studies in Philosophy 13, 1988b, 32–53.
Nussbaum, Martha C. 'Equity and Mercy', in P. A. Tabensky (ed.), Judging and Understanding, Padstow: Ashgate, 2006, 3–43.
Olfert, Christiana. 'Aristotle's Conception of Practical Truth', Journal of the History of Philosophy 52, 2014, 205–31.
Pakaluk, Michael. 'The Meaning of Aristotelian Magnanimity', Oxford Studies in Ancient Philosophy 26, 2004, 265–8.
Pakaluk, Michael (trans.). Aristotle: Nicomachean Ethics, Cambridge: Cambridge University Press, 2005.
Pakaluk, Michael, Pearson, Giles (eds.). Moral Psychology and Human Actions, Oxford: Oxford University Press, 2011.
Penner, Terry. 'The Unity of Virtue', Philosophical Review 82, 1973, 35–68.
Penner, Terry. 'What Laches and Nicias Miss—and Whether Socrates Thinks Courage Merely a Part of Virtue', Ancient Philosophy 12, 1992, 1–27.
Peterson, Sandra. 'Horos in Aristotle's NE', Phronesis 33, 3, 1988, 233–50.
Polansky, Ron, Stover, James. 'Moral Virtue and Megalopsychia', Ancient Philosophy 23, 2003, 351–9.
Poulakos, Takis. 'Isocrates Civic Education and the Question of Doxa', in T. Poulakos, D. J. Depew (eds.), Isocrates and Civic Education, Austin: University of Texas Press, 2004, 44–66.
Primavesi, Oliver. 'Ein Blick in den Stollen von Skepsis: Vier Kapitel zur frühen Überlieferung des Corpus Aristotelicum', Philologus 151, 1, 2007, 51–77.
Rackham, Harris (trans.). Nicomachean Ethics, London: Loeb, 1934.
Radice, Roberto (trans. and notes). Aristotele, Fisica, Milano: Bompiani, 2011.
Rees, David A. 'Magnanimity in the EE and EN', in P. Moraux, D. Harlfinger (eds.), Undersuchungen zur Eudemischen Ethik, Berlin: De Gruyter, 1971, 231–45.
Reeve, David. Practices of Reason, Oxford: Oxford University Press, 1992.

Reeve, David. *Action, Contemplation and Happiness*, Cambridge: Harvard University Press, 2012.
Reeve, David. *Aristotle on Practical Wisdom*, Cambridge: Harvard Unitersity Press, 2013.
Reeve, David. *Eudemian Ethics*, Indianapolis: Hackett, 2021.
Roberts, Robert, Wood, Jay. *Intellectual Virtues*, Oxford University Press, 2007.
Rogers, Kelly. 'Aristotle's Conception of *to kalon*', *Ancient Philosophy* 13, 1993, 355–71.
Roochnik, David. 'What Is Theôria? *Nicomachean Ethics* Book X.7–8', *Classical Philology* 104, 1, 2009, 69–82.
Rorty, Amelie. 'The Place of Contemplation in Aristotle's Nicomachean Ethics', in A. Rorty (ed.), *Essays on Aristotle's Ethics*, Berkeley: University of California Press, 1980, 377–94.
Ross, David (trans.). *Aristotle, Nicomachean Ethics*, Oxford: Oxford University Press, 1925.
Rossi, Gabriela. 'Nature and Excellence of Character in Aristotle', in G. Rossi, *Nature and the Best Life: Exploring the Natural Bases of Practical Normativity in Ancient Philosophy*, Hildesheim: G. Olms, 2013, 155–81.
Rowe, Christopher. *The Eudemian and the Nicomachean Ethics, Proceedings of the Cambridge Philological Society*, Cambridge, 1971.
Rowe, Christopher. 'Aristotle and Socrates in the Eudemian Ethics on the Naturalness of Goodness', in B. Sattler, U. Coope (eds.), *Ancient Ethics and the Natural World*, Cambridge: Cambridge University Press 2021, 203–17.
Rowe, Christopher. 'Sophia in the Eudemian Ethics', in G. Di Basilio (ed.), *Investigating the Relationship between Aristotle's Eudemian and Nicomachean Ethics*, New York: Routledge, 2022, 122–37.
Rowe, Christopher (ed.). *Aristotle: Ethica Eudemia*, Oxford: Oxford Classical Texts, 2023a.
Rowe, Christopher. *Aristotelica*, Oxford: Oxford University Press, 2023b.
Russell, Daniel. *Practical Intelligence and the Virtues*, Oxford: Oxford University Press 2009.
Russell, Daniel. '*Phronêsis* and the Virtues', in R. Polansky (ed.), *The Cambridge Companion to Aristotle's* Nicomachean Ethics, Cambridge: Cambridge University Press 2014, 203–21.
Ryle, Gilbert. 'On Forgetting the Difference Between Right and Wrong', in A. Melden (ed.), *Essays in Moral Philosophy*, Seattle: University of Washington Press, 1958.
Sauvé Meyer, Susan. 'Living for the Sake of an Ultimate End', in J. Miller (ed.), *Aristotle's* Nicomachean Ethics, Cambridge: Cambridge University Press, 2011, 47–66.
Sauvé Meyer, Susan. 'Clarifying the Human Soul and Its Virtues: *EE* 1219b26-1220a20', in H. Lorenz, B. Morison (eds.), *Aristotle's Eudemian Ethics, Book II*, New York: Oxford University Press, forthcoming.

Schmidt, Ernst A. 'Ehre und Tugend. Zur Megalopsychia der Aristotelischen Ethik', *Archiv für Geschichte der Philosophie* 49, 1967, 149–68.

Schofield, Malcolm. 'Ariston of Chios and the Unity of Virtue', *Ancient Philosophy* 1984, 83–95.

Schofield, Malcolm. 'Euboulia in the *Iliad*', *The Classical Quarterly* 36, 1, 1986, 6–31.

Schofield, Malcolm. 'L'*EE* postérieure a l'*EN*? Quelques preuves tirées des livres sur l'amitié', in D. Dhaerbey, G. Aubry (eds.), *L'Excellence de la Vie. Sur l'EN et l'EE d'Aristote*, Paris: Vrin, 2002, 299–315.

Schollmeier, Paul. 'Aristotle on Practical Wisdom', *Zeitschrift Für Philosophische Forschung* 43, 1, 1989, 130–1.

Sedley, David. 'Becoming Like God in the Timaeus and Aristotle', in T. Calvo, L. Brisson (eds.), *Interpreting the Timaeus-Critias*, Proceedings of the IV Symposium Platonicum, Sankt Augustin: Akademie Verlag, 1997, 327–41.

Sedley, David. 'The Unity of Virtue after the *Protagoras*', in B. Collette-Dučić, S. Delcomminette (eds.), *Unité et origine des vertus dans la philosophie ancienne*, Bruxelles: Ousia, 2014, 65–91.

Segvic, Heda. 'Deliberation and Choice in Aristotle', in M. Pakaluk, G. Pearson (eds.), *Moral Psychology and Human Action*, Oxford: Oxford University Press, 2011, 160–86.

Sherman, Nancy (ed.). *Aristotle's Ethics: Critical Essays*, Lanham, MD: Rowman and Littlefield, 1998.

Sherman, Thomas. 'Human Happiness and the Role of Philosophical Wisdom in the Nicomachean Ethics', *International Philosophical Quarterly* 42, 2002, 467–92.

Simon, Attila. 'Sunesis as Ethical Discernment in Aristotle', *Rhizomata* 5, 1, 2017, 79–90.

Simpson, Peter (trans. and commentary). *The Eudemian Ethics of Aristotle*, New Brunswick: Transaction, 2013a.

Simpson, Peter. 'Aristotle's *Ethica Eudemia* 1220b10-11 ἐν τοῖς ἀπηλλαγμένοις and *De Virtutibus et Vitiis*', *The Classical Quarterly* 63, 2013b, 651–9.

Sluiter, Ineke, Rosen, Ralph M. (eds.). *Kakos. Badness and Anti-value in Classical Antiquity*, Leiden-Boston: Brill, 2008.

Snell, Bruno. *The Discovery of the Mind: The Greek Origin of European Thought*, New York: Dover, 1960, 2011.

Sorabji, Richard. 'Body and Soul in Aristotle', *Philosophy* 49, 1974, 63–89.

Sorabji, Richard. 'Aristotle on the Role of Intellect in Virtue', in A. O. Rorty (ed.), *Essays on Aristotle's Ethics*, Berkeley: University of California Press, 1980, 201–19.

Spencer, Mark. 'Beauty and the Intellectual Virtues in Aristotle', in A. M. Ramos (ed.), *Beauty and the Good: Recovering the Classical Tradition from Plato to Duns Scoto*, Washington, DC: Catholic University of America Press, 2020, 93–114.

BIBLIOGRAPHY 195

Spinelli, Priscilla. 'La cause finale de l'homme: nature et éthique', last accessed in April 2024, https://aitia.hypotheses.org/publications/textes.
Steel, Carlos (trans. and notes). *Simplicius: on Aristotle on the Soul 3.6-13*, New York: Bloomsbury, 2014.
Stewart, John A. *Notes on the Nicomachean Ethics of Aristotle*, Oxford: Clarendon Press, 1892.
Susemihl, Franz (ed.). *Aristotelis. Ethica Eudemia*, Leipzig: Teubner, 1884.
Taylor, Christopher C. W. *Plato's Protagoras*, Oxford: Clarendon Press, 1976.
Taylor, Christopher C. W. 'Aristotle on Practical Reason', Oxford Handbook Online, 2016.
Telfer, Elizabeth. 'The Unity of the Moral Virtues in Aristotle's *Nicomachean Ethics*', *Proceedings of the Aristotelian Society* 90, 1989, 35–48.
Toner, Christopher. 'The Full Unity of the Virtues', *The Journal of Ethics* 18, 3, 2014, 207–27.
Torrente, Luca. 'The Beautiful Action for Aristotle', in H. Reid, T. Leyh (eds.), *Looking at Beauty to Kalon in Western Greece: Selected Essays from the 2018 Symposium on the Heritage of Western Greece*, Fonte Aretusa: Parnassos Press, 2019, 219–28.
Torri, Paolo. 'The Telos of Assimilation to God and the Conflict between Theoria and Praxis in Plato and the Middle Platonists', in M. Bonazzi, A. Ulacco, F. Forcignanò (eds.), *Thinking, Knowing and Acting: Epistemology and Ethics in Plato and Ancient Platonism*, Leiden: Brill, 2019, 228–51.
Tricot, Jean (trans. and commentary). *Aristote. Éthique à Nicomaque*, Paris: Vrin, 1990.
Tutuska, John. 'Aristotle on the Noble and the Good: Philosophical Imprecision in the Nicomachean Ethics', *Ancient Philosophy* 33, 2013, 159–79.
Urmson, James O. 'Aristotle's Doctrine of the Mean', in A. O. Rorty (ed.), *Essays on Aristotle's Ethics*, Berkeley: University of California Press, 1980, 157–70.
Urmson, James O. (trans. and notes). *Simplicius: on Aristotle on the Soul 1.1-2.4*, New York: Bloomsbury, 2014.
Verdenius, Willem J. 'Human Reason and God', in P. Moraux, D. Harlfinger (eds.), *Untersuchungen zur Eudemischen Ethik*, Berlin: Walter de Gruyter, 1971, 285–97.
Viano, Cristina. 'Aristotle and the Starting Point of Moral Development: The Notion of Natural Virtue', in S. Stern-Gillet, K. Corrigan (eds.), *Reading Ancient Texts. Volume II: Aristotle and Neoplatonism: Essays in Honour of Denis O'Brien*, Leiden: Brill, 2007, 23–42.
Vinje, Hilde. 'Complete Life in the *Eudemian Ethics*', *Apeiron* 53, 2, 2023, 299–323.
Vlastos, Gregory. 'The Unity of the Virtues in the Protagoras', in G. Vlastos (ed.), *Platonic Studies*, Princeton University Press, 1973, 221–69.
Vogt, Katja. *Desiring the Good*, New York: Oxford University Press, 2017.

Walker, Alice D. M. 'The Incompatibility of the Virtues', *Ratio* 6, 1, 1993, 44–60.

Walker, David. *Aristotle on the Uses of Contemplation*, Cambridge: Cambridge University Press, 2018.

Walzer, Richard R., Mingay, Jean M. (eds.). *Aristotelis. Ethica Eudemia*, Oxford: Oxford University Press, 1991.

Ward, Julie. *Searching for the Divine in Plato and Aristotle*, Cambridge: Cambridge University Press, 2021.

Watson, Gary. 'Virtues in Excess', *Philosophical Studies: An International Journal for Philosophy in the Analytic Tradition* 46, 1, 1984, 57–74.

West, Ryan. 'Anger and the Virtues: A Critical Study in Virtue Individuation', *Canadian Journal of Philosophy* 46, 6, 2016, 877–97.

White, Stephen A. *Sovereign Virtue. Aristotle on the Relation between Happiness and Prosperity*, Stanford: Stanford University Press, 1992.

Whiting, Jennifer. 'Aristotle's Function Argument: A Defense', *Ancient Philosophy* 8, 1988, 33–48.

Whiting, Jennifer. 'Locomotive Soul: The Parts of Soul in Aristotle's Scientific Works', *Oxford Studies in Ancient Philosophy* 22, 2002, 141–200.

Wiggins, David. 'Deliberation and Practical Reason', in A. Rorty (ed.), *Essays on Aristotle's Ethics*, Berkeley: University of California Press, 1980, 221–40.

Wiggins, David. *Needs, Value, Truth*, Oxford: Oxford University Press, 1988.

Williams, Bernard. *Ethics and the Limits of Philosophy*, Harvard: Harvard University Press, 1985.

Wilson, Alan T. 'Unity of the Intellectual Virtues', *Synthese* 199, 3–4, 2021, 9835–54.

Wolf, Susan. 'Moral Psychology and the Unity of the Virtues', *Ratio* 20, 2, 2007, 145–67.

Wolt, Daniel. '*Phronêsis* and *Kalokagathia* in EE VIII.3', *Journal of the History of Philosophy* 60, 1, 2022, 1–23.

Woods, Michael. 'Intuition and Perception in Aristotle's Ethics', *Oxford Studies in Ancient Philosophy* 4, 1986, 145–66.

Woods, Michael (trans. and commentary). *Aristotle's Eudemian Ethics Books I, II, and VIII*, Oxford: Clarendon Press, 1992.

Zanatta, Marcello (trans. and commentary). *Aristotele, Etica Eudemia*, Milano: Biblioteca Universitaria Rizzoli, 2012.

Index

For the benefit of digital users, indexed terms that span two pages (e.g., 52–53) may, on occasion, appear on only one of those pages.

actuality, 22–24, 93–94, 98–99, 100–1, 114, 120, 125, 154n.25, 172–73
Additive, xxi, 150
Functionality, xvii–xviii, xxi, xxiv–xxv, 28, 54, 116, 123–24, 159–60
akrasia, 90n.14
akratic, 7–8, 93–94, 100–1, 109–10
Alexander of Aphrodisias, 32–33n.20, 92–93
Anaxagoras, 125, 126–27n.25, 137–38, 138n.59
Anscombe, 111–12
Aristotle, works of
  Categories, 65n.26, 65n.28, 101n.56
  De Anima (DA), xix–xx, xx n.11, 2–3, 7–8, 13–14, 23–24, 40n.41, 51n.87, 112, 112–13n.101, 118–19n.11, 119n.12, 120n.15, 121n.16, 133n.46, 134n.51, 139, 139n.61, 169n.70
  Historia Animalium (HA), 67n.36, 73n.55
  Magna Moralia (MM), 25n.68, 73n.57, 102n.59, 129n.31, 133n.44, 145n.9, 165n.61
  Metaphysics (Met), xxvii–xxviii, 13–14, 20n.53, 21–22, 32–33n.20, 36n.31, 41n.46, 63nn.17–20, 67n.37, 86, 102–5, 109n.83, 115–16, 119n.12, 120nn.15–16, 121–22, 125, 133n.46, 144, 151–53, 156–59, 167–68, 170
  On the Generation of Animals (GA), 119n.12
  On the Parts of Animals (PA), 11–13, 41n.46
  On Virtues and Vices (De virtutibus et vitiis), 45n.60, 46n.70
  Physics, xxv n.17, xxvii–xxviii, 41n.46, 63n.17, 66n.32, 91–93, 92n.20, 99n.48, 101n.56, 119n.12, 121n.16, 133n.46, 144, 151–53, 157, 158, 169, 170
  Politics, xxv n.17, 7–8, 25n.68, 63n.20, 128n.29, 145n.9
  Posterior Analytics, 40–41, 40n.44, 86–88, 89–90, 92–93, 99n.47, 101n.57
  Prior Analytics, 47–48, 53–54, 100–1
  Protrepticus, x–xi, 47n.72, 53n.100, 77–79, 96n.35, 117n.6, 119n.12, 121–22, 131n.36, 145n.9
  Rhetoric, xxv n.17, 52n.91, 52n.95
  Topics, 65n.30, 108n.79, 148n.16

beneficiary, xxvi–xxvii, 120–21, 123, 131, 132–36
Broadie, Sarah, xvi n.7, 20n.55, 23n.63, 39n.37, 41n.45, 42–43nn.51–52, 46n.65, 51n.87, 74n.64, 77–79, 82n.97, 111–12, 118–19n.11, 120n.14, 124n.19

Burnyeat, Myles, 86n.2, 88–95, 100–1

choice, xxvi, 63n.17, 77–80, 93–95, 98–99, 102, 130, 131, 136–37, 145–46, 163, 167–69, 177–78
cleverness (*deinotês*), 73
common books, xiv–xv, xv n.6, xxii–xxiii, 58n.1, 73n.57, 74–75, 92–93, 115–16, 118–19n.11, 129–30, 137–38, 166, 179

decision (*prohairesis*), xxv, 12n.35, 42–43n.51, 45–46, 45n.61, 51, 62–64, 65n.27, 66–69, 73, 74n.64, 75–77, 84, 111–12, 120–21
deliberative capacity (*bouleutikon*), 7–8, 120–21
Democritus, 50n.83
Dependency
 Functional, xxiv–xxv, 28, 36–37, 43–44, 48–49, 56–57, 58–59
 Ontological, xxiv–xxv, 28, 36–37, 56–57, 58–59
dependent virtue, xvi, xxiv–xxv, 28–29, 34–35, 36–37, 53–55, 56–57, 85n.1, 171
divine
 cultivation of the, 122, 130, 134–36
 in us, 116n.4, 131–34
 objects, xx, 118–19, 121–22, 123–24, 127–28, 132–34
dominant reading/interpretation, xxvii–xxviii, 124n.19, 138–39, 153, 154–55
doxa, 44–45, 46–47, 49–51, 92–94, 112
doxastikon (*see* calculative part)

emerging tasks/functions, xxiv–xxv, 28, 29, 37, 54–57, 76n.68

emotion, xxv, 60, 62n.14, 74–75, 80–82, 83, 91–92, 99, 100–1
emotional, 52–53, 62n.14
endoxon/endoxa, 38–39, 148n.16

for the most part, 11–13, 65–66, 66n.32, 87n.5, 87–88n.7
Function Argument, xviii n.10, xxiii–xxiv, 1, 13, 18–21, 26, 118, 146

habituation, 35–36, 39, 62–64, 66–67, 84, 105, 109
haplôs. *See* without qualification
Heraclitus, 52n.92, 115n.2
hierarchy, xxiii–xxiv, 1, 8–9, 104–5, 109n.83, 171–72
highest good, 34, 104–5, 124–25, 126
honour, 77–79, 82–83, 162–63

inclusive reading/interpretation, xxvii–xxviii, 124–25, 138–39, 153–55
induction, 15, 41n.46, 42–43, 64–65
Interdependency
 Functional, xiv, xvi, xxv, 58–59, 61–62, 71, 76, 80
 Ontological, 58–59, 71, 74–75
involuntary, 90–91
Isocrates, 45–46, 47n.72, 53n.98

knowledge
 explanatory, xxvi, 85–86, 88–89, 94–95, 114
 mathematical, 15, 20n.52, 21–22

megalopsychia (magnanimity), 65n.29, 68–69, 76n.69, 82–83, 160–63, 164, 170
magnanimous, 162–63
mutual entailment, xiii–xv, xvii–xviii, 19n.51, 28n.3, 58–59, 71
reciprocity of the virtues, xiii–xiv, 58–59, 71

natural goods, 77–80, 82n.99, 130, 131, 132n.42, 136–37, 163, 167–69, 176
nature
  contrary to/against, 91–92, 102–5, 106, 108–9
  by nature, xxv, 4–5, 9, 20–21, 27n.1, 35–36, 43, 55–56, 62–64, 65n.27, 66–67, 69n.45, 72–73, 77–79, 103n.62, 125–26, 128, 140n.63

on-off, xxii, xxvii–xxviii, 144, 150–51

pain, xxv, 32–33, 65–67, 75–76, 81–82, 83, 90, 129–30
part/parts
  calculative (*logistikon* or *doxastikon*), xxiii–xxiv, 2–3, 10–13, 25–26, 29–31, 54–55, 73, 119–20
  generative, 2–3, 4–5
  irrational, 2–4, 5, 8–9, 10–11, 76–77, 102–3, 136–37, 168–69
  non-rational, 5n.11, 5n.13, 8n.21, 9, 10–11, 54–55, 63n.18, 132–34
  nutritive, 2–5, 7–8
  part by part, 13n.36, 56, 60n.7, 146–47
  perceptual, 2–4
  rational, 3–4, 5n.13, 7–8, 10–13, 29–31, 33n.23, 54–55, 74n.64, 110–11, 119–20, 132–34
  scientific (*epistêmonikon*), xxiii–xxiv, 2–3, 10–13, 25–26, 29–31, 54–55, 119–20
  vegetative, 2–3, 4–5
perception, 2–3, 29–30, 40–43, 89n.12, 92–93, 101n.57, 110–11
phantasia, 112–13n.101

Plato, works of
  Clitophon, 21n.56
  Cratylus, 45n.63, 49–50, 51n.87
  Epinomis, 31n.16
  Euthydemus, 21n.56, 75n.66
  Gorgias, xiii n.1
  Laches, xiii nn.1–2, 36n.30, 61, 61n.11
  Laws, xiii n.1, 76n.69, 134–35
  Meno, xiii nn.1–2, 21n.56, 36n.30, 61, 61n.12, 75n.66, 99n.47, 105n.70
  Phaedo, 75n.66, 99n.47
  Phaedrus, 105n.71
  Philebus, 49–50, 51n.87, 95n.28, 117n.6
  Protagoras, xiii nn.1–2, 33n.22, 36n.30, 61, 105n.71
  Republic, xiii nn.1–2, 21n.56, 25n.69, 36n.30, 52, 71n.50, 75n.66
  Statesman, xiii n.1, 11n.30, 117n.6, 174n.9
  Symposium, 104n.67
  Theaetetus, 33n.22, 52n.92, 75n.66, 95n.28, 99n.48, 105n.71, 115n.2
pleasure, xxv, 32–33, 65–67, 69–71, 75–76, 81–82, 83, 90, 129–30
potentiality, 22–24, 98–99, 100–1, 114, 119n.12, 120
Protagoras, 61

reciprocity of the virtues. *See* mutual entailment

scalar, xxi, 150–51, 171
sleep/asleep, 16, 22–24, 91–92, 99, 100–1, 108
Socrates, xiii–xiv, xiii n.2, 58–59, 61, 74–75, 94n.25, 95–96, 108–9

Solon, 138n.59
sophos, 55–56, 142–44, 177
superexcellence, xxii, 143–44, 145–46, 149–50
superlative value, 143–44
syllogism, 36–37, 42, 47–48, 53–54, 87n.6, 97–98, 99, 100–1, 102, 106–8, 112

technê (expertise), xix, 21–22, 27n.2, 31n.14, 32–33n.20, 40–41, 44–45, 96–97, 97n.39, 102–4, 110–11, 112–13n.101, 115–16, 138, 139, 148–49
Thales, 137–38
theoretical
 capacity (*theôrêtikon*), 9–10, 116, 120–21, 122, 128, 129–30, 132–37, 168–69
 domain, 42, 85–86, 115–18, 131–32, 139
 study, 127–28
 virtue, 30–31, 126–27n.25, 130n.34, 134–35, 139–40, 142

understanding
 demonstrative, xxvi, 87–88, 89–90, 93–95, 102–3, 114
 scientific, 85–86
unity
 hierarchical, xxiii–xxiv, 1, 25–26
 psychological, xxiii–xxiv, 1, 4, 25–26
 teleological, xxiii–xxiv, 1, 25–26
unqualified. *See* without qualification

vicious
 acting, 108–9
 actions, 106–8
 agent/person, 8–9, 47–48, 68n.39, 109–10
voluntary, 90–91, 96–97, 120–21
 involuntary (*see* involuntary)

wholeness, xxvii–xxviii, 151–53, 159–60, 167–68, 169, 170
without qualification (*haplôs*), 47–49, 72, 86–88, 90–91, 92–93, 114, 150–51, 164, 167